FATAL
SYSTEM
ERROR

For E.F.O.

CONTENTS

FATAL SYSTEM ERROR

THE HUNT
FOR THE
NEW CRIME
LORDS
WHO ARE
BRINGING
DOWN
THE INTERNET

JOSEPH MENN

PublicAffairs
New York

Published in the United States by PublicAffairs™,
A Member of the Perseus Books Group

PublicAffairs books are available at special discounts for bulk purchases in
the U.S. by corporations, institutions, and other organizations. For more information, please contact the Special Markets Department at the Perseus
Books Group, 2300 Chestnut Street, Suite 200, Philadelphia, PA 19103, call
(800) 810-4145, ext. 5000, or e-mail special.markets@perseusbooks.com.

Designed by Pauline Brown

Typeset in 11.5 point Caslon by the Perseus Books Group.

Library of Congress Cataloging-in-Publication Data
Menn, Joseph.
   Fatal system error : the hunt for the new crime lords who are bringing
down the Internet / by Joseph Menn.
      p. cm.
   Includes bibliographical references and index.
   ISBN 978-1-58648-748-5 (alk. paper)
   1. Computer crimes. 2. Computer hackers. 3. Internet fraud. I. Title.

   HV6773.M46 2009
   364.16'8—dc22

                                                        2009037731

FIRST EDITION
10 9 8 7 6 5 4 3 2 1

INTRODUCTION

WHEN I FIRST MET BARRETT LYON in 2004, I was covering Internet security for the *Los Angeles Times* from an office in San Francisco. His story was so good—and met a journalistic need so deep—that I had a hard time believing it was true.

For more than a year, I had been grappling with an onslaught of urgent but complicated stories. Seemingly every week brought a new computer virus that shot around the world. Many had real impact, shutting down large company networks or overstuffing mailboxes with spam until they started rejecting legitimate messages. Even so, the problems could be hard to explain before the deadline for the next day's newspaper—especially if the viruses took advantage of obscure software holes in ways researchers were still struggling to understand.

It wasn't just that the technical explications were tricky. There were few heroes, except for a handful of almost unquotably nerdy researchers. The villains were usually shadows. When someone did get caught in those days, it was typically a maladjusted teenager.

Yet something important was happening. As the world connected to more computers and depended on them for more things, the bad guys were wreaking havoc. Worse, the viruses unleashed for mischief's sake were getting supplanted by those that were about making money.

Then came a new series of Internet attacks, much easier to understand technologically, that illustrated the new thuggery in bold strokes. Assailants unknown simply overwhelmed business websites with so much bogus traffic that the sites failed. To stop, they wanted $30,000 or more wired to countries in Eastern Europe.

I called around to the victimized companies, looking in part for something to make the tale even better, so that any reader could follow along and learn. I quickly heard about cyber defender Barrett Lyon.

He was young and unassuming, yet enormously bright and articulate. He had actually chatted with the attackers. Yes, he knew some of their names. He didn't happen to have a record of those chats, did he? Sure he did. Don't suppose the cops had taken much interest in the case, since they normally throw up their hands at cybercrime? Why, yes, they had—the FBI, the Secret Service, and the national authorities in the U.K. and Russia. The saga grew until it gave a panoramic view of organized crime's brazen new initiative.

Of course, the sort of attack that Barrett specialized in warding off was merely one dramatic aspect of a bigger and rapidly metastasizing problem—technology advances that were helping criminals even more than they were helping consumers. Online scams and identity theft soared, and an entire underground industry grew. Enormous data heists from such places as the information broker ChoicePoint and retailer T.J. Maxx generated plenty of headlines.

By 2009, 30 percent of Americans had become identity theft victims, companies and individuals were losing an estimated $1 trillion a year to Internet criminals, and confidence in the electronic economy and the stability of the information infrastructure was fraying. Now it wasn't only about cash, but about international politics and cyberwarfare as well.

Even if someone were dedicated to sorting out what was going on and where it was leading, there wasn't much help to be found. Few with any knowledge had an incentive to talk. Not Microsoft or the other software companies, whose flawed products made penetration by criminals so easy; not most security firms, whose services were falling farther behind; and not law enforcement agencies, which were catching less than 1 percent of the bad guys.

Private researchers could explain how one virus differed from previous versions, law enforcement could complain about how the trails from identity theft crimes went overseas and grew cold, and a handful of academics could hold forth on the politics of Eastern Europe. But even as fears rose to the point that President Barack Obama devoted a speech to the vast dangers of cybercrime, cyberspying, and cyberwar, almost no one could give a full picture.

Once more, Barrett Lyon could. By then, I learned, he had penetrated not just the Russian mob but the American mob as well, and had gone undercover again, this time wearing a wire for the FBI. Only now does that work become public.

In turn, he and I also met British agent Andy Crocker, who followed his leads and plunged deeper than any previous Westerner into hacking in the former Soviet Union—and whose adventures have never been recounted. Together we retraced the greatest international cybercrime prosecution in history, as an officer from the Russian MVD put it to us in a vodka toast.

Their combined stories shine by far the brightest light yet into a shadow economy that is worth several times more than the illegal drug trade, that has already disrupted national governments, and that has the potential to undermine Western affluence and security. This book is about the triumph of two men who went where none like them had gone before.

But it is also a warning about disaster well along in the making. By mid-2009, word had spread far enough in secretive government circles about the exploits of Barrett Lyon and Andy Crocker that they were flown to Washington to lecture more than a hundred top spies for the U.S. and its allies. Yet those officials still weren't getting the most important message. And both heroes had quit working for their governments.

Cybercrime is too important to be left to the professionals. Read this book and understand why.

PART ONE

1

WARGAMES

FLYING DOWN TO COSTA RICA, Barrett Lyon couldn't wait to meet his new clients in the flesh. It was two days after Christmas 2003, and the twenty-five-year-old computer whiz from near California's Lake Tahoe figured to be welcomed like a conquering hero. The early-morning flight banked away from San Francisco International Airport, piercing the winter clouds as it gained altitude. Barrett looked over at the pretty brunette by his side and felt he was on the cusp of a new and better phase in his life. BetCRIS—short for Bet Costa Rica International Sports—was not only treating him to the trip, it was paying for his girlfriend, Rachelle Sterling, to come along. It was their first plane journey together, and her first outside the country. He hoped it would go a long way toward easing the tensions of the past six weeks.

Barrett now realized he must have seemed irrationally obsessed with BetCRIS, defending an unseen company in Costa Rica against invisible enemies in yet another country. Most of the time all Rachelle saw was Barrett's six-foot, two-inch frame hunched over the boomerang-shaped desk in their cramped Sacramento condo. For twenty or more hours a day Barrett stared blearily into the computer screens he used to track electronic assaults. He even blew off the family Thanksgiving he had promised her so he could try to get his programs and configurations working better. He had been too focused to thank her for bringing him the leftover turkey, let alone to explain everything he was doing.

To Barrett it was a battle for the ages, one that reminded him of *WarGames*, the 1983 movie memorialized in the poster on his wall. In the film, a bright but unschooled teen looking to play games online stumbles into a government supercomputer, nearly launching World War III. Barrett thought he had skipped the initial blunder and gone straight to the fun stuff, trying to short-circuit a cyberbattle that was costing real people their jobs and fortunes.

BetCRIS took in hundreds of millions of dollars every year in sports bets, making it one of the largest gambling houses and among the first to seek a legal haven offshore while catering to U.S. customers. But a vicious attack kept crashing the website during the peak season, keeping bettors away and costing BetCRIS as much as $5 million a day in lost business. Barrett didn't know if the technologically savvy thugs had been hired by the sportsbook's competitors or were operating on their own. In either case, they were trying to extract money from the company in exchange for going away—a perfect protection racket for the cyber age. If the bad guys succeeded at Bet-CRIS, they would be fools not to attack hundreds of other companies.

The previous spring, the first hint of a problem with the BetCRIS website hadn't been enough to worry the company's general manager, Mickey Richardson. Inside the seven-story building in Costa Rica's capital, San Jose, behind the black glass that kept out the heat and the gazes of the curious, the phones were ringing as usual. But bets placed over the 800 number were a minority of the business. For more than a year now, most of the money had come in over the Web, placed by bettors in their homes and office buildings. Over that spring week, however, BetCRIS began hearing complaints that the Web pages were sluggish. "What the hell's wrong with the site?" barked Mickey, who was usually nice when his money wasn't involved. Technician Glenn Lebumfacil checked the logs and saw that while there was a crush of visitors to the website, they weren't real customers. Personal computers from around the world were coming to BetCRIS.com and immediately leaving again. As to why, Glenn had no idea. The mysterious slowdown continued for days.

Checking his email one morning, Mickey got the surprising explanation—along with an extortion demand. An anonymous hacker crowed that he was subjecting Mickey's site to a denial-of-service attack, in which a deluge of fake requests for information overwhelms a Web page. Unlike the teen hackers who had shut down the likes of Yahoo! and eBay during the dot-com boom for bragging rights, the emailer didn't want attention. He just wanted $500 pronto, via the online payment service e-Gold.

"Big deal," Mickey said aloud. He could spend that much on a good night at the local sushi bar. Mickey paid. *That was a cheap wake-up call,* he thought. The next time might be more expensive. So Mickey phoned the most tech-savvy people he knew and asked where they turned for defense. When he got to top oddsmaker Don Best Sports in Las Vegas, his business allies there couldn't say enough good things about the kid from California who had saved them from a similar assault a year earlier—an intense but affable surfer named Barrett Lyon.

Mickey called Barrett and ran through what had happened. Since the problem wasn't dire—BetCRIS was up and running—Barrett gave him some free advice. He told Mickey to buy a couple of machines from a Massachusetts company that specialized in thwarting unfriendly Web traffic, Top Layer. Mickey paid $20,000 for the equipment, and Barrett talked Glenn through setting it up. *If this ever happens again, we won't have a problem*, Mickey thought. Some months later, Mickey began hearing rumors from his cronies. New computer attacks were hitting the competition, and after some initial defiance, most of the offshore bookies were paying up. "These fucks are brutal," one warned. "There's no way to stop them." A few sites that didn't pay got shut down for nearly a month. Their bank balances were pummeled as gamblers turned elsewhere and revenue vanished. A couple of sites never opened again, leaving angry bettors with no way to recover the money from their accounts and howling about fraud.

Now the extortionists wanted $30,000 or more for a year's freedom from attacks. Mickey chuckled to himself, thinking it had cost him only $500 and the new gear. Then his turn came around again. The Saturday before Thanksgiving, an email arrived just before 8 A.M. "Your site is under attack," it said, demanding $40,000 by the following noon in exchange for one year of peace. One of the biggest betting weeks of the year was about to begin, boasting special professional and college football games, with basketball to boot. "If you choose not to pay for our help, then you will probably not be in business much longer, as you will be under attack each weekend for the next 20 weeks," the author wrote.

Mickey asked Glenn if the Top Layer gear was up to the challenge. "We should be safe," his technician said. "I think our network is nice and tight." Glenn had no idea how exponentially more powerful the bad guys had gotten in the past half-year. They had taken over hundreds or thousands of PCs for a "distributed" denial-of-service, or DDoS, so that the malicious traffic came from everywhere at once. Once they were turned into zombies, under the control of an unseen master, the computers could attack in multiple ways. Top Layer's equipment was designed to stop only a few basic methods. After Mickey failed to answer the attacker's first email, a massive denial-of-service attack wiped out the Top Layer machines in just ten minutes, crashing the BetCRIS site. The onslaught also wiped out Digital Solutions, the Internet service provider for BetCRIS and about half the other gambling companies in Costa Rica. Digital Solutions soon had no choice but to drop BetCRIS from its network, temporarily dumping the site into oblivion.

Glenn felt sick to his stomach. Another email came in from the attacker, this one offering a scant hour to pay before the price of safety went up. Mickey begged for more time, inventing a family emergency. As an old-school expatriate tough guy in an industry full of tough guys, Mickey had already decided to fight back. "I'm stubborn," he told his deputies. "I want to be the guy that says, 'I didn't pay, and I beat them.'"

Going to the U.S. authorities wasn't an attractive option. The feds wouldn't have any jurisdiction unless BetCRIS had operations in the U.S.—and if BetCRIS had operations in the U.S., the feds would want to shut the company down themselves for violating American gambling law. Mickey tracked down Barrett, who was already working on behalf of some BetCRIS rivals. Barrett was in the Arizona desert, laying down the digital equivalent of a firebreak at a satellite-based Internet service provider that was the chief alternative to Digital Solutions in Costa Rica. This one had the grand-sounding name of the Phoenix International Teleport. Most customers called it the PIT, and that was a lot more fitting. It consisted mainly of a server farm inside a trailer on an Indian reservation. The PIT hoped that tribal sovereignty would protect it from any legal complications that might arise from letting gambling transactions flow through the trailer's machines and the enormous satellite dish parked outside up to the sky, then back down to Earth in Costa Rica.

Barrett told Mickey to call Top Layer, which he did to no avail. Mickey's attacker, meanwhile, warned that Mickey had better wire the protection money fast—and now the price was $60,000. "Sorry moron but I am just having so much fun fucking with you," he wrote. Mickey called Barrett again on Sunday, more desperate now. "Some advice you gave me," Mickey complained. "They're killing me. If I don't get this fixed, I'm going to have to lay everybody off. Do you have any idea how many families depend on this place?"

This time, Barrett felt he couldn't say no. He had seen similar assaults before, even before Don Best, but on a much smaller scale. While still in high school, Barrett had created his own company, TheShell.com. It hosted a form of group conversation known as Internet Relay Chat. Long the preferred method of communication for hardcore technology enthusiasts, IRC "channels" could nonetheless degenerate into popularity contests as geeks tried to impress one another. A quirk of the format was that if a channel stopped running and was emptied out, a rival could start it up elsewhere under the same name and take control. Likewise, a hacker annoyed with another user could usurp that user's nickname, causing all kinds of havoc. The way to stop a channel from running and seize power was to shut it down with a denial-of-service attack. By necessity, Barrett figured out how to fend off such attacks while still a teenager, well before temporary shutdowns of big-name sites made national news. After those dot-com assaults, the blue-chip firms providing the fattest targets for thrill-seekers paid dearly to improve their defenses. Smaller companies with fewer resources remained exposed.

The dark art's advances stunned Barrett. Instead of relying on a few machines, the cutting-edge extortion gangs such as the one assaulting BetCRIS had thousands and thousands. They had begun weaving together the networks in 2003, when they or their business associates released computer viruses of a previously unseen strength and sophistication to take control of unsecured computers. With little public attention, viruses were morphing from an occasional annoyance to a key criminal tool. Usually without the knowledge of victimized PC owners, the viruses marshaled armies of machines for broad-based denial-of-service attacks, spamming, and whatever else the underworld marketplace found profitable.

Barrett saw this as an enticing contest of wits and brawn, a chance to match his expertise and technology against enormous might. There was also an ethical appeal. Barrett figured that since BetCRIS and its peers were legal in the countries where they were based—and since bookmaking companies in England were publicly traded on the stock market—they all were aboveboard. Their enemies, on the other hand, were cartoonishly thuggish. "In a case if you refuse our offer, your site will be attacked still long time," one wrote. It sounded so much like a joke that Barrett read the message out loud in the voice of Boris Badenov. But he knew that BetCRIS wasn't smiling. For a libertarian-leaning philosophy major, helping the gambling site was an easy call.

From his work at the Phoenix International Teleport and from talking to Costa Rica companies by phone, Barrett figured that he had a real challenge on his hands. Both the PIT and Digital Solutions were small Internet service providers, and the opposition had already displayed enough firepower to knock them out. He would have to assemble enough bandwidth that he could function like an ISP himself—and that was just to get in the game. He called PureGig, a powerhouse service provider that was also based in Phoenix. PureGig weighed the risk of getting pummeled against the benefit of learning how to handle denial-of-service attacks on customers. It promised to help.

As BetCRIS went up and down, Barrett threw together what he could with the gambling firm's hardware and what was at PureGig, along with programming he wrote on the fly. His code diverted some of the bogus traffic, and he hunted by eye for suspect clusters of Internet addresses that he could block. But the hackers randomized the locations that their queries appeared to be coming from. They went after specialized computers at BetCRIS, including the routers and Web servers. And they acted more like real customers would, using software to download data-rich images that clogged the pipes while being harder to filter out.

Now the lead attacker knew that Mickey had been stringing him along, and he was genuinely angry. "I don't care how long I have to destroy your business," he wrote. If the grammar was poor, the message was clear. The day before Thanksgiving, the attacker turned up the volume well past what Barrett or PureGig had expected. When PureGig's other customers started suffering, the company took down Barrett's operation so they both could recalibrate. The enemy went after Digital Solutions as well, knocking off even the bookies who had paid up. Those firms leaned hard on Mickey to pay and stop bleeding them for his pride.

The surge left Barrett battling for thirty-six hours without rest until he brought the website back up. It was slow, but it was up. "Shit, I think this is working," Barrett shouted in Sacramento. He called Mickey. "Check the site," Barrett told him. "Yeah?" Mickey said. "Hold on. . . . Yeah, it's loading!" Mickey said, clicking around as a customer might, then yelling into the next room. "Hey, guys, we're back up!" Soon BetCRIS was full of happy men giving each other high fives. Then an underling couldn't get past the page he was on. "Uh, Mickey?" he said.

Mickey could barely speak. "I know you guys are trying," he told Glenn Lebumfacil and Dayton Turner, who normally ran the computer networks at another firm in the BetCRIS building. "I don't want to yell at you guys. But I have to yell at *somebody*."

Mickey's other employees started to slip away from the meeting. "This isn't worth it," one muttered. "We must have paid six figures, for what? My clients are gone, and they might not come back." Mickey knew what they were thinking, and he called together the staff of two hundred for a pep talk. "I know this seems pointless," he told them. "But we have to do it this way. If we pay these assholes off, they'll be back for more later. We don't answer to anyone!"

Instead of spending Thanksgiving on the couch watching football, Mickey stayed in the office, his wife's dinner uneaten. "Just tell me,"

Mickey pleaded with Barrett, "do you really think you'll be able to fix this? Because otherwise, I'm out of business." Barrett said he could do it. He kept slogging away, looking for patterns in the attacks. There were only so many ways that the zombies could move, and he programmed his machines to stop them all. Though it went back and forth for more than two weeks, the attacks finally stopped crippling BetCRIS.

By the time of Barrett's trip south in late December, the site was up most of the time. One of Mickey's tormentors sent a final email, mocking him for losing so much business during the fight and spending an additional $1 million fending them off—more than they had sought in the first place. "I bet you feel real stupid," he wrote. Factoring in equipment, bandwidth, and fees to Barrett's small company, Network Presence, the estimate was on the money, Mickey acknowledged to himself. The intensity of the experience bonded all of the defenders together sight unseen, and Barrett felt that he really knew the guys at BetCRIS, that they were friends.

• • •

COSTA RICA WAS STILL WARM when Barrett and Rachelle landed in San Jose. Glenn met them at the airport and took them to the Hotel Corobici. The balconies jutted out over an angled internal courtyard with hanging plants—not bad for the Third World. There was a decent-sized pool and a casino, which reminded Barrett that gambling was perfectly legitimate in the country. Then Glenn escorted them to the BetCRIS building, San Jose's tallest. Nicknamed the Hive, it sat across from a park with a large lake and a fountain, stands of bamboo, and jogging paths. Barrett noticed the armed man in a suit posted outside the Hive's front door but said nothing to Rachelle.

Every company inside was connected to gambling in some way. BetCRIS owned the building and occupied the top two floors, with a pit that made Barrett think of a stock exchange. Instead of computer monitors showing stock trades, though, the area was lined with banks of televisions tuned to every conceivable sporting event. Native Costa Ricans and fast-talking expatriate employees with New York, New Jersey, and Philadelphia accents were constantly taking bets over the phone or tending to the wagers over the Web. "There he is!" Mickey shouted as soon as he saw Barrett. "Goddamn, you're young! What are you, in high school?" Mickey himself was still in his thirties, though his bad teeth and the extra weight he carried under his Hawaiian shirts made him look older, a bit like an overfed Jay Leno.

He put his arm around Barrett and introduced him around. Barrett had talked to the members of the core group by phone several times daily during the onslaught. Canadian Dayton was about the same age as Glenn and Barrett, and like the others self-taught. Dayton was less serious than Glenn, sarcastic, and a bit of an adventurer. Barrett liked him right away.

On the phone, the head of BetCRIS's beleaguered Internet service provider, Brian Green, had been all business, with a barky voice and an alpha-male personality kept barely in check. The Digital Solutions CEO was a major figure at the Hive, and Mickey called him his partner. Brian was short and overweight, a Danny DeVito with gold chains.

Brian asked Barrett and Rachelle if there was anything they wanted to do while they were in Costa Rica, which did a brisk business in tourism. When he mentioned deep-sea fishing in the Pacific, the couple said that sounded like fun, and Brian said he'd be glad to take them. The next morning, he and his bodyguard-driver, Leo, picked them up, and they drove for hours to Los Sueños, a posh coastal resort with palm trees, azure-blue swimming pools, and rooms with enormous flat-screen televisions. They met Brian's regular choice for boat charters, the captain of the good ship *Spanish Fly*. The fishing was terrific. Rachelle snapped photos of Barrett hoisting a sailfish so big he needed help to hold it. They also caught marlin and tuna, which the boat captain, Bimi, turned into sushi on the spot.

As they sailed and fished, Barrett got to know a bit about the others on board. Bimi's past profession, it emerged, was cocaine smuggling. He'd done time in jail, but the government hadn't found all his money. That evening, Barrett couldn't help but notice the scars on both of the bodyguard Léo's knees. "Pistola," Léo explained, his crooked forefinger pulling an invisible trigger. With Barrett's rusty Spanish, it took a while for him to work out the basics of what had happened. Léo had been a bank security guard in Panama. A robber came in, the shooting started, and the robber didn't go out. Léo had killed the man. Barrett took in the story with awe.

Two days later, Dayton took Barrett and Rachelle on a bus journey into the rain forest, followed by a boat trip down a river, and finally a long ride on horseback. Then they took breathtaking runs down a zip-line through the rain forest canopy. That night Mickey took everyone out to a steak dinner served with an Opus One cabernet sauvignon blend. Barrett grew so sick with food poisoning he had to leave halfway through.

In the following days, Barrett grew more at ease in the clubby atmosphere that reigned among the elite in the BetCRIS building. All the insiders had nicknames. Mickey called Brian "Fruity." He inducted Barrett as "Smart Kid," and Barrett joined the other men swapping stories in Mickey's modest office overseeing the betting floor. Mickey was hardworking and gruff with less-favored underlings, and he and the others were especially dismissive of the Costa Ricans they depended on for cheap labor. Yet Mickey also came across as a self-deprecating and sincere family man. He had the minivan to prove it, even if it was chauffeured.

Around Rachelle, Brian was on good behavior. But it seemed a real effort for him to avoid foul language and sexist remarks, and Rachelle saw through it immediately. She thought he was a sleazebag, and she didn't get a good feeling from Mickey either. She hadn't known what to expect, but in retrospect it made sense to her that people who did what these men did for a living, where they did it, would have some rough edges. Rachelle was glad these people would stay in Barrett's world—she was just there on vacation. Barrett and Rachelle spent New Year's Eve at Mickey's house behind a locked automatic gate. It wasn't extravagant on the inside, and Mickey's three kids seemed to have the run of the place. Outside, the adults shot off the commercial-grade fireworks they had picked up in town and toasted the entry of 2004.

While he was enjoying himself, Barrett was also contemplating a big move, one that would push him further into the arms of Mickey and his cohorts. Barrett wanted to start his own company, and he needed some financial backers. Mickey appreciated what Barrett could do, had experience running his own business, and obviously had cash to spare. Maybe he and his circle weren't Boy Scouts, but they had no problem taking risks.

• • •

BARRETT HAD ALREADY COME PRETTY FAR, especially for a kid with a profound learning disability. As a child in the Sierra foothill towns of Rocklin and Auburn, California, Barrett had been bright, inquisitive, and happy, often leading other children in games and playing the peacemaker. But during first grade, he struggled with spelling and wouldn't learn to read. The next year, school officials gave him a battery of tests and informed his parents that there was nothing wrong with him—he just didn't want to learn. At the school's urging, Barrett's father, Bruce, a naturally intense lawyer, kept his son up late night after night, forcing him to study. Barrett tried so hard that he finally told his mother that he thought it would be a relief to die. With that, Barrett's mother, Pat, brought him to the home of a new psychologist for another round of tests. This specialist rendered a different verdict: clear intelligence shackled by dyslexia. Without intervention, she said, Barrett would never graduate high school. "His mind is a Ferrari engine without a transmission," the psychologist explained. Barrett's parents found a school an hour away in Sacramento run by an expert who had developed dyslexia tests for the state of California. They enrolled him for third grade. The school staff found that Barrett had been coping with vision problems so intense that when reading, he saw three lines of identical text. He had been gamely trying to follow the clearest one. Barrett also had great difficulty turning letters into sounds. The staff designed a curriculum just for him and taught Barrett such tricks as putting his finger on the printed page at periods and using it to trace the shape of commas. Imagining a cable running through his head helped with the triple vision. Barrett later found the same techniques gave him the power to visualize in three dimensions things that remained hopelessly abstract to most people, such as what was happening inside computers. Barrett's younger brother Andy, who suffered from attention deficit disorder, tagged along to the new school as well. Barrett still didn't like the work much, but at last he could function.

After the family moved to Auburn, Barrett returned to a conventional school for sixth grade. Bullies picked on him, and it was tricky taking a mix of advanced classes and special-education sessions. When his father upgraded his law office's computers and brought the deposed IBM machine home, though, spell-check and a world of other possibilities came with it. Barrett read a manual about the Internet, took more encouragement from a seventh-grade computer teacher, and soon became so obsessed that he fought with his parents when they set any time for him to turn off the computer and get to bed. His parents would insist that the machine be shut down when they went to sleep. But if they woke up later, the computer was back on. Fuming, Bruce Lyon went outdoors one night and shut off the fuse sending electricity to Barrett's part of the house. When he rose in the morning, he saw that his son had snaked extension cords together to reach a working outlet.

Even before the Netscape browser made cruising the Web easy for PC owners, Barrett wanted more than his own machine could give him. He and close friend Peter Avalos set up a server running the free operating system Linux that they could tap into from anywhere. It hosted Web pages and Internet Relay Chat. It stored files and could crunch through prodigious amounts of data at high speed. Even better, it looked after some three hundred domain names that Barrett registered. If he wanted to send emails from any one of them, now he could. Barrett and Peter called their setup TheShell, and they offered its services free to friends. When the number of users ran into the hundreds and they had to add more equipment, they started charging $5 a month. Pat Lyon's problem was adjusting to her son's new friends: people in their twenties whom he had met online and were now inviting him over to take computers apart. Despite her misgivings, the guys all checked out okay. Barrett did get up to mischief, though, as pretty much every teen technology prodigy did. That's why he would later empathize to a painful extent with the hackers he exposed on the other side of the world.

Most of Barrett's misbehavior was harmless. In high school, he and Peter earned credit for managing the school's computer network. Unsurprisingly, they installed a "sniffer" to monitor whatever traffic they wanted. They let on to a favored history teacher that they knew his password, just to see his reaction. The teacher panicked and had an administrator tell Barrett that he had better plug the "security hole" fast. Barrett counteroffered, suggesting that the administrator stop surfing porn from a classroom computer after hours. That was the end of the conflict. Peter went on to the Naval Academy in Annapolis.

Only once in his high-school career did Barrett do something seriously bad, in 1995. Network Solutions, the understaffed firm that registered websites for companies, accepted changes submitted via electronic forms, without making so much as a phone call to the listed owners of the sites. To make sure that those forms were coming from legitimate sources, it checked to see if the submissions came from an email server that belonged to the company in question. But Barrett thought it might be possible to "spoof" a return address on an email by bouncing it off the real server. If he crafted the email in just the right way, it might convince Network Solutions that the request was legitimate.

It would be an enormous security flaw if someone could pretend to be America Online—or the Defense Department—and take control of the relevant websites. The responsible move would have been to warn Network Solutions immediately. But Barrett was curious to see if he was right, and there was a quick way to find out. On "acci-purpose," as he put it later, Barrett tested his theory. He sent trick emails that hypothetically would tell Network Solutions that AOL, Disney, and a few other American mainstays had abandoned their websites.

The sites went down, displaying blank pages to millions of Web surfers as the victimized companies and Network Solutions scrambled to put things right. Barrett had guessed that it might take a few hours to recover, but it took AOL three full days to get back up. *Oops!* Barrett thought. The massive shutdown was impossible for the authorities to ignore, and the FBI was soon on the case. Agents found the bogus electronic forms and traced them back to TheShell.com. They looked up the records showing who controlled TheShell and called Barrett's house, reaching his father. When questioned, Barrett told his dad that it could have been any customer of TheShell who had sent the emails, or even someone just pretending to be a customer. That was technically true, and Barrett, who was still a minor, got away clean. But having the FBI call his house was not a pleasant experience, and Barrett felt badly for the headaches and financial losses he'd caused. From then on, he walked the straight and narrow.

After graduating from high school in 1996, Barrett didn't want to go to college. He wanted to do more computer work. But his father insisted, so he enrolled at California State University at Chico, which was close to home, and expected rigor mostly at parties. Barrett found that being in college was much more interesting than being in class. He drank his share of beer and failed every class but history. After a year, he got his wish to work. Barrett started at a local Internet service provider, then joined a friend at a small security firm, Network Presence. The company specialized in keeping corporate customers safe from hackers.

Barrett often got to work on the "outside team," authorized sight unseen by a customer to test its defenses by trying to break in. He soon showed an unusual flair for thinking like the enemy. A big assignment was to crack into one of the country's largest insurance companies, one that prided itself on security. Barrett set up shop in a hotel room filled with whiteboards a block from the company's headquarters. After running some probes to map what the company's network looked like, Barrett wrote a fake two-paragraph letter from the company to Qwest, persuading the Internet service provider to turn over control of one of the target firm's blocks of Internet addresses. Once inside the company's trusted electronic space, Barrett sent what appeared to be internal emails inviting a dozen key technical employees to sign in to a new internal portal. As they logged in, Barrett captured their user names and passwords before connecting the employees to the old company portal. Those credentials gave Barrett access to the entire network, right down to the desktop of the chief executive.

But Barrett wasn't through. The company was an early adopter of RFID (radio-frequency identification) badges for employees. The badges included photos and coded authentication that the staff swiped through automated card readers at office entrances. Barrett bought an RFID reader and went to a TGI Friday's favored as an after-work hangout, where he surreptitiously swiped employees' badges. Then he bought blank RFID cards, used a picture of himself, and made his own corporate ID. After Barrett's full report to the customer, one of the target company's senior technology executives was so impressed that he visited Barrett at his parents' house, just to see what environment could have produced him.

After maturing on the job, Barrett decided to give college another chance. He enrolled at Cal State Sacramento, put his computers away in a closet, and eliminated the beer issue by signing up for crew, which started practice each weekday at 5:30 A.M. Barrett signed up for a general introduction to philosophy, intending to fulfill a distribution requirement. Even though the course forced him to concentrate on written words, Barrett loved working through the ideas.

Barrett developed a special fondness for the philosophy of ethics and often tried to translate the arguments into the world of computers. In one paper, Barrett used Kant's categorical imperatives—known in rough translation as "do unto others as you would have them do unto you"—to make the case that denial-of-service attacks couldn't be justified, no matter how offensive the targeted content. In his spare time, Barrett worked on photography, a hobby that turned into a post as photo editor at the college paper, where he made assignments and gave grades to students taking a photojournalism class. Rachelle Sterling was a few years younger than Barrett when she showed up at the newspaper office and introduced herself. He suggested she stop by his condo to pick up a camera, and they started dating almost immediately.

Barrett moved on from rowing to cycling, but those endeavors ended when an eighteen-year-old girl ran a stop sign and hit Barrett on his bike, smashing his leg. While laid up, he returned to computers. It was around then that he was chatting with friends about someone else's attempt to map the paths data take on the Internet. Barrett said that the map was nice to look at but that it took too long to generate and was excessively mysterious about how it worked. Barrett declared that he could map the Internet just as well in a single day by building on the route-tracing programs that were a standard tool in the security industry. A friend bet Barrett $50 that he couldn't do it. So while his leg healed, Barrett set out to win the bet, to establish a means for tracking the growth of the Internet, and to make a pretty picture.

Barrett's project won attention on technology websites, and thousands of readers volunteered spare processing power on their computers. After four days of full-time programming, Barrett got the rough outline of the Internet's largest branches in less than a day, and he ran the program again and again to bring out more detail. The hobby lasted years, and the resulting full-color pictures were spectacular. Barrett called it the Opte project; in 2008, it would be accepted as a permanent exhibition at the Museum of Modern Art in New York.

Barrett returned to working part time and summers at Network Presence, where he earned $25 an hour and wore employee badge No. 3. The company's clients included the Navy and the Defense Department, and there was one big perk: the use of a corporate apartment on the beach in Santa Monica, just south of the noisy roller coaster on the pier.

In 2002, Network Presence got a call from the owner of Don Best Sports, the pioneering Las Vegas oddsmaker. "We've got a problem," the man said, reluctant to give away much more over the phone. Once Barrett arrived on the scene, he understood why Don Best wanted things fixed as quietly as possible. A hacker had taken control of the company's database of customers—1,647 names of hard-core gamblers and betting companies, along with their credit card numbers—and encrypted it. A follow-up email promised that Don Best could have its system back for $200,000. Fortunately, the company had a backup system, and it refused to pay. Days later, the hacker responded with a denial-of-service attack that took the company offline.

It was Barrett's first battle with a professional DDoS. There were no quick fixes. But Barrett guessed he could handle that amount of traffic with enough Web servers and hardware. Over the next four days, he worked frantically to build up a server farm so big that it wouldn't have been out of place at a major Internet commerce company. It cost the oddsmaker the same $200,000 the hackers wanted, but it multiplied Don Best's capacity a hundred times over, and it did the trick. Barrett concluded that DDoS attacks were something that could be managed.

Back in Santa Monica, Barrett wondered how to trace the bad guys who had hit Don Best. The answer came unexpectedly. He had just finished a weekend surf session—a beautiful sunny day, with the weak waves typical for the summer season—and was walking back to his apartment. *There were thousands of computers attacking us*, he thought. *One of them has to have some useful information on it.* He started mulling over all the different kinds of software the drones must have had running. Then it hit him: at least some had to be using a basic piece of networking software called the Simple Network Management Protocol in a way that was visible to outsiders. After all, Windows 2000 machines kept SNMP open unless the buyer changed it. The main point of SNMP is to monitor what is happening on a group of connected machines, so that whoever is in charge can modify what they do. But it also keeps track of all Internet connections. If Barrett could get access to the SNMP running on a zombie that had bombarded Don Best and ask it the right questions, he should be able to see where the zombie had been getting its marching orders.

Barrett quickened his step. Back at his apartment, he fired up his molasses-slow dial-up modem and launched a scanning tool. Then he unleashed it on the long list of Internet addresses that had been attacking Don Best. After a couple of hours, he found one with the right kind of SNMP. He interrogated it, then pored over the data it spit out. Eventually, he saw connections that were way out of place— from port 9990, the computer had been talking to an Internet Relay Chat server in Kazakhstan, irc.kamaz.kz.

Barrett joined that channel himself and saw that the administrator of the channel was listed as Oko. He typed in the command for the server to identify Oko and got back: "oko is stran@fbi.gov." A bogus email address, of course, but a valuable nickname to remember, Stran.

Don Best also gave Barrett his first look at how law enforcement pursued hackers. That scared him more than the criminals did.

The company's call for help went to the U.S. Secret Service, which was taking on a major role in fighting Internet crime as part of its mission to protect the national financial system. The Secret Service dispatched an agent to Don Best. The hacker's threatening email had come from overseas, and he had obviously taken over the database from far away, using the company's electronic connections to the outside world. Yet as Barrett and the Don Best employees watched in disbelief, the agent carefully dusted the compromised computer for fingerprints. It was just policy, he explained. As soon as Barrett's sleuthing identified the connection to Kazakhstan, he excitedly informed the agent. The case appeared to die on the spot.

Barrett had earned enough working for Network Presence to buy a condo in Sacramento for $75,000. He and Rachelle, who was starting to work as a graphic designer, moved in together. But Barrett thought he could do better financially, and his entrepreneurial itch was returning. On the BetCRIS job, which was far harder than the Don Best case, he designed new and more sophisticated means to weed out malicious Web traffic. He told his bosses at Network Presence that they should back him in a venture that would do nothing but fight denial-of-service assaults. They said sure—as long as Network Presence got to keep 95 percent of the company.

• • •

THAT OFFER STILL RANKLED AS BARRETT flew down to Costa Rica to meet Mickey and the rest of the BestCRIS team in 2003. The battle for BetCRIS was all but won, and in the back of his mind, he thought BetCRIS or its grateful executives might invest in a new business. When he saw the full scope of the BetCRIS operation, he decided to follow that instinct. All they could do was say no. In January, as his time in Costa Rica was nearing an end, Barrett asked if he could see Mickey in his office. "You know," he said, "I'm thinking of going out on my own, and I was wondering if you'd be interested in helping me out." Mickey didn't seem surprised. "Give me a little time," he said, "and let's meet at the end of the day tomorrow."

The next evening they met again. This time it wasn't in Mickey's understated office but across the hall in a high-end party room, with a bar and a card table, overlooking the park. Mickey sat next to Digital Solutions' Brian Green, looking out at San Jose. Barrett, across from them, saw nothing but wall. "You've been good to us," Mickey said. "We'll take a gamble on you." While Mickey presented it as a huge favor, the deal he proposed was pretty modest. He and Brian would put in a total of $250,000 and each get 40 percent of the new company, with Barrett devoting his expertise and keeping 20 percent. On his own turf, with more time, Barrett might have thought harder about it. He sensed Mickey expected him to make a counteroffer, to bargain a little. But Barrett was far from home and still angry about the lowball offer he'd gotten from his bosses at Network Presence. So instead of haggling with Mickey, Barrett simply took the offer. *I'll just ride this wave,* he thought.

"Terrific!" Mickey exclaimed. Barrett would be chief technology officer. Within a couple months, Mickey and Brian would name as chief executive Darren Rennick, whom Barrett had met a few days earlier. Mickey called Darren "The Weasel" but insisted he was the right man for the job.

Darren, like Dayton Turner, was one of the many natives of gambling-friendly Canada who made the trek to Central America. He was big, friendly, and a bit goofy. He didn't carry himself with the same air of authority that Mickey and Brian did: Barrett found out later that his personal blog was titled "Big Dumb Kid." Though he came off like an overaged fraternity boy, Darren ran a major company in the betting industry, one called Digital Gaming Solutions. Based in the same building as BetCRIS and often called Digital Gaming (to avoid confusion with Brian's Internet access provider, Digital Solutions), it was one of the biggest sellers of software for gambling operations. Darren's programs conducted the electronic equivalent of casino games, including virtual roulette and slot machines, along with sports betting and poker. BetCRIS was one of its dozens of customers, and Brian and Mickey were Digital Gaming investors. Barrett didn't know it yet, but Darren had also been president of an older rival of Digital Gaming that had accused him of making off with its key software. Darren also had helped get another big Costa Rica bookmaker, BetonSports, off the ground.

Mickey had already gotten Barrett together with some of the other extortion victims in town, and now he and Brian helped make those men into customers. Barrett, meanwhile, concluded that there wasn't enough bandwidth in all of Costa Rica to absorb the attacks heading for the gambling sites, no matter how good he got at culling bad traffic. On January 12, he and Glenn Lebumfacil flew to Phoenix to set up a data center that would handle the Internet onslaught heading for BetCRIS and any new clients.

When the plane took off, Barrett's new company had one customer: BetCRIS. When the plane landed, it had a half dozen more, and Barrett had seventeen by the end of the first week. Even as Barrett was plugging in the computers, a San Jose bookmaker called VO-Group came under attack. The CEO tracked Barrett down on his cell phone. "How soon can you guys get going?" he begged. "I'm getting creamed!" Barrett realized there wasn't going to be any more college for a while. He dropped out of Cal State Sacramento just a semester shy of graduating and took to sleeping alongside the computers in Phoenix until he had them in the shape he needed. Two weeks went by before he could get back to Sacramento for more than a night at a time.

Barrett named his company Digital Defense International. After one of Mickey's people complained that there might be copyright issues with that word, Barrett came up with Prolexic Technologies Inc., a play on the word dyslexic. A Google search on Prolexic yielded zero hits, and the word captured Barrett's feelings that his dyslexia gave him an advantage, not a disadvantage. Barrett hired Glenn, Dayton, and a few others. Soon he needed more computing power. As a backup to the PureGig facility in Phoenix, which he knew from his Opte project, Barrett contracted for so-called domain name services from UltraDNS Corp., which managed the master computers that steered everyone looking for a site name ending in .org to the right numeric location. That proved a wise choice. In a final push, the hackers went after Barrett's clients' domain name servers in March 2004. After that onslaught failed, the hackers seemed to lose heart. On some days, their computers still sent thousands of times more hits than normal to BetCRIS. But the surges grew less and less frequent.

Unfortunately for Barrett, the same focus that supercharged his technological guile also left him with a bad case of tunnel vision. For all of his dedication in pursuing the bad guys, Barrett remained shockingly naïve about much in the business world, including the people he had chosen as partners. He didn't stop to think how they had come to be in their positions atop a questionable world of expat gambling pros. Rachelle thought the negatives were obvious. These people had moved to Costa Rica to get around U.S. laws, and anyone that dedicated to avoiding the rules was probably prone to cheat partners as well. But Rachelle and Barrett had only been dating a year, and he hadn't come to rely on her judgment when it came to other people. Barrett also had made it clear that he would choose his career over her. She couldn't count the number of times he had canceled dates in order to work. Besides, she didn't want to stand in his way. She kept her misgivings to herself. In Barrett's defense, the U.S. government hadn't caught up with reality. The rulebooks remained vague on whether citizens broke the law when they wagered overseas, and in any case the police arrested no one. Barrett was setting out to infiltrate the murderous and well-connected Russian mob, with only the murkiest of ideas about its danger. But he had already unwittingly penetrated the U.S. mafia, just as the two forces were accelerating their rivalry over which would reap the most massive spoils from the Internet. Through their offensive and defensive actions, the governments of both world powers would play major roles as well, raising the stakes to a level that intelligence officials would call an undeclared global war.

It was *WarGames* for real.

2

HaRdCORE
VS. EXE

THE ATTACKS ON BETCRIS trailed off early in 2004, granting Barrett Lyon a respite from the essentially constant hand-to-hand combat. He used the time to build the infrastructure to support a rapidly growing roster of clients needing protection. As the Super Bowl approached, virtual gambling houses inundated him with pleas for help. The extortionists would crash one site, then use it as a powerful argument to make others pay up. "We decided to take down some sites today so you understand how important it is for you to make a deal before it costs you more money and you start to lose customers," wcagain@ok.kz wrote to Heritage Sports from Kazakhstan. "Try going to www.jazzsports.com. . . . These are just a small example of the hundreds of sites that will be down this Sunday and Superbowl Sunday."

Barrett would take on a new customer and see if the digital dam he had set up would still hold. If not, he would rearrange his system to keep it functioning until he could get new equipment shipped to

PureGig in Phoenix. Once the gear arrived, he would fly to Arizona and spend however long it took to install it, making more than a dozen trips in a few months.

Barrett was winning. But in his heart, mounting a successful defense didn't feel like enough. The bad guys would just move on to weaker targets, raking in more cash and perhaps reinvesting it by rounding up new captive computers or better programmers. Thinking back to what he had done after helping Don Best, Barrett wondered if he could track the hackers at least partway to their lairs. He told Rachelle he wanted to look deeper, then turn over whatever he learned to the authorities. "Why can't you be happy with saving your customers?" she asked. Barrett reflected for a moment. Trying to do some good in the world was part of it, but that sounded ridiculous. So he told her with equal honesty: "It's an ego thing now. I want to beat these guys."

Barrett wasn't expecting any help from law enforcement. In 2004 very few U.S. hackers had been arrested, and the ones who had been caught were usually dumb teens who had broken into websites and then bragged about it on Internet Relay Chat channels, where officials could secretly track them by the nicknames they used to log on.

He had never heard of police arresting anyone for online extortion, and the bad guys most likely weren't in the U.S., making any prosecution orders of magnitude more difficult. Moreover, if they were hurting anyone in the country, it was mainly people breaking the law to gamble. Barrett called the FBI anyway. When he got an agent on the phone, he explained that at least some of the zombies used in the attacks on BetCRIS and his other customers were American. Beyond that, it was likely that the same machines would be used at some point to go after U.S. companies. The agent listened, asked a couple of pro forma questions, and thanked him for his time. This looked like it was going to be a solo job.

On those nights when he made it back home to Sacramento, Barrett would go back to thinking like a hacker. He studied infected machines and saw that the program that had infected them in-structed each machine to check back in with the attacker through the instant-messaging system ICQ, shorthand for "I seek you." Barrett lifted the ICQ address and messaged the hacker himself but got no response.

Then Barrett tried doing what he had done after the smaller as-sault on Don Best. He told Dayton Turner to check for zombies that were running Simple Network Management Protocol in the open. Once he found one, he could see where that machine had been con-necting. Sure enough, Dayton found an IRC server that was com-manding the army of robots. As in the previous attack, it was in Kazakhstan. Other robots, or "bots" for short, were reporting to IRC servers on the ironically named fbi.pp.ru and on mazafaka.ru, an ad-dress notorious for the hackers using it. Both names had the .ru end-ings designated for sites in Russia. Barrett pronounced the second address aloud. *At least these guys have a sense of humor,* he thought. From another infected machine, Barrett picked up a password that would allow him and Dayton to get into the Kazakhstan chat chan-nel. They joined and watched as hackers in the channel monitored attacks in progress against BetCRIS and other sites, including Microsoft.com. Barrett was tempted to call Microsoft and warn them, but he told himself he would do the software giant a bigger favor by staying focused and taking out its enemies.

Barrett and Dayton decided to see if they could learn about the assailant by going undercover. They crafted a character that they thought would have the most plausible reason for showing up, unin-vited, on a private chat channel on the other side of the world. They logged on as "hardcore," an imaginary hacker from Dayton's Vancou-ver hometown who had been out of the scene for a while. They made hardcore smart but not too smart. Hardcore would have a modest supply of bots under his own control, 250 or so, and be a decent virus writer interested in joining forces.

It helped that most hackers, especially those living abroad, had a well-deserved sense of impunity. Many governments didn't care if their citizens attacked foreigners, and even committed local authorities were ill equipped to handle technology-intensive investigations. Police in the West also lacked expertise, and they ran into all sorts of bureaucratic hurdles when they wanted to work undercover. As a private citizen, Barrett had no such issues.

Just to be on the safe side, he checked in again with the FBI. This time he got a visit from an agent in the Sacramento field office, Matthew Perry. Barrett showed the fortyish agent the chat channel and explained how the attackers used it to compare notes and to issue commands to the zombie computers. It was different from anything Perry had seen before, and he was enthusiastic about something so unusual for the Sacramento office. Looking over Barrett's shoulder, Perry asked what else he could learn. Barrett said he might be able to find out how big the ring was, how many zombies they controlled, and who else they were attacking. He would just have to lie in order to get into their world, and he would have to run traces and other programs the feds needed warrants for.

Perry said he couldn't sponsor anything illegal, but if it were for the greater good he wouldn't ask how Barrett got his information. Perry coached him on what he should try to get out of the hackers, and he gave Barrett an agency code name—Plato.

Some hacking groups overlapped, with freelancers working a job for one group and then another, so it wasn't unheard of to run across the trail of a fellow electronic criminal. When hardcore first logged on to the IRC channel, Barrett and Dayton saw that one member of the gang directing the robots used the online handle "eXe." That rang a bell: one piece of the code installed on an infected machine had included the title eXe. "hi," Dayton wrote to him in the channel. "yes, im here."

"are you from quakenet?" eXe responded, referring to another hacking group. Dayton paused, wondering if a false yes would expose him. So he hedged: "originally, ya." eXe started quizzing him in rough English, asking "what you doing here?" and "do you have your a bot?"

"I just came to see if this was still around . . . looks like the scripts have changed a little."

Other chatters were suspicious and hostile. "part plz our server," wrote a hacker using the handle "uhdfed." When hardcore didn't go, uhdfed launched a miniature denial-of-service that forced Dayton off the network. But Barrett and Dayton kept coming back. Depending on which of the hackers were logged on, they would chat for as long as several hours. They developed the best rapport with eXe. They offered to lend their own zombie computers to the crew's DDoS efforts and to improve the attack programs. "I could rewrite it," Barrett told eXe at one point. "I did it last semester in school for a test—just to see how fast I could scan large groups of machines."

Soon afterward, as he grew more comfortable with hardcore, eXe began making mistakes. He logged on from his home Internet service provider. A private file transfer gave away his true Internet address. The late-night conversations turned social—eXe asked for Britney Spears videos—and he let slip his real first name, Ivan, and that he was a twenty-one-year-old college student in Russia.

When Barrett told Perry what he was finding out, the agent didn't seem as excited as Barrett had hoped. All the same, Perry told Barrett he had to be sworn in, over the phone. "Sworn in for what?" Barrett asked. "To become an agent of the FBI," Perry told him. Not an FBI agent, mind you, but an agent of the agency. Someone else got on the line, and the officials recited the terms of their agreement. The point of it all was that Barrett was now clear to break the law, as long as he didn't get caught. Oh, and if it ever came up, the FBI would deny that it had any such deal. Overall, Barrett's experience with the FBI mirrored that of more established private security experts and, for that matter, the agency's allies in law enforcement: the communication went only in one direction, and there would be little to show for it.

• • •

IT WAS A DIFFERENT STORY with the authorities in Britain. They were interested enough in what Barrett was doing that they tracked him down before he'd even heard of them.

After testing the waters with the bookies in Latin America, the Russian gang had attacked similar companies based in England and Australia, where gambling firms are legal. Soon they or their rivals had hit almost every significant U.K. betting firm at least once, and the matter grew to be a top priority for the London-based National Hi-Tech Crime Unit.

While the U.S. was still floundering for an answer to technology crime, Prime Minister Tony Blair had made it a major emphasis. According to NHTCU Deputy Chief Mickey Deats, the Queen herself had realized the essential role that electronic commerce would play in the growth of the world economy. In the late 1990s she told Blair that she wanted England safe for online business, and that meant trying to get a modicum of control of the Internet. Even if the inherently risky architecture of the Net presented a monumental technological challenge, Blair saw no reason to give up on law enforcement.

In September 1999, as the dot-com boom was in full swing, Blair's office issued a report declaring that the government would strive to make the United Kingdom "the best environment in the world for e-commerce." It recommended that the country establish an Internet crime unit to fight fraud and hacking. The NHTCU came into being in April 2001 as an offshoot of the National Crime Squad, which took the top-rated 5 percent of local police detectives for seven-year assignments.

In October 2003 the elite unit fielded a call from Canbet Ltd., an Australian-owned betting company in the southern English city of Portsmouth that was experiencing a DDoS attack. While working the Canbet case, the agents discovered what Barrett had done to protect companies from similar assaults. One emailed Barrett out of the blue, asking if they could send someone across the Atlantic to "chat."

Three NHTCU agents flew to Los Angeles to meet Barrett. They included Bob Lewis, a former Royal Air Force noncommissioned officer; Andy Robbins, a computer forensics man; and Mat Proud, a white man with brown dreadlocks and serious technical expertise. Proud looked even less like a cop than Barrett did, and Barrett guessed he was on loan from British intelligence.

Two FBI agents hosted the get-together. They explained that the bureaucratic framework for international cooperation required Barrett to give his information to U.S. officials, who could pass it along. When the FBI agents made it clear that they were only there to facilitate, Barrett was again disappointed by their lack of enthusiasm.

Lewis immediately surprised Barrett by saying that the NHTCU had a different sense of mission. Yes, they wanted to punish the bad guys. But whether they succeeded or failed in that attempt, they also had a "duty of care" to protect U.K. citizens and businesses—a goal they could pursue through advocating policy changes or education campaigns. Their first job in any case was to learn as much as they could about what was happening. "We're here," Lewis continued, "because we want to make sure that England is the technology center of Europe. The Queen has decided that the U.K. will be one of the top players in information technology, and any threat to that is a direct threat to England." Barrett saw one of the FBI men rolling his eyes, but he felt instantly in tune with the Brits. They reciprocated by insisting he remain in town overnight, paying the fees to change his airline ticket and treating him to a hotel room.

Barrett outlined what he had learned about the technical aspects of the extortion ring and what he was getting from his first chats with eXe. He kept the NHTCU agents updated by email afterward as his team tracked attacks to new servers and as the types of assaults morphed. The British agents urged Barrett and Dayton to get the nicknames of as many people in the chat channel as possible, along with any clues to their physical location. At the end of February 2004, Barrett turned in more than thirty pages of analysis and IRC transcripts. He gave the paper a title designed to get law enforcement to pay attention: "DDoS Terrorism Report."

Like the FBI, the U.K. agents couldn't make free use of common hacking tools, such as the scanners that look for openings into computers, and they were careful not to advise Barrett to use them. Instead, the British said they would gladly accept any information and wouldn't press too hard to learn how it had come to them. In one email telling Barrett that his captured code had led them to a new chat server, Proud added: "The powers that be ask me to remind you that we can only use stuff that's legally obtained in our investigation ;-)," closing with a winking smiley face. Proud said nothing about what Barrett could use in his own probe.

• • •

THE ULTIMATE "GOTCHA" CAME shortly after the L.A. meeting, when eXe was chatting on another IRC network that Barrett monitored. Barrett looked up eXe's profile information on that network and saw a private email address for the hacker. That address ended with "security-system.cc." Hoping to get lucky, Barrett checked the registration records for the domain "www.security-system.cc." It listed a Russian company Barrett had never heard of as the site's owner. Then lightning struck: the records also listed the full name and address of a contact person at the company—a contact person named Ivan. Barrett couldn't believe it. His enemy had bought a vanity website and used his real identity. It was like robbing a bank and going out and buying a sports car the next day. It would have made sense only if Ivan had intended to start a legitimate business with the new site.

"eXe made a HUGE mistake!" Barrett informed the Hi-Tech unit and the FBI in an email March 13. He pasted in the goods from the Web address tied to the private email account.

Registrant:
Fizitheskoe lico
Maksakov Ivan
30 let pobedi 45 43
Balakovo, Saratovska 413864
RU
+7.8453323464
Email: x3m1st@bk.ru

The email handle was hacker license-plate-speak for "extremist." That was within shouting distance of the nickname eXe.

The NHTCU forwarded Barrett's coup to an agent in Moscow, who would use it to press the Russians for action. The Russians had already traced the Balakovo server to an Ivan Maksakov.

Even then, Barrett didn't expect much to come of it. He thought it was cool that he had figured out who the bad guy was, and that at least the United Kingdom cared enough to send a man to Russia. After the handoff, he would occasionally hear from the NHTCU guys by phone or email. They wanted to get new lists of IP addresses, to check on technical questions, or get Barrett's guesses about the roles of the other people in the chats. They were upbeat about how the case was progressing, but it dragged on and on.

A year later, Russian media broke the news that Maksakov and two other men had been arrested.

3

IN TOO deep

As the U.K.'s Hi-Tech unit followed the trail in Russia, Barrett was up to his neck in a different adventure.

On his return trips to Costa Rica during 2004, Barrett was treated not as a valued contractor but as a full-fledged business partner. The bookies welcomed him deeper into the inner circle of his new sponsor, Mickey Richardson. They came to trust him, blabbing over drinks about things outsiders never learned—like the fact that Mickey's real name was Mickey Flynn III. Much of the Costa Rica gambling crowd, it turned out, had one name up north and another where it was warm. Many had women, even wives, arranged the same way.

Originally from Pennsylvania, Mickey had been in Central America for years, working his way up in the business. Barrett got the sense that he wanted to make it so big that he could return home in triumph, impressing old-timers like his dad, Mickey Flynn Jr., the son of a county commissioner. Flynn Jr. served in the Navy and worked in a steel mill before buying the Union Grill in Washington, Pennsylvania, during the 1960s. That restaurant became a landmark in the town not far from Pittsburgh, serving college students and the local political elite alike. Flynn even had photos on the wall of Bill Clinton eating lunch. But Flynn accepted bets there as well, and he was moving more than $1 million in wagers every month.

Mickey's men told tales about their pasts, celebrating themselves as risk-takers and sometimes including run-ins with the law. They often fell into what Barrett thought of as wiseguy routines, tributes to mafia movies they all seemed to have watched over and over. Once an older visitor came from the U.S. and was welcomed with great respect and the honorific title "Don." Barrett believed it was all in fun.

While Barrett was a "white hat" security hacker, as those in the trade called crime-fighters, he still had the disrespect for authority that predominates among hackers on either side of the law. He liked elements of the Costa Rica crew's attitude. But a few of the tales nagged at him. Mickey, it emerged, had been a bookie during his college years in New York. In some of his stories he was in fights; in others he had gone to jail. Mickey told one about how he had been drinking in public during a spring break trip to Coney Island. When the cops told him to throw the booze away, Mickey took off running instead. The police gave chase, beat him, and dragged him off to jail. His father refused to bail him out, Mickey said with pride.

Prolexic's other big investor, Brian Green, didn't drink, and he appeared to be a recovering alcoholic. In his wilder days, he said, he'd been passed out in a gutter in the Dominican Republic when a local beauty queen named Daisy rescued him. Her family helped him get back on his feet before they married and moved to Costa Rica. Brian came across as aggressive, ready to jump into anything. One story he told involved a man who cut him off on the highway. Brian chased him, bumped the other car until it pulled over, then kicked the door in and slugged the man. Brian thought that was hilarious.

Barrett mulled over what stories he could tell on himself, and came up only with his teenaged hack of Network Solutions, the one that shut down AOL.com and Disney.com. Somehow it didn't measure up. An uneasy feeling began to bubble inside Barrett, one that said he didn't belong with this particular strain of rebels, as entertaining as they might be.

While Brian didn't operate any betting endeavors directly, he was a gambler of some repute himself. He would often leave Digital Solutions in the care of his partner and disappear for a few days—either for sex trips to the Philippines and other locales or to compete in major poker tournaments. Brian played several times a year and on occasion walked off with more than $100,000. He won the April 2001 Limit Hold 'Em event at Jack Binion's World Poker Open, getting four clubs among the five shared face-up cards to complete a queen-high flush on the final hand. A year and a half later, he won another limit tournament at the Bellagio Five Diamond World Poker Classic, finishing off his last opponent with a pair of jacks.

Of the scores of competitors in such tournaments, only Brian was calculating the size of his entry fee in $25,000 Lucent telecommunication switches, which he needed to keep building out Digital Solutions. He would return bragging that he had won several switches' worth of cash, or gloomily complaining that he had lost as much.

Barrett got bits and pieces of Brian's story over many months. The most relevant part seemed to be that Brian was lucky to be alive—that at one point there had been a contract reported out on his life. Brian said he had been helping out at an old-school sportsbook after one of the owners died and the other went to prison. The one in prison thought Brian had tried to sell the company out from under him and "some people from New York helped" by explaining Brian was only trying to pay off gamblers who had gotten stiffed. Brian admitted to doing "a lot of drugs" in those days, and he made other enemies as well, including a Central American bookie named Steve D. Budin.

Brian had helped set up communications for Budin's SDB Global in Panama. The second-generation bookie had moved offshore with the approval of his backers in Brooklyn. Brian installed expensive multiplex machines to handle large numbers of toll-free calls. The equipment didn't function as promised, and Budin suspected Brian was up to something else.

Budin strong-armed one of Brian's assistants, who thought he was going to be killed. The assistant blurted out that Brian was designing software to siphon money away to extra-fortunate bettors. "It was going to be a back door that allowed you to put in bets after the game has started," a time-honored scam known as past posting, Budin said in an interview. Brian said he hadn't planned on stealing anything, but his life improved after he allied with the people at BetCRIS. It didn't hurt when Budin was swept up in a 1998 federal gambling indictment that also named several other offshore bookies. After Budin's father was arrested, Budin returned to the U.S., pleaded guilty to a reduced charge, and remained in his home country.

The stories were scary, but the worst ones seemed anchored in the past. Brian was sober now, with the possible exception of his sordid vacations, and presumably had cleaned up his business dealings as well. Besides, Barrett thought, he had to have his act pretty well together in order to win as much as he did in poker tournaments.

• • •

IN PRINCIPLE, BARRETT DIDN'T HAVE a problem with gambling on cards or sports. But the more he saw in the San Jose building, the happier he was not to be participating himself. Some of the bettors on the other end of the transactions were down big. The really high rollers got through to Mickey when they called. Everyone was identified by an account number to preserve confidentiality. But when someone picked up the line and shouted out that one of a handful of numbers was calling, everyone knew who it was. Actor Bruce Willis, Barrett learned, had lost millions of dollars.

Many of those working the phones and manning the website had been traditional bookies back home. Part of that job was getting tough with losers who didn't pay up. There was some talk of cars that had blown up, taking bettors with them. The people inside Mickey's organization carried some risk as well, depending on their job descriptions. The street-level employees in the U.S. were known as agents. The agents sent cash to Costa Rica and collected cash from there by way of runners, who often physically traveled back and forth. The agents acted like bookies, but they carried no risk as long as they followed the odds set out by the company. More accurately, they carried no risk in the ordinary sense of having to pay out more than they took in. The risk came with the extension of credit, which many of the betting houses did not offer. The rougher firms, including BetCRIS and one called Casablanca, did allow clients to get in the hole. And the agents could get in trouble for giving too much credit. If they allowed a bettor who was way down to make a new gamble on credit, and that bet won big—the bettor was out of the hole, and the agent might be held accountable for giving him the chance.

On the sports side of BetCRIS, players in most of the professional leagues were betting on their own games. The company didn't do much to hide that, stating on its website: "whether you are in business, politics, professional sports, or the movie industry, it is our professional obligation to keep the details of our client's financial and personal affairs strictly private." Once an insider wagered, the bookies knew how to bet themselves. As Darren Rennick explained it to Barrett, sports stars often bet against themselves. Then Mickey would adjust the line on the odds and secretly bet the same way as the athlete at other, unsuspecting sportsbooks.

In the increasingly popular electronic poker and casino games, much of the play seemed harmless for non-addicts. The new games were wonderful for the sportsbooks, though, because they could be played at any time, while betting on sporting events built toward a specific date and hour. BetCRIS and others urged winning sports bettors to try their luck at the poker tables, where they often lost everything back. "It's a playground for degenerates," Mickey said approvingly of the newfangled games. Free-standing electronic casinos could have the same rough methods for collecting debts that the sportsbooks did.

There was another catch to playing poker or the slots. With a football game, everyone could tell who won and who lost. In card games, the players were relying on the companies to tell them who had "received" which cards. Costa Rica and other favored countries regulated little if at all, and the companies relied on software from a few suppliers, including Darren's Digital Gaming. The poker outlets pledged that they were depending on random-number generators to keep the game fair. But true random numbers are surprisingly hard to manufacture. When Barrett asked Darren how exactly Digital Gaming spat out those figures, Darren would mumble a nonsensical answer. In any case, there was nothing to stop a company from ignoring a preselected hand and simply replacing it with a better one.

Darren had been around the scene for years. He had been an executive at BetonSports and at publicly traded software company IQ-Ladorum. After he left that firm and started Digital Gaming, IQ-Ladorum sued the new company in Costa Rica's courts, accusing it of stealing IQ-Ladorum's code for running casino games. The legal system in Costa Rica worked differently from that in the U.S. One day when Barrett was working in the Prolexic offices, on the third floor of the San Jose building, Darren came running up, yelling that Digital Gaming was being raided on the floor below. More amused than alarmed, Barrett wandered down to see the local equivalent of the FBI standing around with machine guns. They also had great-looking hats. Barrett complimented one of the agents on his, then offered to buy it. The cop was not amused, and Barrett realized the situation wasn't funny after all. *Those are machine guns*, he thought. *This is real.* The raid stemmed from the IQ-Ladorum suit. But nothing came of the raid or the civil case, and Barrett heard later that some of the government officials had been paid off. After that, a spooked Darren got more involved in Prolexic and less involved in Digital Gaming.

Barrett divided his time between countries, working a week or two in San Jose and then a month or more in the U.S. With Mickey's blessing, Barrett leased office space for Prolexic in Sacramento, where Rachelle was still in school. Barrett thought he got a great deal on the property. Some of his new hires lived in the area, while the others could work remotely. Soon, however, Darren and the others started pressuring Barrett to move the company. They scouted locations in L.A. and in Chicago, where Barrett was speaking at a security conference.

Mickey had introduced Barrett to many of the men atop the offshore gambling fraternity, so it didn't seem unusual when he asked Barrett to meet one more during a trip to Los Angeles— Ron Sacco, who he said had founded BetCRIS a long time ago. Sacco had a thoroughbred horse ranch outside L.A. and was clearly a big success. Darren set up a dinner for the three of them at a top steak house in Beverly Hills. Barrett, being poorly briefed in more ways than one, showed up wearing his usual flip-flops. The maître d' had no intention of letting him inside, until Barrett mentioned whom he was meeting. Then he was ushered to Sacco's private table in the back.

Sacco was an eccentric with wild, curly white hair, hazel eyes, a gold tooth, and a laugh that came out the side of his mouth. At six foot one and 190 pounds, Sacco was probably an imposing presence a lot of the time. But the oddball way he carried himself reminded

Barrett of actor Will Ferrell's impression of Harry Caray, the old Cubs announcer. Still, Barrett could tell Sacco had something on the ball. He said he had checked Barrett out by calling his nephew, who by an odd coincidence had been Barrett's college rowing coach. Over their steaks, Sacco said his father had been a San Francisco barber. Now here he was in his sixties, talking about a potential new phase of his entrepreneurial career, opening physical casinos in Costa Rica and Mexico. And then there was the Opus One wine and his personal booth in the steak house: pretty impressive, especially after Darren pointed out Jennifer Aniston at the next table.

Barrett asked how he had happened to hand off BetCRIS to Mickey. Sacco paused for a second, then said he had been jailed for a time over a tax issue. Mickey was running another bookmaking operation, YaBet, at the time, and Sacco asked Mickey to handle BetCRIS in his absence. He had done a great job. Mickey built the operation's website up from almost nothing to the source of more than half of BetCRIS revenue, and Sacco said he now considered Mickey a son. As the meal wound down, Barrett asked Sacco for some advice about the business world. "Just work hard," Sacco told him, "and don't let anyone take it away." Then he sped off in his Porsche convertible.

● ● ●

AS BARRETT HIRED MORE STAFF and bought more machines, the bills started coming in, and he still hadn't seen any of the $250,000 that Mickey and Brian Green were supposed to be investing. They wired offshore money directly to a few big vendors, but Prolexic needed a bank account of its own in the U.S.

His backers wouldn't even let Barrett get a corporate credit card. That was a real problem, because Barrett couldn't get a regular card himself. Years before, a thief had broken into Barrett's condo and taken checks and other documents. Barrett soon became one of the 9 million U.S. residents victimized by identity theft each year. He filed a police report and negotiated with bill collectors who would learn that Barrett wasn't responsible for a given debt, then just resell the job to another collector. Having done nothing wrong, Barrett still hadn't earned his way back to credit-worthy status in the eyes of the rating bureaus. In a rising panic, Barrett asked Mickey again and again for the money to pay Prolexic's bills.

After hearing Barrett plead poverty one too many times, Mickey gave him a phone number and told him to call a man named Maurice. Barrett didn't know whether Maurice was a banker, an accountant, or something else, but he called right away. The conversation was a lot shorter than Barrett had anticipated. "Do you know the Good Guys store behind the Serramonte mall, south of San Francisco?" Maurice asked. Barrett said he did. "Meet me in the parking lot at 2 o'clock."

Barrett agreed, but he didn't like the feeling he was getting. As Barrett waited in the nearly empty lot, Maurice pulled up in a battered old Lincoln, made sure it was Barrett he was talking to, and handed over a manila envelope with a brick of money inside. Barrett hadn't imagined getting his business funded more or less directly by gamblers' losses, and he felt like a rube. He quickly ran through the alternatives to taking the envelope. Barrett had employees to pay and company expenses that rivaled his mortgage. He didn't know any venture capitalists who could invest. *I'm just some guy in Sacramento with no money and no credit*, he thought. *I owe people and the network is crashing. Besides, how do I say no at this point without getting killed?*

Barrett felt he was in too deep to do anything else. His business was legitimate and doing well, and that's what he focused on. Barrett still didn't see that in addition to its potentially profitable work warding off the Russian mob, Prolexic was valuable to Mickey and his crew for a more basic reason: as a means to launder gambling proceeds back into the U.S.

Barrett took the money and went shopping for a safe.

After Darren's wife lost her purse in an L.A. mugging, his interest in moving Prolexic there evaporated. Chicago didn't generate much enthusiasm for the gambling crowd either. Instead they urged Barrett to take a look with them in south Florida, where Mickey and Brian had just spent time on the yacht of Sean "Diddy" Combs, who Barrett guessed was a BetCRIS customer. After Barrett objected that the company would struggle to get top-notch job candidates and technology partners in Florida, his patrons decided to show him a good time.

Mickey, Brian, Darren, and Barrett all took thousand-dollar rooms at the trendy five-star Shore Club on Miami's South Beach in September 2004. In case the layout wasn't enough to convince Barrett he was on to a good thing, the executives treated him to massages and room service. He had automatic entrée into Skybar, the hotel's hot nightclub, past scores of people lined up to get in. Barrett had to walk through another nightclub filled with models just to get to his room.

Outside by the pool, the group lounged in cabanas with large beds while waitresses served them. One night, Mickey and Brian decided to take the fun further. Both married with children, they went off with $2,000-an-hour prostitutes while Barrett and Darren stayed behind and talked. *Not my kind of people*, Barrett thought again, but the scenery sure was nice. Darren told Barrett that the company was moving to Florida, period. Barrett figured that sooner or later, Darren and Mickey would realize that it was a mistake. But Mickey and his crew were interested in Florida as a way station for flights from Costa Rica. It was perfect for them in other ways too, Barrett later concluded. It had U.S. amenities, but the rules and the women were almost as loose as those in Costa Rica.

Within weeks, Barrett and Darren found an office in Hollywood, Florida, and hired contractors to set it up. Barrett moved Glenn Lebumfacil and Dayton to the new offices, along with his former Sacramento neighbor Joe Daly. Networking specialist Terry Rodery joined later and was amazed that such a small group defended so many companies against ever-growing firepower. That wasn't by Barrett's choice: he just couldn't get Darren to spend what Barrett wanted him to on staff and equipment.

As the months passed in Florida, Barrett had more time to chat with Darren about Brian and Mickey. One day Darren warned Barrett that both of their patrons would likely be jumpy and unpredictable for the next few weeks. When Barrett asked why, Darren explained that Ron Sacco had won permission from the court to return to Costa Rica.

"So what?" Barrett asked. "I thought Sacco had handed off BetCRIS to Mickey?"

"Oh," Darren replied. "Maybe that's the official story. But not really."

Sacco still owned it, Darren explained. That included BetCRIS itself, and whatever it invested in Darren's Digital Gaming software company—and presumably what it put into Prolexic as well. That fancy party room atop the Hive in Costa Rica? That was Sacco's office. As a matter of fact, Mickey's gated mansion, the one where Barrett and Rachelle had celebrated New Year's Eve, was Sacco's too.

For all any of them knew, Sacco would come back, kick Mickey out of the house, and fire everyone at BetCRIS. "He could do anything." Darren said. "He does kooky things."

Barrett felt queasy. No wonder Sacco wanted to meet him. Now he remembered that Sacco had done multiple stints in jail, for what had been described to him as petty crimes and tax screwups. Even now, though, Barrett didn't peer too deeply into the mouth of the gift horse. He didn't so much as conduct a thorough Google search on the man who appeared to have been running the show the whole time. Now that he had gone this far, he just didn't want to know.

● ● ●

IF HE HAD DONE SOME DIGGING, Barrett might have discovered that the FBI had identified Sacco more than a decade earlier as the largest single bookmaker in the U.S.—and one enjoying the protection of the Gambino crime family, for many years the most powerful and feared of New York's five major mafia clans.

Sacco was born in 1943, grew up in San Francisco, and attended Balboa High School. Back then, people gambled the old-fashioned way, handing cash to the local bookies in bars, union halls, and barbershops like the one his dad worked in. Sacco's rap sheet would eventually boast more than a dozen convictions, almost all related to gambling. The arrests stretched back at least as far as 1970.

Known as "The Cigar," Sacco had no shortage of mob contacts. Sacco's Los Angeles operation was run for years by Kale Kalustian, who took bets from the likes of Frank Sinatra and movie studio owner Marvin Davis. Kalustian's less appetizing contacts included a New York mafia transplant indicted in 1978 for the murder of made man Frank Bompensiero. Sacco's business partners in the Bay Area included Bobby Stapleton, who had multiple ties to the Gambinos back east.

Sacco's big move came in the early 1980s, when Tony Spilotro, the Chicago mob's muscle in Las Vegas and the model for Joe Pesci's bloodthirsty character in the movie *Casino*, was trying to consolidate West Coast bookies. With Spilotro's apparent blessing, FBI agent Joe Davidson told an informant, "He became THE bookmaker." Spilotro was later murdered, and Sacco went independent for a time before settling down with the Gambinos, the FBI believes. By 1988 Sacco was handling $1 million in bets a day through offices in Las Vegas and East Los Angeles.

Sacco had grown too notorious to stay in the U.S. without constant surveillance and frequent jail time. But he figured out how to get customer-friendly 800 numbers to ring inside the Dominican Republic in the late 1980s, so he moved there and started the company that would become BetCRIS.

Things went well for Sacco in the Dominican, as the expats called it, largely because the corruption made business so much easier. Sacco soon had a mainframe computer and forty phone lines to handle calls from Las Vegas. Players respected his operation for paying out on even the largest bets. Employees in the U.S. collected wagers and dispensed winnings, while those in Central America got paid with the arrival of overnight packages of magazines that had $100 bills stapled inside. The math was easy. A good operation would collect a 10 percent fee on payouts. As long as he kept the point spread moving, so that bets were evenly balanced on both sides of a game, Sacco couldn't lose.

Sacco was never convicted of mob charges, and his lawyers always denied that he was the mafia's man. But Sacco processed more bets than anyone else in the U.S.—eventually some $100 million a month—and the FBI said his collection efforts in a dozen big American cities would have been impossible without mob backing. "Sacco was just a front man," said Jim Moody, former head of the FBI's organized crime squad. Overall, Moody said, gambling was the mafia's largest single source of money.

Steve Budin said that in general, bookies immigrated to Latin America to avoid having to pay off the mob as well as to avoid the police. The mob would have real power over those in Costa Rica only if they still had homes in the U.S. or made in-person collections there. After it was pointed out that both criteria applied in Sacco's case, Budin paused. "I wouldn't argue" that mob connections were a prerequisite to reaching the heights that Sacco did, Budin said. He wasn't just another guy in the business. "He was the original. He was like Christopher Columbus."

After his business alliances, the biggest factor in Sacco's success was his commitment to new technology. But experts assisting with Sacco's upgrades repeatedly betrayed him. In the 1970s, the feds picked up one "phone man"—a specialist in making operations harder to trace through calling records—and the man squealed. A decade later, Sacco hired Fred Valis and Dan Hanks as technicians and cash runners. Unfortunately for him, Valis and Hanks were professional informants who had set up narcotics deals for the Drug Enforcement Agency, tapped Heidi Fleiss's phone for a competitor, and sold a list of jurors in O. J. Simpson's murder trial to the tabloids. They promptly went to the FBI and asked to double up with government salaries while they served as moles.

Sacco's henchmen bragged to Hanks about double-crossers getting bludgeoned to death, and he came close to meeting the same fate. After a bitter ex-girlfriend ratted Hanks out, Sacco's men fished around in Hanks's home mailbox and found his phone bill. They dialed the 415 number they saw listed most often and reached the San Francisco office of the FBI. Fortunately, the thugs went to Valis with their accusations. "Prove it to me, and I'll kill him myself," Valis said. A Bay Area newspaper reporter helpfully published a fictional article about a body turning up, and Sacco thought Hanks dead until he showed up in court more than a year later.

The FBI brought an indictment and convinced the Dominican authorities that Sacco's ring was violating their laws as well. More than a dozen employees were arrested in January 1992, and seized records gave the feds a good look inside the operation. But the ever-generous Sacco himself was not arrested. Instead, Sacco gave an interview to *60 Minutes*, describing Valis and Hanks as "two pieces of puke." Asked directly, he also acknowledged fielding an offer to handle bets for John Gotti's Gambinos. "I don't want to talk about that," he stammered. The media splash may have been too much for the U.S. and Dominican authorities to put up with. Later, Sacco would complain that the problem with the Dominican was that there was actually too much corruption. First one man wanted a payoff, then his brother would come, then still more relatives. In 1993, Dominican police finally arrested Sacco at a high-end resort. They put him on a plane to the closest U.S. territory, Puerto Rico, where marshals awaited. Sacco pleaded guilty in 1994 and did a five-year stint.

Sacco's operation moved to Costa Rica while he was in jail, and he joined it there on his release. The reunion was brief. On a trip back to the U.S. in 2000, Sacco was picked up for money laundering and gambling. He got out after twenty-one months, in January 2004, when BetCRIS paid his fine. Identifying him as a "consultant," the company later told the court Sacco would return to Costa Rica to work at Darren's Digital Gaming. Under the terms of his release, it was important that Sacco not be connected to BetCRIS. But he was still calling the shots there, at times even answering Mickey's private phone number.

• • •

DESPITE THE MOUNTING EVIDENCE before him, Barrett was, like most Americans, oblivious to the ways in which the U.S. mob had bent the Internet to serve its own ends.

The Five Families had experimented with identity theft and Web fraud, but Internet betting was the easiest payoff. As the most powerful of the old-school mob men who came up through street bookmaking, Sacco was in prime position when cable television sent the poker game Texas Hold 'Em into millions of American living rooms. Some shows featured closely watched celebrities like Ben Affleck playing cards, while others helped create new celebrities: amateurs such as the improbably named Chris Moneymaker, who paid $39 to start playing in a tournament feeder game online at PokerStars.com and made it to the top in Las Vegas. Moneymaker's $2.5 million win in the 2003 World Series of Poker drove millions to their computers to join in. Annual online poker revenue soared from $90 million in 2002 to $2.4 billion in 2005. With poker illegal outside of regulated casinos, organized crime just followed the money. BetCRIS and other outfits already handling sports bets overseas simply added poker software from the likes of Darren Rennick.

A younger generation of fraudsters got to the same place after cutting their teeth on other tech-related cons. They moved to the Caribbean or Central America, skipped sports, and went straight to Web poker and other casino games. By far the biggest poker company would be PartyPoker, a runaway success that would take half the available market. While it would come to be valued in the billions of dollars, that company had leaders trained in mob scams or mass fraud.

One such training course was at the side of reputed Gambino soldier Richard Martino. His operation ran from the early 1990s until 2002, raking in $650 million with phone and Internet scams, the biggest haul in Gambino family history. The Martino racket went through several iterations as law enforcement cracked down on its techniques. It installed rogue "dialers" on home computers that called expensive overseas numbers. For a time, companies in the scheme also stuck consumers with unwarranted phone charges through 800 numbers. A later Web version of the scam was much simpler, an early system for credit card fraud. Internet visitors were asked to supply a credit card number proving they were eighteen in order to get free tours of membership porn sites—including HighSociety.com, Cheri.com, and Playgirl.com—owned by a company named Crescent Publishing Inc. Then they were charged as much as $90 a month by a revolving cast of businesses with names unrelated to the sites.

After hundreds of consumer protests, the Federal Trade Commission sued Crescent in August 2000. But the full extent of the scheme didn't emerge until federal prosecutors brought criminal charges in 2003 and filed a more comprehensive indictment in 2005. The second indictment named Martino, alleged Gambino captain Salvatore Lo-Cascio, and four Gambino associates. Facing insider testimony, all pleaded guilty.

Though he was not named in the court filings, Yishai Habari, a major traffic broker to porn websites, almost certainly was involved in the fraud. Along with the indicted Harvest Advertising, Habari's WebMedia Interactive Inc. sought to bring Web surfers to Crescent websites, according to officials, employees, and porn publishers. Habari directed projects at the Martino operation, employees said, and his company and Harvest were based on the same floor of the same building in New York. "It was my feeling that they were one and the same," said the FTC's lead attorney on the case. A Crescent employee from before the FTC case said Habari was a significant part of the operation at least as far back as 1999. She asked not to be named out of concern for her physical safety. In late 2000, San Francisco businessman Gary Kremen and attorney Charles Carreon flew to meet Habari and negotiate whether he would steer visitors to Kremen's Sex.com. After a sushi lunch, Habari took them to meet with Martino, and Carreon said it was clear that Martino was in charge of their business.

Because the FTC suit didn't extend much beyond Crescent, Martino and Habari continued to operate with relative freedom for some time. Investigators who worked on the case said they were most concerned about working upward and arresting the full-fledged Gambino mobsters collecting money from the scam. All the same, Habari left the country as the probe accelerated.

While he might have had reason to worry about the law, Habari had no reason to worry about money. He could deliver Web surfers to the sites that were willing to pay. For that reason, he had been popular in the world of Internet porn, and some of his friends and associates were now moving from porn to poker, where their sites also needed high-volume traffic.

• • •

AMONG THE CONVERTS WAS Habari's old friend Ruth Parasol, who was on her way to becoming the richest self-made American woman. More than anyone else's, Parasol's path to epic riches illustrates the Internet's windfall potential for a post-Sacco generation unconcerned with moral issues.

In high school, even her friends called her Ruthie Ruthless. Her prep school in Marin County, the wealthy, wooded enclave just across the Golden Gate Bridge from San Francisco, was filled with characters. There were plenty of richer kids, several teens from famous families, and some close to the raven-haired Parasol's league in great looks. But the laid-back style in most of the cliques at Marin Academy was to play down one's natural intelligence and camouflage material ambition.

Not Ruthie Ruthless. One of the most polarizing figures there, she didn't give a damn who knew she was on the make or what they thought of her. She proved it in the way she designed her page for the 1984 senior yearbook. Others chose casual pictures of themselves cavorting with friends, listing all the great memories they would carry forward from high school. Parasol picked a single photo of herself in jewelry, furs, and full makeup, offering a pout just short of a sneer. Underneath, she wrote her caption: "Diamonds are a girl's best friend."

Parasol got her brash attitude, as she would her start in business, from her flamboyant father, Rick. A heavyset Holocaust survivor, Rick developed federally subsidized housing for the poor but preferred the ostentatious good life for himself. He rode around San Francisco Bay in a noisy speedboat named "Rude," joined by topless women he found on the Internet, irritating the more circumspect members of the upper class. All the while, he was married to an understanding Swedish housewife. Family life "was like an Ingmar Bergman movie and a Woody Allen movie at the same time, with a little Hugh Hefner thrown in," said Ruth Parasol's youngest sister, Ricarda, who went on to front a goth-rock band.

Rick Parasol's serious money came from phone sex lines. Ruth followed him into the family business, joining a variety of allied phone scammers who, like Mickey Richardson and Ron Sacco, were second-generation hustlers. After graduating from the University of San Francisco and arming herself with a law degree from Western State University, Parasol and her father teamed up in the 1990s with Ian Eisenberg, a Seattle king of the phone-sex business. The FTC sued Eisenberg in 2000 for running a fake "rebate" check scam in which tiny print on a $3.50 check said that by cashing the check, the recipients agreed to make Eisenberg's company their Internet service provider for as much as $29.95 a month. Ruth Parasol advised Ian Eisenberg and his companies, which took in $27 million before the FTC stopped the scam. Then Parasol funded an associate turned rival of his, Seth Warshavsky.

Ruth Parasol and Warshavsky invested millions in phone-sex companies that were sued by North Carolina and Nevada for improper billing and collection practices, such as threatening to seize the home of a woman in her sixties who denied making any calls. Beset with scams, the U.S. barred phone companies from cutting off customers who refused to pay 900-number bills. The Parasols and Warshavsky stayed one jump ahead of the law, moving quickly to put porn on the less-regulated Web. Quietly funded in part by the Parasols, Warshavsky became the best-known operator of Web porn through his Internet Entertainment Group. He bragged of the first widely accessible live sex shows on the Web and distributed the famous sex video made by Pamela Anderson and rocker Tommy Lee.

Ruth Parasol co-founded IEG, according to a close associate, but made sure her name stayed out of the papers. That fit a lifelong pattern of using her legal knowledge and smarts to plot in the shadows: she has never granted a media interview in her life. Warshavsky defrauded many of his business partners, and several former employees accused him of routinely overbilling customers. Ruth Parasol made sure she wasn't one of his victims. By 1996 the Parasol family owned 49 percent of Warshavsky's business, and they sued him, claiming he reneged on an agreement to buy out the family's share. Before Warshavksy's scheme collapsed, Ruth negotiated a favorable settlement in 1997. "She got a good deal," according to an attorney involved in the talks. "She got their dough out and moved on down the road." Facing massive debts and a criminal probe, Warshavsky eventually fled to Thailand.

•   •   •

ONCE AGAIN, PARASOL MOVED AHEAD of the curve. She read up on gambling law, consulted some of the top experts in the field, and figured out that online casinos could probably operate safely in other countries while taking money from gamblers in the U.S., where most betting was prohibited. The same year she got the settlement money out of Warshavsky, Parasol set up her first online poker business, Starluck Casino, which would grow into the multibillion-dollar sensation PartyGaming Plc., the parent of PartyPoker.

By 2001 Ruth Parasol's Caribbean casinos said they were handling 3 million visitors a day. But the combined company known as IGlobalMedia had also attracted complaints, especially about the house's frequent wins at blackjack and its roulette promotions, which offered double payouts for anyone betting on a single number.

Mysteriously, customers said, they would never win with that number, even if they played hundreds of times. After a while, the ranks of Parasol critics grew to include industry opinion leaders like Las Vegas actuary and casino consultant Michael Shackleford, also known as the Wizard of Odds. "My results clearly showed they weren't fair," Shackleford said. IGlobalMedia executives didn't deny it, instead saying they had changed their ways. "We recently had our software developers run analysis on our games, and they did find some bugs and they have corrected them," Chief Operations Officer Mario Wells wrote to a mathematician who complained.

The big breakthrough for Parasol was her early realization that Texas Hold 'Em could erupt in popularity. "IGlobalMedia casinos were low budget and not very reputable, but they made a good decision to go into the poker market while it was still young," Shackelford said. "Kind of like eBay, they cornered the market."

With card games, PartyPoker didn't have to cheat. It took a small percentage of every pot, known as the rake. That made it the only sure winner in every hand. It was the perfect formula for investors: the only challenge was getting as many players to wager as much as possible.

Just being early wasn't enough. Parasol had to promote her websites and draw in surfers, even if it meant paying a lot to other sites that referred them. For that, she turned to allies from her porn days. Later, when PartyPoker owner PartyGaming went public, its prospectus briefly noted that Parasol had been involved with "adult sites." It said nothing about her partnerships with a series of rip-off artists who deceived tens of thousands of consumers and bilked investors out of tens of millions of dollars. Parasol's personal spokesman, Jon Mendelsohn, said she "severed her ties" to the porn business in about 1995.

But Parasol kept at least her personal connections. She stayed in touch with Ian Eisenberg and others well known to law enforcement. She was also friends with Habari, close enough friends to give him a big hug when they saw each other at a Las Vegas porn-business convention. She recommended Habari for a crucial job near the top of the PartyGaming hierarchy. Once there, he oversaw a plan to provide PartyGaming's interface to other poker sites, so people who thought they were playing at Empire Poker or other competitors were really spending their money at PartyPoker. He controlled where PartyPoker spent its massive advertising budget, mostly online, and compensated other websites based on how many players they converted. He also gave some a cut of whatever the players eventually lost at PartyPoker, a brilliant move that cemented PartyPoker's lead and left hundreds of thousands of people trying their luck at a company with the barest of regulatory oversight. In its prospectus, PartyGaming credited its dominance over competitors largely to the online sales and marketing campaign.

In separate industry presentations during 2005, the thirty-eight-year-old Habari was identified as director of marketing at PartyPoker and director of online marketing at PartyGaming. But because of Habari's past, the company decided he wasn't the sort of person they wanted on the roster when it came time to court investors at the mammoth initial public offering (IPO), former employees said. Habari left full-time employment at Gibraltar-based PartyGaming just before the IPO, so the company didn't have to disclose his shady background. By then, the company claimed more than half of the world revenue for regular table games. It had more than 400,000 active players and regularly hosted 70,000 at a time.

PartyGaming reinvested much of what it earned, spending heavily to advertise on Google, Yahoo! and other search engines, in sports publications, and in mainstream media to reach the largest possible American audience. In a 2003 stunt, PartyGaming held a live poker tournament onboard a cruise ship. It was broadcast as part of the World Poker Tour, which aired on the Travel Channel. PartyPoker began to buy millions of dollars' worth of commercial time on the channel. The authorities took note. They might have great difficulty in prosecuting overseas gambling companies based on their interactions with customers in the U.S., their largest market. But they could at least follow the money as it came back to America for marketing.

In mid-2003, the Justice Department wrote to the National Association of Broadcasters, warning that accepting ads for offshore casinos could constitute aiding and abetting illegal activity. The officials wrote that "broadcasters and other media outlets should know of the illegality of offshore sportsbook and Internet gambling operations since, presumably, they would not run advertisements for illegal narcotics sales, prostitution, child pornography or other prohibited activities." Most broadcast and cable outlets stopped accepting the ads. In 2004 the Justice Department went so far as to seize $2 million that PartyPoker had sent to the Travel Channel's parent company for additional airtime. The *Sporting News* and the major search engines would later fork over millions to end the threat of federal legal action.

But Ruth Parasol wasn't easily deterred. PartyGaming switched gears and sponsored television shows in the name of PartyPoker.net, an ostensibly nonprofit, educational site about poker that just happened to remind visitors about the main site, PartyPoker.com. The company became one of the chief backers of televised tournaments, where viewers could watch mountains of money getting passed back and forth over green felt emblazoned with the PartyPoker.net logo. Hold 'Em developed such a grip on the popular imagination that the 2006 James Bond film *Casino Royale* kept the fictional icon in a poker tournament for nearly a third of the movie.

PartyGaming nimbly took advantage of the craze. Its 2005 IPO proved to be the biggest on the London stock exchange in four years, vaulting PartyGaming past the likes of British Airways to a market value of $8.5 billion. Even after that offering, the company was majority-owned by just four people: two technologists from India and Parasol and her husband. The couple together owned 32 percent, worth more than $2 billion, and they sold out much of their stake before legal problems once again caught up with Parasol's business. In 2005 Parasol entered the Forbes 400 list of the richest Americans at No. 164—that year's highest rank for a woman without a fortuitous inheritance or marriage.

Barrett encountered Ruth Parasol just once. Prolexic had major poker firms in London as customers from its early days, and Barrett traveled there several times. Darren timed one trip for both of them to coincide with a casino industry conference. Staying at the swank Sanderson hotel, they were drinking one night off the lobby in the Purple Bar, a heavily draped watering hole that felt like the inside of a jewel box. Darren spotted Parasol and went up to shake her hand. PartyGaming had been hit with denial-of-service attacks too, but Darren didn't take the opportunity to pitch her on Prolexic's security services. Instead he set about hawking betting software from his other company, Digital Gaming, unintentionally underscoring his priorities. Darren did at least introduce Barrett to Parasol, who struck Barrett as very pretty.

"Nice to meet you," Parasol said, giving a remarkably firm handshake for a woman. Then she turned on her heel and went back to her circle.

Yishai Habari, Parasol's Gambino-connected henchman, escaped close scrutiny. In 2009, as CEO of Israel-based phone betting company 777Mobile, Habari was invited to speak at a London conference on fighting crime in online gambling. Speaking at the same conference were a detective from Scotland Yard and Lord Erroll, the leading voice on cybersecurity in British Parliament.

Parasol was far from the only tech-oriented crook or fellow traveler to make it big in the online poker business. BoDog founder Calvin Ayre, to give another example, made the cover of *Forbes* as a billionaire despite being fined for improper stock sales at a previous company. It was all too easy for the unprincipled to dodge the patchwork regulations of the Internet age and reap the giant payouts.

4

THE TURN

THROUGH 2005, BARRETT LYON struggled with the ethics of working at a company he was belatedly realizing was funded by illegal activity. He told Rachelle that gambling per se wasn't that bad and that he was putting ill-gotten gains to the best possible use—defending companies against extortionists bent on destruction. Ruining businesses was a lot worse than setting the odds in a football game. Rather than argue the point directly, Rachelle asked questions, playing to Barrett's abiding interest in the philosophy of ethics. Was it a problem that he was also earning money for people like Mickey Richardson and Brian Green, who cheated on their wives and might cheat him as well? What if some of that money was going to mobsters with guns who killed people? Would that be a problem? Yeah, it would, Barrett said.

Sensing Rachelle could be a problem for them, Darren Rennick and Brian put obstacles between her and Barrett. As her graduation date neared in mid-2005, they took Barrett to dinner and urged him not to let her move to Florida. He ignored them, and the couple re-united. Cohabitation brought a healthier lifestyle and a ready reality check. Brian had kept a room in Barrett's apartment for his trips to the U.S., at times bringing home a stripper he called "the Brazilian" for the night. When he stopped coming, Barrett cleaned out Brian's nightstand and found it full of syringes. *What the fuck?* Barrett thought. *I sure hope this means Brian has diabetes.*

Even as Barrett worried about his sponsors' ethics and manage-ment skills, the outside world's opinion of Prolexic soared. Neither the FBI nor the U.K. team had ever told Barrett to keep mum about his help with the case against the arrested Russian hackers. His under-cover work earned him a front-page *Los Angeles Times* feature in Oc-tober 2004, making Barrett semifamous. Magazine writers and television crews showed up in his Florida offices, and the *New Yorker* wrote its version of the Ivan Maksakov tale the following year. The squad in London also continued to vouch for the young company.

There were other security firms that tried to fend off denial-of-service attacks, generally as part of a broad and expensive overall protection service. But none did what Barrett's small company was doing for anywhere near the low price he charged. And none of them could boast that they had put a Russian extortionist behind bars.

The press and endorsements made it easier for Prolexic to garner non-gambling clients, especially such electronic payment processors as StormPay and e-Gold. The cyber gangsters DDoSed those firms with a vengeance, even though they liked to be paid through such services. They could always find another route for their cash, like the emerging favorite Webmoney, which was based in Russia.

E-Gold was one of Prolexic's oddest clients. Officially based in the West Indies, the company declared itself exempt from the ex-haustive regulations governing U.S. financial institutions. E-Gold's gimmick was that each account was backed by actual gold, though it was extraordinarily difficult to collect it. Otherwise, it functioned as other Internet currencies did, relying on a network of outside merchants or individuals who traded traditional currency for e-Gold funds, taking a cut in the process.

Customers needed just a functional email account and a name of their choosing to open an e-Gold account. Even the name could be transparently bogus, unless cruel parents really named their children Mickey Mouse, Donald Duck, and Bud Weiser. For that reason, thieves flocked to the service, along with hackers and child-porn purveyors, many of whom would accept nothing else. E-Gold founder Douglas Jackson arrogantly put his real offices in Melbourne, Florida. But his customers had so much faith in their perpetual anonymity that they voluntarily listed as the "purpose" for transactions such things as "dumps," which was shorthand for mass credit card information. E-Gold's own employees, meanwhile, allowed transactions to continue in accounts that they had labeled "child porn," "scammer," and "CC fraud."

Prolexic defended e-Gold against massive DDoS attacks beginning in the fall of 2005. When e-Gold went offline a couple months later, some customers contacted Prolexic to find out was happening, and Prolexic in turn called e-Gold. The executives there explained that they were too busy to talk; their offices were being raided. The U.S. eventually indicted the company and its founders, winning guilty pleas in 2008. E-Gold's records contained some valuable email and IP addresses, which helped in a number of hacking prosecutions. Many of the criminals also used their familiar handles on e-Gold. "Segvec," for example, was thought by federal agents to be a Ukranian carder, someone who stole credit card information or turned that data into cash or goods. He turned out to be Albert Gonzalez, a key Secret Service informant later accused of stealing data on tens of millions of credit and debit cards from T.J. Maxx and other national retailers. Prolexic also protected a few porn and counterfeit pharmacy sites. Darren wanted the company to sign up "high-yield investment programs," known as HYIPs, which were large pyramid schemes, but Barrett wouldn't do it.

Barrett and his crew brought customers into their own infrastructure while they filtered out the bogus traffic of one type and another. They would often try to find out the Internet location of the servers directing the attack, then call the authorities or the service provider and ask them to disconnect the offending computer. As their reputation grew, more big companies started helping as soon as Prolexic called.

Because Prolexic's defenses almost always worked, there wasn't much need for the full-fledged infiltration that marked the BetCRIS case. An exception came after an assault on a Canadian company called Proliflik, which sold out-of-copyright DVDs over the Internet. Proliflik bid and won the right to advertise next to Google searches on the phrase "vintage movies." Then a competitor from Japan warned Proliflik to stop its ads, or else. When Proloflik ignored the threat, someone launched one of the most obliterating DDoS attacks Prolexic ever faced, just before Christmas 2005.

Barrett was on Christmas vacation with his family at Lake Tahoe when the attack occurred. Without an Internet connection of his own, he trudged to a Starbucks to use its wireless hookup. Barrett set to work and traced the attacking machines to Japan. They appeared to be coming from servers running the operating system Linux that had been compromised through a flaw in the Web programming language PHP. The attack was strong enough that it began to crush other Prolexic customers sharing the same equipment, and Barrett had to take Proliflik offline, all while sitting on the damp coffee shop floor when no tables were free. Two days later, Terry Rodery found the Internet Relay Chat channel directing the attack. Just as Barrett and Dayton Turner had done with the BetCRIS bot attack, Terry joined the channel himself. He lurked there until another human being logged on and began issuing commands to the more than 70,000 bots in the channel.

Posing as a teen hacker, Terry accused the man of taking over bots that he had woven together earlier. "Why are you stealing my boxes?" he demanded, using slang for the captured computers. "They are not mine, not yours," the man responded, soon adding, "Sorry, but I have to DDos." He went on to say that he was punishing a shop for selling pirated material. "I do this for money," he wrote. Terry said he wanted to get into DDoS for money as well, and said he could get together a few hundred bots. "I'll ask my employer," the other man wrote. "He tell then what to do and pay for you."

Barrett wrote a report on his and Terry's work to inform other network administrators and posted it to a major email list for those in such positions. A Secret Service agent in Los Angeles responded and said he would ask his counterparts in Japan to get the plug pulled on the server, and the attackers' machine vanished from the Internet. It was one of many times that the agency went outside official lines to cut off the zombie networks known as botnets, earning it a better reputation in the business world than its larger rival, the FBI.

The two agencies had overlapping turf in cybercrime, leading to bureaucratic battles that further handicapped the federal government's weak response to the crisis. Both had some successes worth crowing about, and both had some embarrassing failures. The FBI had more people, while the Secret Service had better expertise. Perhaps because that agency was smaller, it was more nimble and less hidebound, in the same way that Apple often develops niftier software than the far larger Microsoft. In terms of style, the Secret Service was more likely to share information and work harder at cooperating with other officials and private companies. The FBI took in reams of information and let little back out. That's why the U.K. National Hi-Tech Crime Unit stopped inviting the FBI to its conferences and asked the Secret Service to come instead.

The Secret Service's unofficial help with Proliflik was part of a broader trend that emerged in response to widespread frustration at the inadequacy of official channels. When the authorities were helpful, it was often on the sly. And a number of private groups and individuals were coming to the fore. Some compiled public blacklists of attackers' addresses that could be blocked from accessing websites. Others tried to trace the patterns, linking certain botnets to preferred methods of attack and favorite hosting providers. Big security firms like Trend Micro and Symantec gradually got better at sharing information with their peers as well.

When Barrett emailed around about the Proliflik case, he heard back from someone new: Rob Thomas, of a secretive nonprofit security company called Team Cymru. Cymru (a Welsh word pronounced as if the vowels were backward, Cumree) had former military operatives, police veterans, and private security experts on board. It too had a mailing list, but someone could get on it only if several people had long-standing relationships with the candidate.

Team Cymru kept the lowest possible profile, which was why it had so many sources of information deep within companies most affected by the botnet phenomenon. Under wiretapping laws, telecommunication companies could share information with Cymru about their customers that they couldn't share with law enforcement. Once it got that data, though, Cymru could advise others. Invaluable raw transcripts of IRC chats went to law enforcement, lists of possibly compromised account numbers went to banks, and databases connecting blocks of suspect IP addresses with their service providers were made available to those who needed access.

Thomas told Barrett the group was tracking some nine hundred separate botnets, watching not just which viruses were responsible for assembling them but also which individuals. As the authorities continued to stumble, Team Cymru and its allies would grow in importance, eventually providing one of few obstacles in the major criminals' path to power.

During a lull in the Proliflik battle, Barrett resumed his vacation by taking Rachelle for a wander around the curio shops in the Tahoe town of Truckee, California. The couple had grown closer as Barrett fought with the Russians and worried about his own patrons, and they had talked about marriage. In a jewelry shop, Rachelle admired a vintage ring: Barrett bought it and proposed. Rachelle hadn't lost her faith in Barrett's ability to navigate the treacherous waters of his business life. But she wanted him to sort it out, definitively and soon. The same was true of his marriage proposal; on the right track, but half-assed in execution. She hesitated, then said yes.

• • •

BARRETT TOOK EVERY OPPORTUNITY to make Prolexic bigger and more legitimate. If he succeeded, perhaps he could sell it to a straight-arrow security company, and none of the shady beginnings would matter. Just four of the twenty-nine customers brought on in the year beginning November 2005 were gambling companies. Other clients included the U.K. Royal Mail, State Farm Insurance, top domain name registrar GoDaddy, and the Royal Bank of Scotland.

Barrett urged his fellow executives to drop all of the gambling clients. The closest he came to succeeding was when Mickey suggested they delete from the company's website references to protecting gambling sites from getting obliterated near the Super Bowl. Writing to Barrett, Darren, and Brian, Mickey said, "I don't think it is a good idea to have people think the company is gaming related."

Though the Maksakov stories in the press helped broaden the customer base, Darren hated them, telling Barrett that it made some clients uncomfortable to hear that he had gone to the FBI. "It definitely hurts business when we put those guys away," Darren told him. Barrett just shook his head.

Revenue climbed to $3.4 million in 2005, and the company turned its first profit. But the spending was excessive—it cost $1 million for the move from Costa Rica—and there often didn't seem to be enough money. Barrett could never get a look at the company's books, even as a partial owner, and he didn't like the way Darren ran the place. Often away at his other enterprises, Darren promoted or transferred several Prolexic employees away from their capabilities. He kept members of the team divided against each other, telling all that he was their biggest supporter. Barrett came to believe he wanted them beholden to him and unlikely to compare notes.

Personal loyalty was a major concern for Darren. For the company's chief financial officer, he picked an old friend, Keith Laslop, whose brother had been Darren's roommate at a Canadian college. In addition, Laslop's father had worked at Darren's old companies, including BetonSports. Laslop came off as a likeable guy, despite the British accent he kept after spending six years in London. But Barrett couldn't figure out why he was getting far more than double Barrett's compensation.

Meanwhile, Barrett was learning more than he wanted to about his investors. In February 2006, Mickey and Ron Sacco flew into Miami on a private plane. The plane, Barrett gathered, made it easy to move cash back into the country. Mickey was on his way to help his bookie father, who had been arrested again in Pennsylvania. Complaining that Dad was getting sloppy as he aged, Mickey griped metaphorically, "I should have taken away his keys."

Indeed, Mickey Flynn Jr. had been given multiple chances. He'd been arrested in August 2003 on charges of bookmaking and participating in a "corrupt organization" with multiple bookies. Though he could have faced twenty years, Flynn pleaded guilty to bookmaking and conspiracy and got off with probation. This time police had caught him in a probe of a mob associate named John Conley. The gambling baron did business with Pittsburgh's Genovese mafia branch, according to state officials. When Conley got out of prison in 2005, he started passing Flynn more than $1 million in bets monthly. A large part of that went to BetCRIS, according to a federal prosecutor. After the arrests, police found guns including an AK-47 assault rifle in Flynn's house, along with more than $500,000 in cash. Flynn pleaded guilty to conspiracy and running a gambling business in the fall of 2006 and this time got two and a half years in jail.

While they were in Miami, Sacco and Mickey commandeered the Prolexic conference room for a meeting with a bunch of tough guys smoking cigars. The meeting, Barrett learned, concerned Florida's plan to legalize slot machines in more places, which the group feared would cut into their illegal betting business.

Every time Mickey came through town, he would meet with Howie, an older man with a walrus mustache who held the cash. Often, the group would head to Café Martorano in Fort Lauderdale, a "South Philly Italian" restaurant with a pronounced mobster shtick. On the walls hung pictures of the chef with stars from *The Sopranos* and plasma televisions running old mob movies. Martorano himself professed admiration for connected men, including his uncle Ray "Long John" Martorano, who was shot to death on a Philadelphia street in 2002. "My uncle was a man's man," Martorano told the *Philadelphia Inquirer* in 2007. "He did 20-something years and kept his mouth shut. You tell me somebody who'll do that today."

Ron Sacco might have been the sort of man Martorano admired, but Barrett didn't feel the same way. In another restaurant once with Barrett and Joe Daly, Sacco had tried to compliment their light-skinned Latina waitress by telling her he preferred his coffee "sweet and not too dark, like my women." Barrett had wanted to crawl under the table. Barrett dined again with Sacco in Las Vegas during an industry conference. Sacco's wife came too, and she complained that she had only $200,000 to decorate their new home. Barrett couldn't help wondering how big a house he could buy with just her beautification budget.

He told Rachelle she had been right all along. These were not the good guys. As she slept in one weekend morning, Barrett spread rose petals through the condo, lit candles, and poured champagne. He woke her and proposed marriage again. This time she said yes with enthusiasm.

• • •

As he continued to update others in the security community with his research, Barrett's profile grew. In March 2005 he was invited to speak about botnets at what would become the first of an annual series of gatherings called the Peering Forum. Conveniently held at a hotel in Miami, the invitation-only convention drew the people in charge of operating the biggest pipes in the Internet infrastructure. Nobody outside of their insular world knew their names. But their deals to exchange traffic with one another, known as peering arrangements, were what kept the bits going to the right places. If one provider sent about as much traffic to another as the other way around, they typically struck a deal without money changing hands. If one sent a lot more than it received, it usually had to pay for the freight.

In ordinary circumstances, the peering chiefs were predominantly libertarian and firm believers in network neutrality, the doctrine that all Internet traffic should be treated the same. But the authorities were doing close to nothing to stop criminals who were abusing their access to the Net, and the group didn't want to be facilitating mass fraud or worse. In the real world, the peering bosses had more power over the Internet than the government. If they acted together, they had the best chance of cutting off the providers who served the worst cybercriminals.

Barrett's talk, "In the Trenches of Cyberwarfare," included the Maksakov story and updates from the denial-of-service struggle. He impressed the crowd, and a number of listeners came up afterward to introduce themselves, including Jay Adelson, the founder and chief technology officer at giant hosting and connection provider Equinix. He was also approached by Paul Betancourt, who said he was from the Miami office of the FBI and would love to chat more. Barrett hadn't grown much more impressed with the FBI since his days in California, but at least this agent cared enough about Internet crime to come to a conference for hard-core technologists. Betancourt dressed in slacks and an untucked shirt with a collar, dark sunglasses perched on his hair. *Straight out of Miami Vice,* Barrett thought. Betancourt offered to take Barrett shooting at the FBI range, and Barrett accepted, giving him some advice on a few technology cases in return. Betancourt got in touch with Barrett's old FBI handler in Sacramento, Matthew Perry, and told Perry that he would be in charge of the informant from now on. Betancourt bumped Barrett up in the hierarchy of those who helped the agency, telling him that he was now part of a council of elders who could advise the FBI on a wide range of topics, not just cases he was personally involved with.

Barrett knew that Darren was no fan of the FBI. He had faulted Barrett for working so closely with the feds on the Russian case, even though the agency had mainly passed Barrett's information on to the British. But Barrett felt that was Darren's problem. He told his CEO that the new FBI man would be stopping by the office for some further education. Darren cursed, then spent a long time getting rid of anything in the suite that described Prolexic's clients. Barrett blanched.

Within a few months, Darren's concerns made a lot more sense. Over Barrett's objection, Prolexic had been protecting some gaming companies by hosting their traffic on machines in the U.S. With gambling on sports banned in most of the U.S., that sure felt like it made Prolexic an accessory to criminal activity. And Sacco wasn't the only customer with an alarming reputation. In early 2005, Prolexic was hit with a subpoena by prosecutors in New York who wanted information on another rough bookmaker, Casablanca, best known for its Wager-Web site. An executive there emailed Prolexic and said that the subpoena followed the arrest of one of the gambling firms' U.S. agents. "We have had a problem with the New York police," the man wrote. He asked Prolexic what it had given the cops. And to make sure the "problem" didn't continue, he suggested ending the current contract with Prolexic in order to "create a new one under a different company name."

Meanwhile Brian's Digital Solutions, a major Prolexic client from the young company's beginning, was in bed with all manner of questionable offshore firms. Worse still, Darren had Digital Gaming Solutions paperwork spread around his office, had demonstration software loaded on his computer there, and was selling the programs right out of the U.S. office. To Barrett, the Digital Gaming business was a cancer. He repeatedly asked Darren to keep it away from Prolexic, getting only vague promises in response. "You need to get the DGS stuff in the office OUT, I am sick of this crap," Barrett exploded in a final email to his boss. "Please make sure you only use your Prolexic laptop and clear out any DGS stuff on it."

In the end, what pushed Barrett over the edge was simply bad management. He had developed a new method for assessing the risks to clients from a denial-of-service attack. Barrett sold it to the Royal Bank of Scotland for $100,000, then told his bosses he needed to take some vacation. Rachelle's grandmother was dying, and the couple flew together back home to Lake Tahoe. Instead of letting lower-level staff help the bank with the installation, Darren told Barrett he needed to see the job through. Since business hours in the United Kingdom were 1 A.M. to 9 A.M. California time and Barrett didn't want to disturb Rachelle's family, he checked into a hotel to work through each night. When the trip was over, no one thanked Barrett for his trouble.

"No more," Barrett swore. He demanded that the company hire a service team. He wrote a letter detailing his ideas for the company and sent it directly to Brian and Mickey. The letter called for a return to California, where there were better job candidates and a potential customer base of technology companies that would give Prolexic a boost in credibility. Barrett also criticized strategic decisions by Darren and Laslop.

Brian and Mickey secretly forwarded Barrett's letter to Darren. But Barrett had invoked what he felt was his prerogative as chief technology officer and begun monitoring the other executives' email. Darren critiqued Barrett's letter for Brian and Mickey in writing, and much of what he said was predictable. Then Barrett saw Darren's main argument for keeping the company in Florida: that location, he wrote, would "keep Barrett in check."

• • •

BARRETT BEGAN THINKING HARD about the ramifications if he simply quit—and about the ramifications if he didn't. If he quit, the company he had started would go on, but might be outgunned by criminals who had reinvested in research and adopted newer techniques. More innocent companies would be slammed with DDoS attacks. And he would be abandoning his friends, including Glenn Lebumfacil and Dayton Turner, whose wives worked in Costa Rica and couldn't move to the U.S.

If he stayed, he would be working to enrich crooks, perhaps helping them to launder money, and he might be criminally liable himself for that and for helping the gambling-firm customers in the U.S. Barrett no longer saw the bargain he had made with the devil, working for crooks against a bigger enemy, as worth the moral price.

In March 2006, Barrett offered to buy Prolexic for $5 million, part of it in cash and the rest to come from a slice of future earnings. His co-owners said no, perhaps because they wanted to keep using

Prolexic for their own purposes. Then Barrett resigned as an officer and employee and suggested he sell back his 20 percent stake for the bargain price of $200,000. But Darren, Brian, and Mickey refused to buy him out. Barrett remained invested and on the company's board, still potentially liable for all that was going on.

To contemplate his next step, Barrett took his long-delayed vacation, flying with Rachelle to Hawaii. Visiting his high school friend Peter Avalos, now in the Navy and stationed on Oahu, Barrett wrestled with what to do. He talked for hours with his friend and his fiancée about how to extract himself. He could do something new. But that would leave Ron Sacco and Mickey in charge of an illegal gambling empire, one that probably broke kneecaps or worse. Even if all Sacco was doing was paying tribute to the mob, that money was still going to fund murders. And evidence that could help the government take down Sacco was on his company's computers. He didn't walk away from chasing the Russians, even though he hadn't been hired for that. So why should he walk away now? Barrett not only wanted out; he felt an obligation to help law enforcement pursue his investors. It might not be as satisfying as seeing Maksakov in handcuffs. But it was the only right thing left.

Barrett decided to expose the criminals around him. On his last day in Hawaii, he assembled his courage. Waiting in the airport for their flight home, Barrett called Paul Betancourt at the FBI. "Paul," he said. "I've got a whole bunch of stuff to tell you." Barrett laid out much of what he knew about Mickey and Sacco, the parking-lot cash transfers, and the gambling transactions that were running through Prolexic's machines. "That's *really* interesting," Betancourt said. But he hadn't been working gambling cases, and he didn't seem focused on what Barrett was saying. Barrett guessed that the FBI already had a lot of this information and that Betancourt wasn't allowed to tell him so.

In his high-rise condo in Florida, Barrett had been sketching out ideas for a new business he could start after making a break from Prolexic. A noncompete agreement in his employment contract meant that he couldn't do denial-of-service jobs. But Prolexic had succeeded largely because it had both enormous amounts of bandwidth and clever techniques that Barrett and his crew used to maximize the efficiency of that bandwidth.

Barrett thought about what else would benefit from the fattest pipes and smart engineering and was also in a market destined to grow. Once he pondered it that way, the answer was obvious: Internet video. As an added bonus, that would keep him well clear of the bad guys. "It's nice when people aren't trying to destroy your network," he told a friend. "And working in security makes you paranoid." Barrett called around to his contacts until he had a pretty good idea how sites handled the demand for connectivity from millions of people watching their videos. It seemed awfully basic. So he started working out how it might be done for less money.

When Barrett knew he had something good, he got in touch with a venture capitalist who had come to check out Prolexic, Perry Wu. After a series of conversations, they co-founded a company called BitGravity. Instead of relying on investors that Barrett now knew they would have to research before trusting, Barrett and Wu decided to bootstrap the business by themselves. Barrett contacted some of the major Prolexic suppliers and told them that he had a new idea. If they could lend BitGravity some gear, it would pay them when it could. If the company got as big as Barrett thought, it would become a big customer. Normally that kind of pitch would get an entrepreneur nowhere. But the people Barrett called knew what he could do, because they'd seen it before. Barrett started off with $250,000 worth of equipment, for which he paid nothing upfront. Barrett and Rachelle moved back to Northern California. They settled in the Bay Area town of Pacifica, picking a condo with a view of the best surf break within half an hour of San Francisco.

Barrett's departure could not have come at a worse time for Pro-lexic. The company was about to take on its most unusual client, an anti-spam firm based in Haifa, Israel, and in Silicon Valley's Menlo Park, where venture capital firms had invested $4 million in it. Blue Security Inc. had a radical idea for stopping spam. Over the course of a year, it compiled a list of 450,000 email addresses of people who wanted to be protected. Blue Security then contacted major spammers, telling them to purge Blue Security's clients from their target lists. If they refused, the security company warned, the free software on its clients' machines would send "opt out" requests simultaneously to the spammers, in effect launching a vigilante denial-of-service attack on the mass-mailers. Impressively, many of the spammers complied, and some longtime spam foes hailed Blue Security as the culminating triumph of tech-savvy volunteerism that could save the Net from a host of ills.

Much remains murky about what followed, including exactly which spammers fought back. But Blue Security clearly had not thought everything through. For starters, it had assured clients that the email addresses they provided would be encrypted for their privacy. The idea was that spammers willing to purge their lists would have to submit their own roster to Blue Security for cleaning. But it was child's play to do that and then compare the two lists, making it apparent which intended recipients were working with Blue Security. Those people then began getting emails with threats like "You cannot participate in illegal activities and get away with it" and "You will end up receiving this message, or other nonsensical spams 20–40 times more than you would normally . . . just remember one thing when you read this, we didnt do this to you, BlueSecurity did."

In a series of instant-message chats with Blue Security, a spammer calling himself Pharma Master, presumably one of the many specialized in peddling counterfeit medications, threatened worse: "u started with my and my people and my staff, you shall get hurt first to feel who we are . . . how about each time you play games I'll hit your company? . . . I wish you can have 10 million of users so my people can infect them and with the short period we'll be recording the ddos ip's and make sure to infect this users and make them ddos you." And in a spammer IRC channel monitored by security professionals, the bad guys egged each other on: "Guys, download the DB [database], spam it, compile your lists with it and trade it around. Use them as froms, mail your anti [spammer] DB with them, do whatever you want. Let this database leak to the point all these stupid ass fucks have to get new e-mail addresses. Adios bluefreaks."

Blue Security did next to nothing to prepare for the easily anticipated DDoS attacks against it. Its main website was hosted in a conventional facility, sharing a server with many other companies. In early May 2006, one or more spammers knocked Blue Security offline. The company then redirected people trying to reach its main website to a blog hosted at TypePad.com, where it could update clients on what was happening. This was, to say the least, inconsiderate. The DDoS assault naturally followed the switch, taking down not just Blue Security's blog but 2 million others associated with the popular TypePad blogging software. A similar fate befell Toronto Web services company Tucows, which provided domain name services for Blue Security. Hundreds of thousands of other Tucows clients were shut down. Twelve hours later Tucows dropped Blue Security like a hot potato, ending the attack but leaving Blue Security without a website that anyone could find.

Only days later did Blue Security do the obvious thing and hire Prolexic, which got Blue Security back in the game for more than a week. It wasn't an easy task. Not only did the spammers continue their industrial-strength DDoS attack, they sent unsolicited mail that appeared to come from Prolexic, which prompted many spam filters to start rejecting legitimate Prolexic emails. Yet the defenses held, according to Joe Daly, which is why it was very strange to hear Laslop's end of a phone conversation with the head of Blue Security on May 16. CEO Eran Reshef said that he was giving up. When a surprised Laslop relayed the news, Daly didn't get it. "Why? They're up right now," Daly told his boss. Laslop said he thought Reshef's life had been threatened.

Blue Security's site stayed up long enough for it to post a cryptic goodbye message. "We determined that once we reactivated the Blue Community, spammers would resume their attacks. We cannot take responsibility for an ever-escalating cyberwar through our continued operations." The company stopped doing business, and the previously media-friendly CEO never gave any interviews about why he quit. It could have been death threats, fear of legal repercussions, or concern for the fate of Blue Security users. But perhaps Reshef knew what would happen next. Less than twelve hours after his unsigned farewell, the spammers launched a major attack on UltraDNS, the company that provided domain name services and backup bandwidth to Prolexic.

That assault put away Blue Security's website and downed hundreds of other Prolexic customers as well. While the apparent order of events—a surrender followed by a catastrophic attack—left some room for quibbles, it appeared to reasonable observers that Prolexic had been beaten, badly and for the first time. "Goliath Wins," proclaimed the *Washington Post*. Prolexic itself was down for hours, to the alarm of the security community. "If they can take down prolexic and KEEP them off-line, we are in trouble," wrote one regular poster to an anti-spam discussion board at volunteer security group CastleCops. "The guy behind prolexic is a magnitude 9 genius. Let's hope that is enough."

But Barrett had been quietly gone for more than a month. A day later, after Prolexic got back up, Darren penned his own postmortem on Prolexic's site. "We understand that once customers of Blue Security started receiving real threats of viruses/worms/DDoS/etc. attacks against their own networks, Blue Security realized that they were putting many other businesses in jeopardy by continuing the fight with the spammers. Not wanting to escalate the war on their customers, Blue Security, understandably but regrettably, decided to exit the anti-spam business on May 16th. . . . Currently Blue Security has taken their site offline, to avoid themselves being responsible for any further attacks on their customers. Whether or not you applauded Blue Security for taking the fight to the spammers, I'm sure you'll agree that it is a sad day when criminal spammers win. Blue Security will be missed."

Things might have been different if Barrett had been there. At a minimum, Prolexic would have gone in fully armed. That's because Prolexic's initial deal with UltraDNS allowed it to rely on all of that company's bandwidth, which could have absorbed the attack that felled Prolexic in May. But UltraDNS wasn't happy with the terms of that deal, since it let Prolexic resell UltraDNS connections for less than what UltraDNS charged its own customers. In fact, UltraDNS had been watching Prolexic grow with no small amount of jealousy, and it had recently introduced its own denial-of-service offering, sending a sales executive to court the same gaming firms in Costa Rica that had been Prolexic's early customer base. Not long before Barrett left his company, UltraDNS complained that some of the attacks on Prolexic customers were putting too big a strain on its resources. It said the best solution would be to "quarantine" Prolexic customers on specialized UltraDNS equipment, ensuring that other customers wouldn't be crushed by any overflow. "We really need to talk about getting your zones moved to a new set of dedicated ip addresses and servers so that we have a better shot at managing during a ddos," wrote UltraDNS founder Rodney Joffe in February 2006, before Barrett moved back to California. Barrett thought for about a second before saying no:

isolating Prolexic meant it could rely on far less of UltraDNS's resources during an attack. In case Prolexic's differences with UltraDNS escalated, Barrett drafted a contingency plan for Prolexic to get more bandwidth on its own.

As soon as Barrett left, UltraDNS made a renewed quarantine push, and this time Prolexic agreed. "Those guys were and are jackasses," Daly said of the top brass at UltraDNS. "They removed us off the servers. It was death for us." A former UltraDNS employee admitted that the quarantine was rough treatment, despite what the company said at the time. "We didn't have the best deal with them," the former employee explained. "They were offering us as a package deal at way below what we charged." The quarantine left Prolexic hopeless before the onslaught from Blue Security's enemies. Barrett never said so in public, but the truth is that Prolexic might have beaten the spammers if he had still been on board. Though it's impossible to know for sure, it certainly would have been an epic battle, and possibly something that changed the momentum in the war against the robot hordes.

• • •

BARRETT'S EXIT WAS JUST AS MESSY on the corporate side. Equinix, the big data-hosting company, offered to buy Prolexic for $10 million in July. Prolexic's backers refused, and Barrett called a meeting of Prolexic's board to argue the point. He got nowhere; Darren called the offer "terrible." The issue of gambling clients, meanwhile, grew increasingly important as legislation to explicitly ban online wagering gathered steam in Congress. As passage looked more likely, Barrett called for another board meeting to consider whether all gambling customers should be dropped. "I feel the company is tainted by the associations with online gambling and no matter how ambiguous the laws may be, Prolexic must eliminate any risk it may have in the future by making a clean and precise separation from gambling business now," he wrote on October 20, 2006. When no such meeting was scheduled, Barrett quit the board.

Unless they just wanted to frustrate Barrett, or to keep control of Prolexic to launder money, it's unclear why Darren, Mickey, and Brian wouldn't sell to Equinix. From early on, they had sought the opportunity to cash out. All the way back in May 2004, soon after Darren took over day-to-day control of Prolexic, he arranged a group meeting at the posh St. Regis hotel in Los Angeles with a man named Jonathan Strause, who had co-founded a small consulting and banking firm, Bellwether Group, that specialized in mergers and acquisitions. That firm was soon hired on, for at least $300,000, to develop a business plan, and Strause in turn arranged meetings with Wedbush Morgan, a bigger L.A. investment bank. It gradually emerged that Strause, for all his Wharton business school and McKinsey & Co. credentials, had previous connections to both Darren and Mickey.

After another meeting at the Clift Hotel in San Francisco, Strause had a few drinks and explained to Barrett that not everything he did was traditional. In fact, he had a sort of gambling hedge fund for investors on the side, which he directed toward what he thought were sure things. Strause also worked with Mickey to take over a bankrupt company that took bets on virtual horse races. Later, Mickey would tell Barrett that Strause had succeeded Darren in running Digital Gaming.

In 2008, Prolexic's backers finally sold the firm for $10.5 million to a publicly traded Philippines Internet company called IPVG, which ran data centers and did outsourcing for Fortune 500 companies. One of its units was a Prolexic customer that also resold Prolexic services. Once again, personal ties played a role. IPVG's deputy chairman was Roger Stone, a friend of Darren's who had been CEO of gambling software firm IQ-Ludorum. A number of maneuvers watered down Barrett's expected cut of the proceeds before that sale closed. Of the initial $3.5 million payment, for example, $1 million each was designated for repayment to Mickey and Brian for "loans" to Pro-lexic. Considering that Mickey and Brian had initially put up just $250,000 in total, the sale produced an extremely healthy return. Then again, the mafia has always done well in the protection business, and in this case, the protection was real. IPVG defaulted on its final payment, leaving Barrett with $400,000, a third of his promised payout.

5

CRACKdOWN

IN MID-2006, A MONTH AFTER giving all the information he had on Mickey Richardson and Ron Sacco to Paul Betancourt and quitting Prolexic, Barrett finally heard back from the FBI agent. Betancourt had been interested after all, but needed time to research what Barrett had told him. "It all checked out," Betancourt said. He began asking a lot of questions, building a case against Prolexic's investors and some of its clients. He and Barrett would talk almost every day during the next year. Barrett ran down all of Digital Gaming's and Digital Solutions' customers for Betancourt, and as Betancourt nosed around, he found one that was already in the crosshairs of a gambling probe being run by the district attorney in the New York borough of Queens. That investigation, involving a private, password-protected site called Playwithal.com, was farther along, so Betancourt decided to piggyback. "They wanted to use the Queens case as an excuse to get financial information on the people around Prolexic," Barrett said. "They looked at it as a huge smorgasbord of bad stuff."

Barrett had spent several years protecting companies. He'd helped crack one Russian gang and educated government officials, technologists, and others about what else they could do. But there didn't seem to be any more progress in the fight against criminal hackers abroad. Rather than walk away, he figured he could at least hurt the U.S. mob by pulling the rug out from under his partners. A close observer might conclude that the U.S. government, following reasoning of its own, had come around to a similar position. The American mafiosi who had moved illegal gambling to the Internet were more vulnerable than the criminals doing damage from overseas. They faced a national law enforcement apparatus that had useful regulations on the books and that already knew who the key players were. And the bad guys hadn't managed to go completely "virtual." Bettors could make deposits and collect winnings through online accounts. But a lot of the clientele were old-timers like those Sacco grew up around, people who wanted to hand their cash to a guy in the neighborhood and get paid the same way. That meant a human trail of agents and runners who could be caught and occasionally turned into cooperating informants.

Barrett's change of heart came just as the Justice Department turned aggressive against some of the sports outfits. The feds had previously made a smattering of arrests of mobsters with gambling operations in Costa Rica. Justice officials believed that the 1961 Wire Act prohibited at least sports betting and probably other forms of gambling online, but not all lawyers agreed. As a result, the government carefully picked cases to prosecute. It generally stuck to sports and often targeted either companies with mob ties or the most aggressive promotion—or both, as in the case of BetonSports. Steve Budin of SDB Global was arrested in 1998, paid a big fine, and avoided jail. In a confessional 2007 book, Budin described working for unnamed Brooklyn investors, whom he never had to finger in court. In 2002, New York and federal officials unveiled a sixty-eight-count indictment against seventeen Gambino family members and associates, including boss Peter Gotti, who succeed his nephew John atop the clan. Prosecutors said a Gambino captain, Anthony Ciccone, played a leading role in extorting money from actor Steven Seagal and helped run the New York operations of Pelican Sports, a Costa Rican book, in 2000 and 2001.

BetonSports drew fire by shouting from the rooftops. The longtime Prolexic customer blew more than $10 million a year on advertising and marketing, buying space in *Maxim* magazine and time on Howard Stern's radio show. When the 2002 football season started, the company pushed the envelope even more. It hired a Florida firm, Mobile Promotions, which covered a motor home with the BetonSports Web address and related artwork and drove it to the parking lot outside a Tampa Bay Buccaneers game. A Tampa Bay police detective joined a group of fans who walked in to get BetonSports material. Employees helpfully registered him as a BetonSports client, accepted a credit card deposit to open an account, and dialed Costa Rica for him so he could place his first bet. Police busted four Mobile Promotions staffers. The feds likewise used the ban on promoting gambling to go after publications, radio stations, and Internet sites that took virtual casino and sports betting money for advertisements. In 2007, Microsoft, Google, and Yahoo! settled claims that they profited from gambling ads by agreeing to turn over a total of $31.5 million in cash and public-service warnings.

In July 2006, federal agents arrested David Carruthers, CEO of publicly traded BetonSports, as he changed planes in Texas en route to the company's Costa Rica headquarters. Notwithstanding the unusual prominence of the target, the indictment followed the pattern by focusing on sports and activities in the U.S., including the ads on Stern's radio show. Carruthers had also spent a fair amount on public relations, which apparently backfired. He had led an industry lobbying group and even written a piece in the *Wall Street Journal* calling for legalization.

The indictment also named as defendants London-based Beton-Sports itself, which handled more than $1 billion in bets annually, and company founder Gary Kaplan, making much of his criminal history as a bookie in New York and Florida before he moved abroad in 1995. Kaplan was caught in the Dominican Republic in March 2007. After that, BetonSports pleaded guilty, filed for liquidation, and agreed to help prosecutors in their case against Kaplan and Carruthers, who was kept under house arrest until he pleaded guilty to racketeering in April 2009. Kaplan pleaded that August, agreeing to a mammoth $43 million fine and a sentence of more than three years.

Mere weeks after Barrett quit Prolexic's board, the company's name made its first appearance in court records. A sweeping indictment named a Lucchese crime family associate, more than two dozen other people, Prolexic, and Brian Green's Digital Solutions. New York Police Commissioner Raymond Kelly announced the arrests on November 15, 2006, saying they dismantled "the largest illegal gambling operation this department has ever encountered." During the period when the ring was under scrutiny, it processed a mammoth $3.3 billion in bets, more than most casinos. Atop the enterprise was well-known professional gambler James Giordano. Phone taps showed he had a network of 2,000 bookies who kicked their action up through more than 100 agents. Among those arrested was an active baseball scout for the Washington Nationals. To get Giordano, agents had to scale the walls of his $10 million compound in Pine Crest, Florida. Authorities seized four Manhattan condos, millions in cash, artwork by Salvador Dali, and a football signed by the 1969 Super Bowl champion New York Jets.

Darren Rennick and Keith Laslop were stunned by the indictment, which accused Prolexic of aiding gambling. Darren told his lawyer that Prolexic had just sold bandwidth to Brian's company, which had been a real vendor of Playwithal's. But they didn't have long to recover from the shock.

With Barrett telling him where to find servers and information related to Digital Gaming and Digital Solutions, Betancourt decided to extend the search and got federal warrants to raid Prolexic's office and its computer rooms in Miami and Phoenix. A week after the New York indictment, five FBI agents and eight local Hollywood, Florida, police barged into Prolexic's office with their hands on their guns. They broke down the door to the office Darren and Laslop shared with Joe Daly, finding only Laslop and Daly. "Take your hands off your desk!" an agent shouted. The squad herded the employees into a central area. When the company's sixty-year-old accountant began to ask a question, a local cop snarled, "Shut up and sit down!"

Police brought staff members into a conference room one by one for encounters with the FBI. The agents spent hours questioning everyone. Did they know of any illegal activity? Who was in charge? What did the company do? "They wanted to make sure we were a legitimate business," Daly said. The agents took half of Prolexic's equipment, including Laslop's computer and cell phone. As word spread, panicked gambling customers began calling, asking what had been taken and what it might show. Laslop was especially concerned about what was on the servers dedicated to gambling firm First Fidelity, owner of YouWager.com. He had good reason to be nervous; First Fidelity's machines housed Web pages marketing its betting business.

After the raid, Darren left for Canada. Laslop, who had been named president in July 2006, stayed behind and tried to convince the FBI that he didn't know anything about what Prolexic's clients did. The company struggled on, its payroll met by loans from BetCRIS, before its eventual sale. The FBI, meanwhile, followed Barrett's leads about Prolexic's unsavory ties. Barrett passed on emails from such clients as First Fidelity showing that bets had been handled on Prolexic machines, and he turned over cash-flow statements proving that Digital Gaming had poured tens of thousands of dollars into the company.

• • •

WHILE SPORTS BETTING OPERATIONS were finally feeling the heat, poker companies still seemed safe in early 2008—at least for the owners. Just like the sports companies, many were controlled by mobsters offshore or by questionable founders who had managed to go public in London. It was the customers who stood to lose: though the companies uniformly claimed to be regulated, in reality they were often corrupt.

PartyPoker's predecessor cheated at some casino games. Many other books didn't pay when they lost big, tried to stretch out payments over long periods, or simply disappeared. There wasn't much the victims could do. In theory, they could appeal to a number of websites that ranked the betting sites by quality or to the industry groups that sanctioned various companies. But both could have secret conflicts of interest. Such bodies as the Offshore Gaming Association and the International Sportsbook Council, it later came out in court, were controlled by BetonSports.

Poker players also worried about automated programs that pretended to be fellow bettors. The major poker sites officially banned these "robots," but they still took a percentage of every pot the programs contributed to, raising questions about how hard the companies tried to weed them out. One of the best-known poker sites secretly deployed bots against its customers to fill up tables and bolster earnings, according to a professional player who gambled there and asked to remain anonymous. Even Brian Green said he wouldn't play for serious money online for fear of getting cheated.

The robots stayed underground until 2005, when a $100,000 contest lured some into the open. A couple of promoters staged the World Poker Robot Championship at Binion's in Las Vegas, and most of those who competed said they had been playing their creations on PartyPoker. Ken Mages, one of the promoters, had written his own robot before signing away the rights. After two weeks of programming, he said, "I could sit down at a 50-cent table, put 50 bucks in the account, go to bed and wake up with at least $75." The most Mages won that way was $250; he never lost. PokerProbot, written by an Indiana car salesman named Hilton Givens, won the top prize and a playoff against a human pro, Phil "The Unabomber" Laak, known for his shades and hooded sweatshirt. It took Laak three hundred hands to win. "It would for sure make money online," Laak said after his victory. At least in the simpler versions of Texas Hold 'Em with betting limits, "bots are better than the average person."

Then there was insider cheating, like that exposed by some players at Costa Rica–based Absolute Poker who were determined, clever, and lucky—at least in their seat-of-the-pants investigation. Before that, they seemed downright unlucky. Todd Witteles, a computer expert and professional poker player, dropped $15,000 to a terrible opponent called Grey Cat. Harvard law grad David Paredes lost $70,000 to a turkey named Nio Nio on a sister betting site, Ultimate Poker. Players compared notes online and agreed that the victors had been betting at all the wrong times, in all the wrong denominations, and still somehow cleaning up. The break came when one of those who had been offended by the results requested a history of the hands that involved Potripper, another improbably lucky soul. The company accidentally sent back not just how those hands had been played, but what everyone had in the hole. The mathematical analysis was damning, number-cruncher Michael Josem told *60 Minutes* in 2008: it was "approximately equivalent to winning a one-in-a-million jackpot six consecutive times."

It got more interesting when the players traced back the player IP address that Absolute Poker had included in the spreadsheet of data—again accidentally, unless, as the *New York Times* wondered, a whistleblower sent the address deliberately. It belonged to a modem controlled by an employee—according to the *Times*, company part-owner Scott Tom. Finally, the company admitted that insiders had been cheating, and it pointed the finger at an unnamed former employee, whom other sources identified as A. J. Green. Responsible for investigating the scandal was the Kahnawake Gaming Commission, which handles complaints for the many poker sites whose servers are officially on Mohawk Indian land within Canada. The commission said groups at Absolute Poker and sister site Ultimate Bet cheated regular players out of more than $20 million over four years. It fined the sites $2 million and told them to repay the losers, but it didn't take away their license, which happened to be held by former Kahnawake Grand Chief Joe Norton, who set up the commission in the first place. Neither the Indian commission nor *60 Minutes* ever got the full story. A. J. Green, alias Potripper, wasn't a former employee at the time of the scandal, but a current employee. He also happened to be a friend and sometime roommate of Scott Tom, leading people inside the company to conclude their top man had been involved in the scandal.

Loose regulation, which varied widely from country to country and remained in some cases entirely absent, meant that much more cheating could exist undiscovered. "It's not only difficult to find out if a company is operating under a well-run regulatory system, it's hard to find out if they're even licensed," said Whittier Law School professor Nelson Rose, who has written books on Internet gambling laws and was an early advisor of Ruth Parasol, the mysterious doyenne of the poker world. Consumers who felt cheated certainly couldn't turn to the government. The Federal Trade Commission deferred to the states. The California attorney general, among others, received complaints about companies vanishing and cheating, said spokesman Nathan Barankin, but couldn't help. "We really don't delve into it, because online gambling is prohibited by federal law," Barankin said.

• • •

IN CONGRESS, NUMEROUS ATTEMPTS to authoritatively ban online gambling, some of which cited links to money laundering and organized crime, all met with failure. One reason was that the established gaming companies in Las Vegas and Atlantic City, which initially saw online betting as a competitive threat, decided it was helping them. Companies like PartyPoker were teaching a new generation of people how to play cards, and a good number of those players decided that tapping away on a screen at home paled in comparison to the fun of tempting fate in person. Every year that online gambling grew—and by 2005 it was past Las Vegas's haul—the sales in Vegas grew too. And of course, if Congress legalized computer gaming, no one would be in as great a position to benefit as the likes of Harrah's and MGM Mirage. Congress was "making a major mistake by not legalizing this type of gambling," warned MGM Chief Executive Terry Lanni. "Almost all wagers going to offshore sites come from the United States." The main gaming lobby moved to an official position of neutrality, while calling for a study of how online betting could be regulated best.

But as Barrett nervously watched in 2006, Congress finally moved to make it clear that Internet betting, even on poker, was illegal. In September it surprised many of its own members by approving a sweeping and poorly worded anti-gambling bill, the Unlawful Internet Gambling Enforcement Act. The bill made it an offense to accept or transfer money for an illegal gambling transaction but didn't define what exactly made a gambling transaction illegal. Senate Majority Leader Bill Frist backed it just ahead of the midterm elections, attaching it to an unrelated bill on port security that passed in the small hours of the morning. It took clearest aim at financial companies that processed transactions for gambling concerns, but analysts said the law also barred the betting companies themselves from accepting U.S. wagers.

A few things had changed to let this bill pass where its predecessors had stumbled. Voters decided the 2004 election on moral-values issues, politicians believed. The number of online gambling addicts who had lost everything was growing. Greg Hogan, for one, went from the president of his Lehigh University class to federal prison after he robbed a bank to pay off a $5,000 online poker debt. But perhaps the most salient reason was super-lobbyist Jack Abramoff. He had fought fiercely against the proposed bans on behalf of a legal online lottery company before getting disgraced in a bribery probe. For the Republican majority, a vote against Internet gambling gave them distance from the Abramoff scandal.

Whatever the motivation, the Unlawful Internet Gambling Enforcement Act crashed poker company stocks in a New York minute. More than $7 billion in market value evaporated in a single day. PartyPoker's parent, PartyGaming, lost 75 percent of its worth in the next four weeks, and the company said it would drop the three-fourths of its business that originated in the U.S., some $4 million daily. Those investors who still had a stomach for the industry turned to gambling companies with few or no customers in the U.S.

After President George W. Bush signed the online gambling ban into law on October 13, 2006, Justice Department prosecutors really turned on the gas, starting with one of the big companies that handled payments, Neteller Plc. Based in the Irish Sea tax haven of the Isle of Man, Neteller had been founded in 1999 by Canadians John Lefebvre and Stephen Lawrence as an Internet payment system like PayPal. It became increasingly important to online gamblers after credit cards and big banks stopped sending money to companies that were obviously in the betting business. That forced many in the U.S. to transfer money first from their online bank accounts to a service such as PayPal, then from that service to the casino or sportsbook.

After a civil investigation in 2003, federal authorities rattled their sabers at PayPal. PayPal had been bought by the Internet auction giant eBay, which was publicly traded and sensitive to bad press. It agreed to stop handling bets and forfeited $10 million in estimated profit from past gambling transactions. That capitulation sent more business Neteller's way, and the company went public on the London stock exchange.

Neteller got even more important when PartyGaming and some of its rivals officially stopped taking bets from the U.S. in late 2006. Some players avoided the ban by using Neteller to help disguise their locations. Meanwhile, some privately owned gambling firms boosted the company when they defied U.S. authorities and openly kept taking American bets. PokerStars, Full Tilt Poker, and their ilk all steered prospective customers to Neteller, which handled more than $7 billion in transactions during 2005. Little got Lefebvre and Lawrence in as much trouble as their company's own statements. Neteller's 2005 annual report bragged that the company handled transactions for 80 percent of the world's gaming firms. In a conference call the following year, executives said that 75 percent of their revenue came from the U.S. In January 2007, after Lefebvre was arrested in Malibu, California, and Lawrence was picked up in the U.S. Virgin Islands, prosecutors charged the pair with conspiring to promote illegal gambling, and both pleaded guilty.

The biggest quarry, though, was Ruth Parasol. The feds started by issuing subpoenas to more than a dozen banks involved in PartyGaming's 2005 IPO. Accountants involved in that probe said the top targets appeared to be Parasol and her three co-founders.

PartyGaming responded to the legal pressure by hiring a lawyer, Mitch Garber, as CEO, and allowing him to sound out the Justice Department about possible settlement terms. Parasol and her husband also hired a lobbying firm founded by Hunter Biden, son of Joe Biden, then head of the Senate's Judiciary Committee. The younger Biden tried to convince Congress to pass a law that would declare that Internet gambling had been legal before 2006. He quit lobbying after his father was named the vice presidential nominee to Barack Obama. Anurag Dikshit, a software engineer and one of

PartyGaming's co-founders, was the first inside the company to crack. He pleaded guilty in December 2008 to one count of violating the Wire Act and agreed to pay an astonishing $300 million fine. Sentencing in the case was delayed until December 2010, suggesting that he was expected to cooperate as the probe continued. Parasol resisted making any plea and forced out Garber. But the board approved a guilty plea from the company itself, convinced that it would position PartyGaming for a return to the U.S. market if poker were legalized. Parasol fought on, burnishing her image by getting increasingly involved with a few charitable funds she established. All the same, she kept Polish and Israeli passports on hand, preserving her options in case a return to the U.S. would be ruled out forever.

The Neteller and PartyGaming probes drew political cover from the 2006 law, which stopped many poker companies from soliciting or knowingly accepting U.S. business. But the law itself wasn't put into much use for more than two years. The regulations took that long to draw up, and they didn't become final until January 19, 2009, the day before President Bush left office. Even then, they didn't make much sense. They ordered the credit card companies and others to reclassify gambling transactions, based on opinions as to whether a given type was legal. But they also told the processors that they needn't bother examining individual payments to see if they actually met the new criteria. However flawed, the law was still an insult to powerful opponents, including American casinos and European countries, and key members of the majority-Democratic Congress that swept into power in November 2008 pledged to finally introduce bills to legalize and regulate Internet poker. The following May, House Financial Services Committee Chair Barney Frank did just that, urged on by Parasol's new lobbyists.

• • •

IN THE CRIMINAL CASE THAT SWEPT up Prolexic, most of the thirty indicted parties pleaded guilty to felonies. Prolexic itself pleaded to promoting gambling and coughed up $200,000. The feds also used the Prolexic raids Barrett made possible to take a fresh look at the Central American operations of Mickey Richardson and Ron Sacco. More help came later, with the documents that changed hands as part of the deal selling Prolexic to IPVG, the Philippines Web company. The paperwork used Mickey's real name in describing him as a key stockholder. And it listed Prolexic's bank accounts, including three that were active. One of those, in Panama, apparently had been set up after the 2006 raids for receiving customer payments. Only one person had authority over the account—a non-Prolexic employee, Karen Molnar, who happened to be the BetCRIS comptroller. (Her LinkedIn page, which used the altered spelling Monar, described her as overseeing "day to day financial operations for the entire company" of BetCRIS.) Figuring that Molnar might be the way to crack the flow of Mickey's money, the FBI peppered Barrett with questions about her and even sent a picture to confirm that they had the right woman in mind. They did.

The feds were even more excited when Barrett told them that Sacco still traveled to the U.S. from time to time. At a minimum, it appeared that if they could find him in the country, they could pick him up for violating the terms of his 2004 parole. The probation ruling dictated that for the three following years Sacco "shall not engage in any form of gambling and shall not frequent any establishment where gambling is conducted." Barrett was an eyewitness to Sacco working in the BetCRIS office during the probation term. "He sat in Mickey's office and worked, and when the phone rang, 90 percent of the time Ron answered," Barrett told the FBI. "He was taking calls and doing bookmaking."

But the FBI might have gotten serious about looking for Sacco just a month or so too late—either that or the agents hadn't bothered to check civil records, which showed that Sacco had gotten roped into a lawsuit in which he wasn't a defendant. In September 2006,

Sacco flew from Costa Rica to Los Angeles to sit for a deposition in a case filed in Los Angeles federal court. The lawsuit involved the estate of a Canadian con man who raised tens of millions of dollars from investors backing his supposedly surefire formula for whitening teeth. The scammer claimed that he lost $40 million of the proceeds betting on sports through a Costa Rican outfit run by one Maynard Garber, no relation to Mitch, who allied with BetCRIS. The estate's lawyers weren't so sure, and they were doggedly trying to trace what had happened to the money. In the process, they organized a raid of the BetCRIS offices in Costa Rica and came up with financial records showing where Sacco hid his funds.

They didn't get much more. In the deposition at a law firm in Orange County, California, Sacco cited the Fifth Amendment and refused to answer such questions as whether he still controlled Bet-CRIS; whether he was known as the Old Man, the Cigar, and the Boss; and whether he took a $2.5 million loan from Maynard Garber or knew that Garber was a convicted felon. (Sacco's parole also barred him from associating with felons.) The FBI apparently had no idea he was in town.

The feds were still on the trail in the fall of 2007, when Darren Rennick called Barrett and told him he wanted to bury the hatchet. They hadn't met in the year since Barrett had quit, but Darren had no reason to think Barrett was so reckless as to have blown the whistle on his own business partners. Now it was three days before Barrett's wedding, Darren was coming through San Francisco, and he wanted to get together. Barrett suspected Darren wanted to snoop around BitGravity and make sure it wasn't really in the anti-DDoS business, which would have violated Barrett's departure deal.

Barrett called Paul Betancourt and asked what he should do. Betancourt was thrilled. He got on the phone to his FBI colleagues out west. Then he called Barrett back and told him to meet some agents right away, that night, outside an address in San Francisco's China

Basin district. When Barrett arrived, he felt like he had just been drafted into a mob movie. Barrett was standing on a dead-end street by an empty warehouse when the agents' dark sedan pulled up. The rear door opened and Barrett climbed into the backseat, next to a man in a suit. "What kind of car do you drive?" the man asked, opening a briefcase on his lap. Inside the case were dozens of key fobs for every type of car, the kind with buttons that lock and unlock the doors. Only these fobs, the agent explained, were actually digital recorders. One click started a recording, and two clicks stopped it. The tiny machine could hold six hours of conversation. Barrett should begin each recording by speaking the date and time, giving his code name, and announcing whom he was meeting.

Barrett took a recorder that looked identical to his real fob and called Darren back. Sure, Barrett said coolly, he could get together the next day. But Barrett still needed to get dress shoes for his wedding ceremony—did Darren mind tagging along as he shopped? Darren didn't mind. Barrett picked Darren up at his hotel the next morning. They spent most of the day together. Darren was his usual self, friendly and silly.

Barrett, meanwhile, was giving the performance of a lifetime. He really did need shoes, and they went to a Burlingame mall, then the Westfield Mall in San Francisco. Barrett wanted to focus on his conversation with Darren—to get him to open up about Mickey and Sacco, where the money had come from, and where it had gone. But first he had to deal with the recorder. The FBI agent had warned him that the key-fob gizmo would get muffled if it stayed completely inside his pants pocket, ruining the recording. The agent suggested that Barrett leave the fob sticking out of his pocket, looking like it might fall out. The way to mask that oddity, the agent explained, was to wear a long jacket that hung over it. Barrett decided to junk all that and just dump the fob with the other stuff from his pants pockets on the table while they ate, hoping that Darren wouldn't examine it too closely. At first they talked about uncontroversial things: Barrett's wedding and where other Prolexic alumni had ended up. They stopped for lunch at a food court in the second mall. After more shopping, they went for a tapas dinner at Medjool, in the Mission District, and Barrett encouraged him to have mojitos.

Thinking again about how he had tried to do the world some good and gotten suckered into working for the mob, Barrett went for the close. He invited Darren back to the house and poured his good wine. Darren began to enjoy himself. He laughed about Sacco buying a thirdhand plane with a Panamanian pilot and about Brian Green, classy guy that he was, traveling to the ecological wonderland of the Galapagos Islands—to go hunting. As Barrett struggled through his own developing buzz to egg Darren on, the chief executive of one of the biggest gambling software suppliers blabbed on and on to the unseen tape recorder on the counter.

BetCRIS had fulfilled the dream Sacco had shared with Barrett at the Beverly Hills steak house in 2004, he recounted. It had opened physical casinos in Ecuador, Peru, Guatemala, Venezuela, and several cities in Mexico. Darren told Barrett he had set up the Mexican operation himself, cutting deals with the drug cartels in order to pull it off. Hazy with his own wine consumption, Barrett wasn't sure whether he had gotten everything the FBI wanted. But it seemed a pretty good start.

The next night, at the wedding rehearsal dinner at the Hotel Vitale, on San Francisco's downtown waterfront, Barrett excused himself to go to the bathroom. Looking over his shoulder, he ducked outside and ran across the street to the same dark sedan, now parked outside of the swank Boulevard restaurant. The agent inside rolled down the window. Dressed up for the special occasion he had just left, Barrett reached in to shake his hand, slipping him the fob in the process. A year and a half later, Betancourt told Barrett that the FBI was drawing up long-shot papers to extradite Darren, Mickey, and Sacco, who had quietly been indicted by a state grand jury in Arizona.

6

FROM SPAM TO IDENTITY THEFT

WHEN BARRETT HAD BEEN WEIGHING whether to leave Prolexic in 2006, he had thought about more than the ethical complications of working for immoral people against immoral people. He was also thinking about whether denial-of-service attacks, which had been on the cutting edge of technology crime three years before, were still such a high priority for the hacking gangs. If they had become routine, then perhaps other companies would do just as well in warding them off. And if the top criminals had moved on to something else, it wasn't clear whether Barrett would be doing the world much good by staying in the fight.

Barrett decided to check back with the criminals who had been state of the art when he got in the game, just to see what they were up to. He went online to see if the Internet Relay Chat channels that had given orders to Ivan Maksakov's bots were still up and running. Yes, they were. And even long after the crime ring was supposedly broken up, infected computers were still registering in the channel, seeking instructions.

Now, though, whoever ran the channel wasn't launching the zombies on denial-of-service attacks. Instead he was telling the machines to send him all the financial information and passwords that were stored on each PC. The Russian gang had moved on to identity theft.

Like everyone else in America, Barrett already knew that identity theft was a major and growing problem. He'd even been a victim himself. But he hadn't known the Russian mob had gotten in on the action.

From the time of the dot-com boom, identity theft had topped each year's list of complaints to the Federal Trade Commission. The burdens ranged from days of aggravation trying to clear a tarnished credit report to major financial losses. In 2005, the issue broke onto front pages across the country after a ring of Nigerian con artists penetrated ChoicePoint, a Georgia-based spin-off from one of the three big credit bureaus and one of the world's largest repositories of private information on consumers. That breach was only disclosed because of a recent California law requiring notification of its residents placed at risk. Even then, ChoicePoint tried at first to warn only Californians, and it continued to mislead the public after that. Among other things, it said such wide access had never been granted mistakenly in the past, when in fact another ring had done exactly the same thing two years before.

But how had Russian hackers joined in? Barrett guessed that they were simply pursuing the highest profit. Since viruses had gone professional in 2003, they had woven together millions of compromised machines. A denial-of-service attack was one of the easiest ways to convert that resource into cash, but now Barrett realized that it was far from the only one.

It had all begun, innocently enough, with spam. Because the earliest email programs had no restrictions on who sent what to whom, people looking to spread their ideas or hawk their products quickly seized on bulk messages as the closest thing to free advertising. Spam actually predates broad use of the World Wide Web. The term, from the Monty Python sketch in which every dish on a restaurant menu has either a little or a lot of the canned meat product, first appeared in an email group in 1993, after an administrator accidentally sent two hundred copies of the same message to every subscriber.

As more people began using email, spam got more effective. A technology arms race ensued, with service providers and stand-alone software companies trotting out different means for weeding out unwanted messages. Not much worked for long, at least on any scale. Filtering out certain words prompted deliberate misspellings. Blocking specific senders just forced them to fake the email addresses in the "from" field. "Challenge" systems sent out automated replies to all correspondents in search of proof that they were human beings, but most consumers didn't want to both download an additional product and annoy their friends.

Those companies routing tens of millions of emails eventually found it most effective to trace spam back to the computers that were spewing the come-ons. They began assembling blacklists of the suspect Internet addresses and sharing them in industry forums and through such resources as Spamhaus, a volunteer and mostly anonymous group in London that launched the Registry of Known Spam Operations, the ROKSO list of the worst offenders, in 2000. The anonymity was by necessity: when the home address of CEO Steve Linford leaked, death threats forced him from the country.

As was the case elsewhere in technology, simple economics drove substantial progress on the part of the spammers. Since it cost just a few pennies to send millions of emails, a tiny percentage of recipients clicking through and buying what was on offer made the financials compelling. A dozen or more of the most prolific spammers made millions hawking penis enlargement pills, get-rich-quick schemes, and counterfeit pharmaceuticals.

When blacklists stopped spammers from using a single computer to reach everyone, the more entrepreneurial bought or rented another machine. Better still, they stayed put and bounced their emails off what are called open proxies. Proxies are in the email-routing software within many large computers. In more trusting days, they were left "open" and therefore would helpfully relay any incoming mail to the next stop. Many administrators never bothered to change that setting, generally because they didn't realize that the spammers were abusing their machines to launder the Internet addresses from which they were spamming, evading the blacklists. Gradually, the people in charge of corporate networks figured out that they were aiding the enemy and began closing the loophole.

At the same time that the business-minded spammers were developing a bigger appetite for open proxies, the world of computer viruses was blossoming. Long the handiwork of teenage computer geeks with an excess of curiosity and a deficiency in common sense, viruses spread faster as more people bought software with security flaws, especially Microsoft products. Because consumers got used to clicking on new kinds of attachments in email, electronic messages became one of the easiest vectors for spreading viruses. There were many others, though, including instant messages, rigged websites, and especially pernicious "worms" that spread automatically, without the computer user downloading or clicking on anything. Some security researchers fed the flames by publicly posting their discovery of new vulnerabilities and even "proof of concept" code that showed hackers how to take advantage of them.

The spammers didn't want to use viruses to delete files, turn machines off, or broadcast love for a stripper, as the Melissa virus did. They wanted to harness that power to take control of machines and open them up to send email. While no one has definitively shown how the leading spammers and the virus writers got together, security experts have concluded that the spammers hired virus authors, or wrote such code themselves, in order to make spamming easier. In any case, the era of amateur viruses came to a rapid close.

The early weeks of 2003 brought forth what would develop into a type of virus more threatening than any that had gone before. The first version of the virus was dubbed SoBig by the security researchers who discovered it. Like other viruses, SoBig spread by persuading recipients to open a mislabeled attachment containing a malicious program. Once activated, the virus looked in the machine for new addresses to mail itself to. SoBig was cleverer than most, because it forged the "from" address in outgoing email so that it often appeared to be coming from a trusted friend. More troubling was the complexity of the program, which used encryption and multiple computer languages. SoBig told infected machines to check in with other computers, whose location would be revealed only at the last instant, to get additional tools and instructions. Worst of all, the system appeared to be commercially motivated, in that infected machines would eventually turn into open proxies. Those who knew where to look could use an email program to connect to the new zombie, and the unwitting machine would spew out thousands of messages while disguising the initial source of the mailing.

In May 2003, a new and improved version of SoBig started spreading. But the initial alarm at a serial offender was mitigated by an unusual twist in the coded instructions: after spreading for two weeks, the worm was programmed to turn itself off. That made the project appear to be some kind of science experiment, where the author was holding himself in check, perhaps due to some moral misgivings. As new versions of SoBig began to appear—labeled SoBig.C, SoBig.D, and so on—the mechanics of the program grew more sophisticated. They hid the second and third phases of infection better and fixed various bugs. SoBig.E sent attachments as compressed or "zipped" files, allowing them to get past gatekeeper software that bars executable programs from getting into corporate networks. By then, security experts realized that the short shelf life of the new versions was one of the most ominous things about them. It meant that the authors—by now generally believed to be members of a highly organized group—didn't want old versions cluttering up the Internet when they released better varieties. They were learning from each assault and refining their work.

On August 18, 2003, someone using a stolen credit card and the online handle "Misiko" posted what he described as a "nice" pornographic picture to several online newsgroups. When others downloaded the file, they unleashed SoBig.F, which in short order would become the biggest virus of all time. SoBig.F sent more than 300 million emails with such subject lines as "Your Details," "Thank you!" and "Re: Approved." SoBig's mail clogged the networks at FedEx and Starbucks and shut down CSX passenger trains.

The programming was by far the best ever seen by the top virus hunters. Those researchers were an odd breed, often self-taught experts like Barrett. Many worked for small companies, like Finland's F-Secure or Atlanta's SecureWorks, that big security firms relied on for help in protecting corporate clients from the latest threats. The global cadre raced to decrypt and analyze the code, and a team from F-Secure got there first. When it did, the researchers found that SoBig.F told infected machines to contact twenty master computers for a new payload on Friday, August 22, at 7 P.M. Greenwich time—just thirty hours away—and then again every subsequent Friday until September 10. Given how fearsome the foundation program was, the experts hated to imagine what the next step would be.

Once the Web addresses of the twenty masters had been identified, Finnish and U.S. authorities tracked them to the U.S., Canadian, and South Korean Internet service providers they depended on, then succeeded in getting most of the computers knocked offline. Microsoft and others joined the chase for the remaining machines as the minutes ticked down. Finally, nineteen of the twenty had been neutralized. While much of the technological world held its breath, the twentieth was overwhelmed with zombie traffic at the appointed hour. When experts succeeded in connecting to that computer a short time later, it was still redirecting infected hosts to Gary Kremen's Sex.com, a harmless pornographic site being used as a placeholder. Hearing the figurative footsteps coming up the path, the virus writers had never put their next phase into play.

SoBig stopped spreading quickly and began to fade from public awareness as 2003 came to a close. Then along came two similar uber-viruses, Bagle and MyDoom. Like their inspiration, both were frequently updated with improvements. These too showed the so-phistication that is a hallmark of organized criminal activity. And both created new legions of zombie computers for spam and other ends. In MyDoom's case, the trimmings included a successful denial-of-service attack on the SCO Group, a software company that had outraged technologists by filing copyright suits against firms using the free operating system Linux. Like some earlier virus-enhanced denial-of-service attacks, MyDoom's assault might have reflected per-sonal taste but was more probably a red herring for investigators and a bid to win some points with technophiles angered by the infections. Prolexic defended against the SCO attack for about five hours. The firepower was so massive that the company told SCO it would cost $200,000 a month to fight off. The company decided to register a new Web address instead.

Bagle had the distinction of being the first truly commercial virus, according to Russia's Kaspersky Labs. It opened a back door, and later downloads through that opening turned the captured computers into open relays for spam. Estimates of the damage from the three giant spam-driven viruses ran well into the billions of dollars. When no one was charged with their release, it underscored how powerless au-thorities were in fighting cybercrime. That failure prompted some ambitious responses by private citizens, in ways both good and bad.

The most notable case of vigilantism run amok was that of a German vocational computer student named Sven Jaschen. The seventeen-year-old was impressed by MyDoom's technical merits and appreciative of its DDoS attack on SCO, which rendered the company's main website unreachable. But he was horrified by the crass financial motivation he saw behind MyDoom. Jaschen asked a classmate if he thought they could build something together that would spread even more quickly and wipe out MyDoom. Sitting in the basement of his home in Rotenburg, across the desk from his computer-repairman stepfather, Jaschen wrote a total of twenty-nine versions of what came to be called NetSky. The virus used the same recently discovered Windows hole as MyDoom and Bagle to enter machines, but then removed the pernicious programs and all traces of the infections.

While the fight was deadly serious, the sides traded insults like children. Bagle.J contained the following text: "Hey Netsky, fuck off you bitch, don't ruine [*sic*] our business, wanna start a war?" And a war is what it was. Each version of all three not only improved from the previous edition but also adapted to the latest moves by its opponents. In clandestine battles fought inside family rooms and dusty studies in homes across the world, each virus used the advances to roust foes from their lairs. In terms of sheer numbers of hosts infected, the underdog NetSky was the most successful of the three. As a result, said F-Secure's Mikko Hypponen, it was more effective in cutting down on the flow of spam than anything that had happened in Congress or the federal courts. Jaschen "saw himself as some kind of Robin Hood."

Most professionals would say that NetSky, like its forebears, was a bad idea to begin with. It tied up resources and complicated the efforts of security experts as they tried to plug holes and fix the damage. And though Jaschen produced the most effective antivirus virus to date, he took a questionable act and then made it indefensible. As he released new versions to keep up with better Bagles and MyDooms, Jaschen added functions that strayed farther and farther from his initial plan. First he included denial-of-service attacks against websites that offered hacking tools. Then he slid more, adding as targets some peer-to-peer sites for file traders and even some universities that had kicked Jaschen out.

Jaschen's next project was a virus called Sasser, which had no redeeming qualities at all. It forced computers to reboot continuously. In May 2004 Sasser shut down most of the train traffic in Australia and knocked out X-ray equipment at two hospitals in Sweden. For several months, Hypponen said, Jaschen "was probably the most powerful seventeen-year-old in the world." Not long after his eighteenth birthday, Jaschen was arrested. He had been betrayed by the classmate to whom he had turned for advice. Even though he was suspected of collaborating with Jaschen, the whistleblower-come-lately was hoping for a $250,000 bounty from Microsoft. Tired of criticism and lost sales due to its security issues—as well as the denial-of-service attacks against it—Microsoft had recently begun offering rewards for the capture of virus writers. For what may have been the most important company on the planet, it was a startling strategy—a lot less Harvard Business School and a lot more Wild West, and a potent indicator of how far the Net had moved beyond control.

• • •

SOBIG'S INTELLIGENCE AND POWER had overwhelmed law enforcement and the growing ranks of security professionals. It suggested that organized gangs working for or with spammers could take control of the Internet at any time. Out of official sight, a small group of researchers decided to dedicate themselves to figuring out who was behind the virus that changed the world.

The team took six months to thoroughly dissect the code underlying SoBig, the changes in each new version, and the timing of those shifts. The crew concluded that the stylistic tics in the program echoed those of one of the worst providers of spamming services in the world, a Russian company that made software called Send-Safe.

Send-Safe not only provided the technology to deliver spam, it offered a list of open relays that could be used in the process for an additional fee. By creating relay zombies, SoBig directly benefited the makers of Send-Safe.

In addition, a major customer that routinely used pre-release versions of Send-Safe had started using computer ports that would be opened by new versions of SoBig a week later. That implied that the same people who had advance knowledge of Send-Safe had advance knowledge of SoBig. The researchers gave their findings to the FBI. When six months passed without any action, the team posted their work on the Net under the title "Who Wrote SoBig," where it attracted attention from other security researchers—and the man the team named as the most likely suspect for leading the SoBig effort, Send-Safe executive Ruslan Ibragimov. The Russian denied involvement, calling it "bullshit" in an online interview.

But Ibragimov also sent an email to the anonymous address posted by the study's authors. "Just read your doc. I'm very impressed ☺," he wrote. The paper stirred up massive opposition to Send-Safe. After a concerted effort organized online, the company's foes succeeded in getting telecom giant MCI to stop hosting Send-Safe's website, an account that had been bringing in $5 million a year. Within days, Send-Safe had been evicted from two subsequent homes, forcing it out of the world of speedy Western technology hosts. It was a rare victory that showed how the concerted effort of professionals and volunteers could do something to blunt the growing clout of the criminals.

In the first interview he granted on the subject, the lead author of the SoBig paper said the real force behind SoBig was not Send-Safe but the big Send-Safe customer. He declined to identify that customer explicitly, out of fear for his physical safety. But he said it was not an ordinary spammer, instead one with special needs. In the context of the conversation, the most reasonable interpretation of his comments is that he was talking about an agency of the Russian government.

The authors of "Who Wrote SoBig?" did more than silence the apparent writer of the first massive spam-financed virus. They inspired others to take up their methods. One of the best was Joe Stewart, who worked for a small South Carolina security firm that has since been bought by SecureWorks. At the least Stewart came up with a compelling lead for anyone investigating the Bagle family of viruses.

In early 2004, a couple of weeks after the first version of Bagle began spreading, Stewart got a tip from an industry colleague in Bulgaria that someone was offering to sell a program that would turn computers into open relays for sending spam. The advertisement, by someone calling himself Oboron, was posted on CarderPlanet, a notorious Russian-language forum for fraudsters. CarderPlanet was one-stop shopping for cybercriminals, offering everything from spam services to tools for computer break-ins.

The sale of an insidious spam program was no longer a startling offer. But out of professional curiosity, Stewart grabbed the demonstration version of the program and reverse-engineered it to get at the underlying code. Oboron's Trojan horse for the computer takeovers turned out to be the same program left behind by Bagle when it broke into a machine.

Of course, Stewart realized, the Trojan could have been written by some third party and sold to both Oboron and Bagle's author. So Stewart kept monitoring the salesman's postings and collecting information on him. As Bagle spread further and further, Stewart saw the salesman's business model change. Instead of just offering the Trojan for sale, the salesman began charging for access to a network of compromised machines, for as little as $200 a month. Oboron's program invoked the same Web address that was used to control drone computers under Bagle's spell, and it had the same ability to block IP addresses of spammers who abused the system or didn't pay.

Stewart gave his research to the FBI. "I thought law enforcement should have enough to go on here to follow up and catch this guy. I know better now," he said. His law enforcement contacts initially reacted with enthusiasm. That was followed by silence lasting weeks, then months, as evidence slipped away and the trail grew cold. "I've learned that law enforcement is pretty much unable to act unless you can hand them 'actionable' intelligence, showing a clear trail of evidence and the perp's name and home address," Stewart said at the time. "I doubt anyone will ever be arrested for writing Bagle."

Still angry at "seeing a few jerks ruin a good thing for the rest of us," Stewart decided to try to identify Oboron on his own. He believes he succeeded. After giving the full report to the FBI and seeing no action, Stewart agreed to have his findings spelled out here.

Oboron initially offered his Trojan for sale on a site called Elitehackers.com. His profile on that site gave the email address Sprutnet@mail.ru. On another forum, crack.ru, one SprutNet listed his email address as zoomoboron@mail.ru. Still elsewhere, a hacker accused an Oboron of not being SprutNet, who had built a good reputation selling malicious software. Oboron replied that he was, and noted that both had used the ICQ instant messaging address 353000. The profile directory maintained by ICQ showed that number was supposed to belong to a twenty-four-year-old woman named Yvonne. But the picture on Yvonne's page was of a young man, who listed as his homepage www.sprutznet.chat.ru/sprutnet.html.

More Internet searches turned up a Web page offering a Trojan claimed by a "Sprutnet" at ICQ number 353000. Checking the source code for that Web page revealed that it had been created in Microsoft Word, and the metadata listed the author of the Word file as "Pavel." One last page contained the prize. On the Russian business-to-individual sales site Plati.ru, a company had registered as SprutNET, of Vladivostok, on Russia's east coast. The company gave for its contacts ICQ number 353000 and email sprutnet@mail.ru. Finally, it gave a name for those who wanted to get in touch: Pavel Ramzinskiy. Perhaps he had taken the risk of combining those two identities to get credit in the Plati.ru feedback system from customers he served in each guise: SprutNET was listed as having fifty-five positive reviews and no negatives. Quality always shines through.

• • •

THE STELLAR WORK OF STEWART and the lead SoBig investigator was doubly futile. While they managed to name suspects, neither was arrested, strongly suggesting a lack of interest by Russian authorities. Second, identifying and stopping a virus author would never again be as important, because soon anyone would be able to cobble one together. In February 2004, the latest version of the MyDoom virus included a copy of the source code for the virus. In July, well after Stewart began his dealings with Oboron, a new Bagle release followed suit. Why would the authors allow their work to escape their control, empowering potential competitors? Researchers weren't sure, but a popular guess was that they were covering themselves in case the original code were found on their computers. If the same code were on tens of thousands of machines, that otherwise critical evidence against them would be worthless.

Whatever the motivation, the mass distribution of high-end virus code meant that hordes of people with lesser skills could take and modify code for ensnaring enormous numbers of computers. At Prolexic, Barrett initially kept track of which computers attacking his clients had been corrupted by which viruses. Then he realized that it didn't matter. So much code was on the loose and readily available that tracking it did little good. By 2004, the eruption in virus code and zombie botnets brought the boom to a community of thousands of hackers and criminals. Many offered spamming services, while others offered the almost equally straightforward denial-of-service attacks for hire.

An awkward German teenager probably did more than anyone else to put botnets in the mainstream. Axel Gembe, aka Ago, dropped out of school in ninth grade and lived with his father and brother in a small Black Forest village. He taught himself to program and developed a worm, called Agobot, to see if he could. Agobot had a lot going for it. It worked well and it was modular, making it easy for him or others with the code to add in new exploits as they became available.

Two related innovations were still more important for the history of online criminality, although neither was Gembe's idea. Both stemmed from the small group of online contacts that helped Gembe in spots, some of whom had ambitions that helped propel hacking into the commercial world. At their urging, Gembe set up a website in 2003 where people could buy modified and improved versions of the program for as little as $50. One of Gembe's associates distributed the Agobot code online, where others could use it, "we suppose to raise his profile," said Frank Eissmann, the lead German police officer on the case. Agobot-derived worms were still spreading five years later, and the move might have inspired the MyDoom authors to release their own code.

The other big innovation was contributed by a British associate of Gembe's, Lee Walker. Walker cut a deal with American Paul Ashley, who hosted e-commerce sites and was looking for help launching denial-of-service attacks for a client. Walker and others provided the Agobot code, expertise, and drone computer networks, and Ashley crippled competitive websites for his client, Saad "Jay" Echouafni, who sold satellite television services. It was the deal that brought DDoS-for-hire into the Western marketplace.

The direct victims in the case included online retailer Weaknees .com of Los Angeles, which was essentially shut down for two weeks in October, costing it $200,000. Attacks on another target, Rapid Satellite.com, battered the systems of the company hosting the site,

Speedera Networks of Mountain View, California, so badly that the websites of all Speedera customers—including Amazon.com and the U.S. Department of Homeland Security—couldn't be accessed for nearly an hour. Speedera estimated its losses at $1 million. The Echouafni case was the first U.S. prosecution of a financially motivated denial-of-service attack. It took months of investigation by experts in several states and England before charges could be filed, although the hackers failed to cover all their tracks. The FBI also had an unusual advantage in that Echouafni was immediately suspected because of a business dispute with Weaknees, which sold TiVo and other digital video recorders. The case did help the German police catch Gembe, who was apprehended in May 2004. Even so, the man with the money got away. Echouafni jumped bail, earning his way onto the FBI's list of Ten Most Wanted fugitives.

Such unchecked innovations transformed hacking from a guild-like activity to a modern industry. For Send-Safe and others who sent billions of pieces of spam, the entry of additional players increased competition and drove down profit. Virus-ruled botnets would continue to spew spam for years, offering services to the highest bidders, and Spamhaus's list of the worst offenders would continue to feature many Russians. But the bigger opportunity lay in emerging fields, especially identity theft. The federal anti-spam law that took effect in 2004, known as the CAN-SPAM Act, only hastened that trend. The law legalized commercial email that wasn't deceptive. But many spammers who were deceptive, and therefore newly at risk, decided they might as well go all the way and start "phishing," or sending spam designed to trick people into revealing their credit card and banking numbers and passwords, their eBay and PayPal logins, and anything else that could be converted into cash.

Phishing began simply as spam with spoofed "from" addresses, messages appearing to come from eBay or Citibank and sent to everyone in the spammer's lists. Most recipients wouldn't be clients of any given financial company, but it didn't take many for the math to work. Even if only one person in a hundred was a customer, millions would get the bait and several thousand of them would bite. As word spread about what was happening and the fraud market grew saturated, phishers moved downstream, even sending mass emails purporting to come from obscure local credit unions in search of new victims. Otherwise, the scams got better and better. The crooks polished their laughable English. Some not only used the wording and images of the real sites they imitated, they linked back to them in case anyone clicked there. They also became adept at faking Web addresses so that even professionals couldn't tell they weren't about to go to a legitimate site to enter their financial information. When it seemed everyone in the world must have been warned about phishing attacks, the bad guys sent fake emails from financial institutions alerting users that they had been phished—and that they would need to reenter security information to reactivate their accounts. Yet many targeted companies continued to send emails with Web links themselves. Small wonder so many millions of Americans failed to internalize the warnings never to click on any Web address contained in an email.

As competition among phishers increased, the innovators invested in efforts to hack into corporate databases, stealing everyone's financial information at once, or getting the same files with "social engineering," more familiarly known as trickery. The number of disclosed hacks into companies soared to 656 a year by 2008, with more than 35 million identities at risk just that year, according to a tally from before the discovery of the biggest breaches. That didn't count phishing victims or those stung by hackers who used security holes and viruses to enslave computers or to install "keyloggers," as Barrett's Russian criminals were doing in 2006. Those programs sent off anything typed, including credit card information, or lay dormant and unobservable until the consumer visited any of a long list of financial websites. U.S. residents were natural targets because they used credit cards far more than Europeans and had higher credit limits.

Competitive forces weren't the only thing driving identity theft into the stratosphere. Free-speech laws meant that writing viruses and other malicious programs—even publishing and selling such programs—was generally protected behavior. Worse, the U.S. courts had held that lousy commercial software—the sort with obvious security holes that allow all manner of attacks—were immune from product-liability suits, on the grounds that they technically aren't sold to customers but licensed, or loaned under strict conditions.

The U.S. banks, however, bear a large part of the blame. They didn't make their cards as secure as European banks did, and they continued such inherently unsafe practices as sending unsolicited credit card applications through the mail and approving credit with minimal identification. The financial institutions were in no hurry to tighten standards because of a little-known fact: retailers, not banks, generally absorbed losses caused by identity thieves wielding pilfered credit card numbers. Many identity theft victims didn't have to pay for the charges or loans made in their names. Visa and MasterCard covered the expenses, then passed them back to the businesses where goods were sold to the wrong person. That setup ensured that the credit card companies, which were often thought to be absorbing losses, actually earned money from many instances of fraud. The merchants couldn't afford to stop accepting credit cards, and they had nowhere near enough muscle in Washington to change the system. Financial institutions spent more than ten times as much on lobbying as retailers did. The federal government might have gotten more serious if there had been a public hue and cry. But it was generally the poorest victims who suffered the most—a third reported being harassed by debt collectors after such fraud—and they had the least power.

Yet in a sense, the credit card industry was leveraging itself too deeply. Because it played down concerns about identity theft, nothing changed. As the first decade of the millennium waned, the crime kingpins shifted focus again, going after ATM and debit cards and stealing directly from online bank accounts. In those cases, the banks were frequently on the hook, and they had to eat a growing, if still undisclosed, amount of losses. The criminals had reinvested their loot and gotten much better in the interim, while U.S. banks by then lagged farther behind their global peers in security. By this point, two things could go seriously wrong with electronic commerce. The first was that as fraud burned more consumers, enough would pull back that they shrank the system. Caution is already slowing growth. The second was that the banks themselves, already half-wrecked by the economic crisis that exploded in late 2008, would be so desperate to reduce their burgeoning fraud write-downs that they pulled back from e-commerce on their own.

Visa, MasterCard, and the banks that collectively controlled those card associations didn't just keep quiet about the epidemic of identity theft: they actively worked to distort the public discourse. In 2005, for example, Visa, banker Wells Fargo, and online payment firm Check-Free Services Corp., all of which profited from Internet finance, paid for a purportedly independent research report following up on a land-mark Federal Trade Commission study two years earlier that certified the pandemic of identity theft. The Better Business Bureau and the FTC were listed as advisors on the 2005 report.

The most startling finding: according to the study's author, Javelin Strategy and Research, "Although there has been much recent public concern over electronic methods of obtaining information, most thieves still obtain personal information through traditional channels rather than through the Internet." The report said 72 percent of iden-tity theft crimes occurred the old-school way, such as via a stolen purse or pilfered mail. Javelin even advised consumers to do more on-line banking, because those who bank online check their records more frequently and therefore tend to detect improper billing sooner. Top federal prosecutors had a different take. Not only should consumers avoid online banking, authorities said, they shouldn't store any financial information on computers hooked up to the Net.

The problem with the Javelin study's conclusions, reported uncritically in the *New York Times*, the *Wall Street Journal*, and elsewhere, is that they were almost certainly false. According to the details in the report, only 54 percent of the victims surveyed knew how their information had leaked. So only 72 percent of 54 percent of the cases were reasonably believed to spring from traditional theft—or 39 percent. Javelin founder James Van Dyke claimed that the majority of unsolved cases were likely to be offline crimes as well. He went on, improbably, to describe phishing fraud as "the biggest non-event. . . . There's scant evidence within the merchants of any large-scale phishing attack. These crimes are under control."

FTC Associate Director Lois Greisman begged to differ. "We have concerns with putting out, frankly, numbers like that," Greisman said, adding that extrapolating from the 54 percent who knew what happened didn't make sense. "I know if I've lost my purse," she said. "A big problem with phishing is that people have no idea they've been phished." Beyond that logical flaw, the vast majority of business was still conducted offline: for that reason, one would expect most theft to occur there. The fact that Javelin's study failed to show that it did reinforced the belief of technology experts that online commerce was already riskier than traditional business and getting more so.

Each year from 2004 on, Internet crime grew dramatically more effective, increasingly organized, and disproportionately led by groups overseas. But the problem was exacerbated by the inaction and dissembling of major U.S. industries and an inadequate government response. CheckFree Services, which played a role in nurturing consumer complacency, eventually would have a direct hand in punishing them for that stance. In December 2008, hackers obtained the company's login credentials at Web registrar Network Solutions and sent anyone coming to CheckFree's site over a four-hour period to a bogus page hosted in Ukraine. That page attempted to install password-stealing programs on the computers of thousands of CheckFree clients.

Barrett Lyon had become the leading defender against a particularly brutal aspect of cybercrime. He had saved dozens of companies. He had taken down a few bad guys and taught the authorities how to catch more. DDoS attacks continued, and would soon find new types of targets, but Barrett realized he was largely fighting yesterday's battle. He couldn't defend millions of people at once. The new war, against mass identity theft and the underground economy itself, couldn't be waged without at least the concerted effort of many governments—and perhaps a rebooting of the Internet's essential architecture.

PART TWO

7

WHATEVER
IT TAKES

WHEN BARRETT LYON handed off what he knew about the BetCRIS attackers to agents from the United Kingdom's National Hi-Tech Crime Unit in 2004, he didn't expect much more satisfaction than he had gotten from the FBI. He was impressed that they had flown to California on the case and that they saw their mission as a broad one: to protect electronic commerce however they could, be it by arrests or education. But prosecutions even in Western countries were extremely rare, and Barrett had personally traced Ivan Maksakov, the hacker known as eXe, to Russia. He had no reason to think Britain could do any more there than the U.S. could.

Gradually, though, Barrett came to realize that the case went to just the right country at just the right time. Prime Minister Tony Blair's government, determined to get Internet security right, had built up a crack national police team with first-rate agents and independently minded managers. One of the three dozen on the elite squad was Andy Crocker, a Welshman who had spent fifteen years in the armed forces, mostly as an instructor of everything from shooting to kayaking. After the army he joined the police department in Surrey, outside London. Starting as a patrol officer, he rose to detective, handling robberies and violent crime. Most of that was easy. Computer crime, when it came along, was more interesting: it was too new for an instruction manual. Andy launched Surrey's tech crime division and devised a still-secret technique for tracking visitors to websites that were likely to interest crime suspects. When Andy took a training course for NHTCU officers, they saw he knew more than they did and pushed to bring him aboard.

Like Barrett, Andy had turned to computers as an alternative to his frustrations at school. For Barrett, it had been the intellectual challenge of understanding the logic of the systems first, followed later by the thrill of competition with enemy hackers. With Andy, it was the other way around. The son of a heating engineer and a housewife in the South Wales seaport city of Swansea, Andy often skipped classes to carouse and fight with his friends. As they drifted into drugs and stole cars, Andy tried to channel his aggression, boxing competitively and joining the army at sixteen. As a balding but athletic suburban police detective two decades later at the turn of the millennium, Andy set up the computer crime department because the quarry were more challenging than the typical violent louts of the sort he had grown up with.

Andy had added enough polish over the years to speak easily with celebrity burglary victims and diplomats, yet he stayed close enough to his roots to pound vodka shots with cops overseas who earned half the salary of a London janitor. Though Andy participated in the elite sport of dressage, running horses through jumps and other obstacles, he was coming from a different place than his rivals. Once the forty-four-year-old Andy was thrown to the ground and dislocated his hip. He refused to see a doctor and competed the next day. He realized he had a serious problem only when he thought he was squeezing both knees into the horse's flanks, urging him forward. The horse felt pressure on just one side and turned instead.

Andy had probed exactly one denial-of-service case when the first gambling company complained to the NHTCU in October 2003. That had been years before at the Surrey police department, when a man hijacked a university's computers for an attack on an Internet Relay Chat channel. Andy worked with cybercrime specialist Steve Santorelli at the London Metropolitan Police, commonly known as Scotland Yard, who made the arrest. (Santorelli later joined Team Cymru, the nonprofit network security group that tracked arch cyber-criminals.) That single case was enough to make Andy the NHTCU's DDoS expert by default when the agency fielded a call from Canbet Ltd., an Australian betting company with a major office in Portsmouth, England.

Andy had not yet heard of Barrett when Canbet reported that it had been shut down by a DDoS and was losing $100,000 a day. Andy and another officer, Trevor Dickey, went on a Monday to the Canbet office, where the company's U.K. boss told them the website had been hammered over the weekend. An email demanded $40,000 to stop the attack, with the sum to be broken into four payments and sent via Western Union to accomplices in Latvia. The company had already decided to pay. Andy told them the easiest way for him to figure out who was behind the attack was to follow the money.

Andy liked the intrigue of the case immediately. It was something truly novel, and the chance to travel someplace new carried the prospect of adventure and good stories for his mates. Andy couldn't get to Latvia by the next day, when the extortionist wanted his money delivered. But some forethought by the NHTCU kept hope alive. Len Hynds, the head of the unit, had realized early on that most serious technology crimes crossed national boundaries. And the official means for getting cooperation from authorities in other countries was a nightmare. A British agent would have to draft a formal "letter of request" spelling out exactly what was wanted. Then the letter would go to one of the top officials in the unit, and then to the crown prosecutor, the equivalent of the U.S. attorney general. From there it went to the top prosecutor in the other country, who would eventually pass it along to the head of the relevant police force, who would hopefully put it in front of a detective, who probably had cases of his or her own that were a lot more pressing. Even with an ally as close and as well funded as the United States, the process usually took months. In a place like Latvia, there traditionally had been no point in trying.

Hynds set out to change the system. He divided up the world and sent his agents out to every country that might be important in a future investigation. The agents took the heads of the national computer crime units out to dinner, learned about their problems, and found out what they needed. Often the NHTCU sent them decent computers to replace their outdated models. And the British agents went home with everyone's phone number and an understanding: When a big case was breaking, the hated letters of request would still be sent. But the right people would be getting a phone call, telling them where the letter was in the process, what was in it, and why it mattered.

After the Canbet meeting, Andy wrote the formal letter, while the colleague who had done the wining and dining in Latvia, Mike Ford, made the phone calls. On Wednesday, Andy and Trevor Dickey flew in and joined a Latvian officer from Interpol, the international police association. They drove through the capital of Riga to the national computer crime division's offices. The headquarters were in a decrepit building that had housed spies from the KGB during the Soviet empire. A plaque on the outside commemorated the Latvians who had been tortured there. Inside, the holes in the floor were so big that a man could fall through them.

Andy had stalled by getting Canbet to negotiate with the extortionist. At his direction, Canbet said that the requested $10,000 payments would attract too much attention: instead, the company asked for ten names to whom it could send $2,000 apiece in a first series of transfers. Andy had guessed that it would take awhile for the extortionist to set up additional mules to pick up the money, and he was right. Then the company said it could only send $6,000 each day.

Andy and the Latvian police arranged with Western Union to flag the transactions and call the computer crime division's offices when anyone came to collect. In the meantime, the locals identified the most likely Western Union outlets for a questionable pickup, and the team put each of them under surveillance. Andy soon started getting the calls. He relayed the physical descriptions of the mules to the teams waiting outside, which followed the men to their apartments and kept on their trail for days to see where they would go with the money. But before they could identify the next handoff, the mules went back to Western Union and picked up more cash. Andy called Western Union and demanded to know why he hadn't been tipped off again. "It's not your money," the manager explained. It wasn't just Canbet that was sending funds to the Latvians—it was dozens of companies from the U.K., Costa Rica, and around the world, most of whom had obviously never gone to their governments for help. "Oh my God," Andy muttered. "Just how big is this?"

After making repeated collections, the Latvians headed for a big office building that housed a local franchise of Webmoney, a service like PayPal or e-Gold that simplified financial transactions but also appeared to be tailor-made for hiding fraud. In November, after Dickey had returned to England for training, the Latvian police swooped in and made ten arrests, bringing the crew in for hours of individual interrogations on metal chairs in the cramped, dingy former KGB redoubt. Andy and his allies couldn't get everything they wanted, because the mules didn't know enough. The Webmoney franchise owner said everything had been arranged over ICQ instant-message sessions with someone inside Russia he knew as Stran, who wanted everything sent to a bank account in the Russian city of Pyatig-orsk. Andy assumed that Stran was still another mule. Nonetheless, he started banging out a letter of request to Russian officials. There wasn't much more he could do from Latvia; it wasn't even clear that the mules had broken any local laws.

• • •

ANDY RETURNED TO LONDON only to discover that the Russians had hit a slew of other major U.K. betting companies, including Blue Square, Ladbrokes, and William Hill. Some had paid up, and several had gone to the NHTCU. Executives from many of the companies also began getting together weekly to compare notes and hear from NHTCU investigators and technologists. Word spread quickly about how Barrett's company had saved some firms in Costa Rica. When that news got back to Andy, he had a colleague send the email that led to the meeting in Los Angeles where Barrett passed on the transcripts of his first chats with the assailants. Barrett told the men that he thought the same ring was behind a wide range of attacks, and they said that if that were the case, they were either extraordinarily efficient or extremely busy.

SportingIndex was typical of the early victims, though it was such an oddity in the gambling world that it was regulated by the U.K. futures exchange, like a broker of commodities. Instead of letting customers bet on which team would win a game, the twelve-year-old London firm predicted the point totals in rugby, soccer, and other matches and then took wagers on whether the real scores would be higher or lower. Bettors could also wander into more remote territory, such as how many times in a televised match featuring soccer star David Beckham the camera would pan to show his wife, former "Posh Spice" Victoria Beckham. At SportingIndex, dozens of employees known as traders—mostly young men in jeans and casual shirts—sat on one of the company's three floors in a brick building in a residential district, each monitoring at least two personal computers and watching four television sets. More than half of the bets came in over the Internet—when everything was working.

One Sunday in January 2004, SportingIndex got an email from JohnHancock99@hotmail.com, who asked for $10,000, then attacked the site for four hours. "This money is a small help for our team. We think that it's not large money for you," the American patriot wrote. The next Friday another attack came, at a low level at first. The next day it got worse, so the company began to switch the numeric addresses that were home to its flagship website. The attacker kept following through each of the moves. With major soccer events coming the following week, SportingIndex information technology director Hugo Smith talked with peers at other targets that had paid $200,000 or more to install traffic filters. Then Smith's supervisor, Andrew Ross, talked to agent Bob Lewis, who worked with Andy at the NHTCU.

"We'll investigate," Lewis told him. "But you shouldn't count on it working. In the meantime, off the record, you should talk to this young chap named Barrett." Ross had his doubts, especially since Prolexic was officially based in "dodgy" Costa Rica. It even crossed his mind that Barrett might be behind the attacks, drumming up business the old-school way. He called anyway. Barrett didn't want to talk about how much he would charge. "First let me take a look at your site and see if I can help you," he said.

Barrett accepted the job that Monday. By Wednesday, the site was still down, the phones were ringing off the hook, and Ross's boss was breathing fire, since a championship soccer match was scheduled to start at 7:30 P.M. At 6:50 P.M., Barrett got the site up again. Ross screamed his thanks over the phone. Barrett seemed as placid as could be. "No problem," he said. "We'll keep an eye on it."

As Barrett worked on defense, Andy Crocker had been continuing to press ahead on offense. He knew there had been little help from Russia in past international crimes, with a few exceptions in drug smuggling and tax cases. To make those cases, he gathered, British agents had to have been persistent, talented, and lucky, finding just the right vein to work in the mammoth Russian bureaucracy.

After a flurry of paperwork, Andy began shuttling back and forth to Moscow, staying two or three weeks at a time. For his first trip, in November 2003, Mike Ford wangled an introduction to Department R, the Moscow police division charged with technology cases. Dept. R belonged to the sprawling Russian Ministry of the Interior, known by the acronym MVD, which operated like the FBI but also ran the police departments in every city. Dept. R had received the letter of request asking for help in intercepting Webmoney transfers to the man known as Stran and in identifying him. And the officers there had indeed been investigating the matter in the intervening three weeks. But they saw no reason to share what they had found.

It was a slap after the enthusiastic cooperation in Latvia, a bad sign about how any joint operations were going to be conducted. Andy was left to drink vodka with the police colonel in charge of Dept. R, while the colonel's men did the work. At the end of the day, the colonel would tell Andy what he felt like telling him, which wasn't much. It didn't help that the bitter Moscow winter was different from anything Andy had encountered in the army, even when he taught skiing to servicemen. Once Andy thought he saw a billowing cloud of smoke emerge from the entrance to the Pushkin Square subway station. He couldn't understand why people were still walking in. As Andy drew closer, he finally realized that the cloud was water vapor condensing as the trapped human moisture inside hit the freezing external air. It was as if the entire subway system could see its breath. The same way a Texas television reporter might try to fry an egg on the sidewalk during a heat wave, a Moscow station's reporter emptied a bucket of water off a roof, then showed it turning to ice and shattering as it hit the ground.

The Cold War hadn't thawed much either. Everywhere Andy went, he saw men from the all-powerful Federal Security Service, or FSB, the spy agency that inherited most of the old KGB's duties in 1995 and had gone on to assume the same dominant role in society once played by the Communist Party. The men didn't bother much with subtlety. After a week's trip to England, Andy returned through the Moscow airport and got a border agent who didn't know he was supposed to make a phone call and then ask Andy some time-consuming questions. As the U.K. detective drove off, traffic police promptly pulled his car over until an FSB sedan could catch up and start following him. Staying at the Golden Ring hotel, across from the towering, Stalin-era building housing the Ministry of Foreign Affairs, Andy saw that FSB agents were constantly tailing him. He and a colleague teased them one day, waiting until the last second before darting across a busy boulevard to the Golden Ring as the crossing signal changed. When they got to the opposing sidewalk, they turned around and smiled. One agent had sprinted after them as cars honked: he angrily lowered his head and went past them. Another hung back and tried to conceal himself behind a lamppost. Andy and his colleague walked to their hotel elevator and were still laughing when the desk clerk ran to intercept them, demanding they show identification. That gave the FSB time to get inside. By way of apology, Andy sent the agents beers in the lobby restaurant that night, but the spies grumpily sent them back.

Barrett had identified one of the servers directing the attacks on BetCRIS as having the domain name fbi.pp.ru, and he saw that the same server was going after the London betting firms. The Dept. R detectives now managed to trace that server to an Internet hosting service in Houston that was known for providing computing facilities to scam artists and other Internet undesirables. Andy asked Houston FBI man Todd Burns to go to the provider, Everyone's Internet, and get the server taken offline. Andy was inexperienced enough to think that would end the attacks.

After a wave of denial-of-service assaults on Christmas Eve 2003, Andy flew to Houston in January to get his hands on the server. The head of the Everyone's Internet office provided records showing that the server had been rented by a man in England who paid with a Visa credit card. That transaction would turn out to be like virtually every other technology deal in the multiyear case: the man's credit card information had been stolen, and he had never heard of Everyone's Internet. Andy found the contents of the confiscated Houston hard drive much more useful. The first pass at the hard drive came up empty. Back in England, though, a deeper forensic probe discovered a connection to the box from a site based in the Russian town of Balakovo, a server called balakovo.pp.ru.

Though the FBI's Burns had been happy to help, just as Sacramento agent Matthew Perry had been willing to listen to Barrett, the FBI as a whole still didn't seem especially concerned that American computers had fallen under the control of a Russian gang and that American hosting and connectivity providers were effectively acting as accomplices. The FBI had agreed to broker U.K. dealings with Barrett, but there was no sign they had done any further digging on their own. The combination of unsympathetic and offshore victims, sheer complexity, and probably unarrestable perpetrators was too much for an agency obsessed with Islamic terrorists.

What happened next in Moscow made Andy want to give up on the Americans altogether. As he wheedled information out of Dept. R operatives, an officer of the FSB summoned them to the intimidating FSB headquarters building for a briefing. Once they assembled, the FSB agent gave them a surprising nugget. Some of the money sent to Stran had ended up in the hands of terrorists in Chechnya.

Located just below Russia's volatile south, the predominantly Muslim nation had a special hold on the Russian psyche, like Vietnam and Iraq rolled into one for Americans. Russia had fought two wars there, and the real power in that country remained in the hands of gangsters.

Chechens had conducted vicious attacks on Russian soil, and they had been blamed for apartment bombings around Moscow that killed hundreds, though in all likelihood those were orchestrated by the FSB.

The FBI needs to know the Chechnya connection, Andy thought. He called the U.S. Embassy and told the officials there that he needed to pass along sensitive information about an ongoing international criminal probe that led to terrorists in Chechnya, some of whom had allied with anti-American jihadists. An FBI agent grudgingly agreed to a meeting in the sprawling, high-security Embassy complex, which had been built during the Cold War to include housing, food, and shopping in case bilateral relations deteriorated. But the FBI agent insisted on hearing Andy talk in the Embassy canteen, within earshot of many Russians, and he didn't bother to bring along a pen. After Andy finished whispering what he knew and what he theorized, the FBI agent borrowed Andy's pen, jotted a few notes on a napkin, and promised to relay the information upstairs. Walking out, Andy cursed and vowed never to work with the FBI again.

• • •

ANDY WAS SOON SIX MONTHS into the extortion case. His superiors at the NHTCU were willing to bankroll the effort because they believed that if arrests were made in Russia, it would send a stunning message that no one was safe after attacking British e-commerce. That did not mean, though, that they were delighted to waste their money and Andy's time. Even Andy's patience was wearing out. With help from Barrett, Dept. R had figured out that eXe was operating the server in Balakovo, well south of Moscow. The Russians knew the server's numeric Internet Protocol address, which matched the one Barrett had found and the one on the Houston machine. Now Andy needed to go get the machine.

But every time he pressed for action, the Russians asked him to fill out another form. He completed so many he lost count. None of them made sense to him, and he couldn't grasp the real reason for the stall either. Until he figured it out, at least he could keep typing and showing them that he wasn't going away. In the afternoons, he walked the streets to Red Square and back, stewing in his own juices and wondering how anyone could live in such a country.

Mick Deats, the No. 2 at NHTCU and Andy's boss, arranged to come to Moscow for two weeks of meetings with the brass at Dept. R in a bid to get things moving. Andy brought Deats in from the airport and got him settled in the hotel. The next morning, before the first of their meetings, the British Embassy called to tell them that Dept. R had canceled.

Enraged and making the best use of Deats's greater rank, the two men protested so loudly that they got some additional information that would have been far more useful months earlier: Dept. R had no jurisdiction outside of Moscow. It might have wanted to expand its mission, but for now doing anything in Balakovo or wherever else the trail led required cooperation from another arm of the MVD, Dept. K. "At least you're still in town," Andy told Deats. "Let's see how far we can get with Dept. K." When Andy reached a Dept. K official, he explained the case and told him that they needed to get to Balakovo and that Deats wanted to meet with the top officers in K. The meetings were duly scheduled—and then duly canceled, one after another, for the rest of Deats's time in the country.

On the eve of his departure, a fuming Deats met with the British ambassador to Russia to complain. As it happened, British Foreign Secretary Jack Straw was scheduled to come soon for talks with the Russian minister of foreign affairs, Sergey Lavrov. The ambassador listened sympathetically. He said he would do what he could, and he began plotting with Deats to get the Russian ministry involved. He even pledged to get Andy's plea into the tightly choreographed chat between the two dignataries as they walked between Moscow buildings.

Andy soon got an invitation to meet General Boris Miroshnikov of the MVD, a former FSB official who oversaw Dept. K and much of the rest of the sprawling organization. This time there was no vodka. Instead there were flags from each country in the middle of the table, as if a small piece of the United Nations had come loose and lodged itself in the Russian administration. Miroshnikov was a bright and powerful man, one of a network of FSB alumni who held key posts elsewhere in government and atop many of the telecommunication companies, which the FSB had free rein to tap. Slim and dressed in a suit, Miroshnikov struck Andy as fundamentally serious but half-amused by the situation at hand. "Obviously, you're not going to go away," the general said. "Everything we've asked, you've done. Please go back to the U.K. and return in two weeks. You will have an office, and you will work with this man, Igor Yakovlev." Igor, a broad-shouldered colonel in the MVD's elite, forty-man Investigative Committee, was now in charge of the case, Miroshnikov said. Not even Dept. K, it emerged, could decide to open a formal case. Only the MVD's Investigative Committee could, though it could ask Dept. K for help.

Andy did as he was told. When he came back to Russia, Igor Yakovlev welcomed him politely into his small office. Igor smiled easily but was built like a bear, with a short shock of dark brown hair and a belly that suggested a preference for drink. He sat back down behind a creaky wooden desk that looked like it had been inherited from a high school. None of the rest of the furniture matched, and the small refrigerator in the corner could have been decades old. Igor told Andy that he had gotten up to speed on the case, but he offered few details at first. Instead, Igor introduced Andy to his staff. Five of the men shared a larger office with only three dirty desks among them.

Andy decided to apply what he had learned about Russian customs during his otherwise unproductive time at Dept. R. Drinking prodigious amounts of vodka on the flimsiest of excuses was important, Andy had gathered. That was partially because Russians were the per-capita drinking champions of the world. But there was a sober point to the practice as well. In darker days, when the country was full of government informers, Russians said the best way to tell who was planning to betray the confidences of a group was to look for the man who wasn't drinking.

So Andy took Igor to lunch, informed him that the Queen would be picking up the check, and suggested a little vodka with their meal. A bottle and a half later, they went back to work. The next day was Igor's birthday, and his family came to visit the office. Two more bottles of vodka disappeared before 4 P.M. The next morning, Andy apologized to Igor for passing out, only to learn that Igor's wife, Sonia, had subsequently passed out on Andy's shoulder. "It's very good you feel you can drink with us," Igor reassured him. "I trust you."

That trust would prove the key to the case. Igor was a competent and ambitious officer who had volunteered for the DDoS case despite having never worked a technology crime. He learned quickly. The two men discovered that they had been in the military at the same time: Andy as an instructor in the U.K. forces and Igor as a political officer in an engineering unit of the Russian army. Back then, in Soviet times, being in the Russian army meant you had enough food and money when others had little of either.

In the late 1990s, as the country's power structure collapsed, that no longer held true, and Igor joined the MVD as a detective, working his way up just as Andy did in the English police system. Among other things, such advancement required knowing the safest places to steer an investigation. Igor's largest case involved a nonexistent insulin factory that had been sold to the Russian government for $20 million. He arrested six men—though, of course, none were the corrupt officials who had approved the purchase sight unseen. Four of the six were acquitted, while the other two were granted bail—an unusual event in Russia, except when money changes hands—and then fled.

With gangsters rolling in money that they flaunted in hotels and nightclubs, Andy no longer wondered why so many police officials were corrupt.

Igor himself, for all his rank, earned only about $500 a month to live in what was then the world's third most expensive city. Igor began inviting Andy for Saturday dinners at his modest Moscow flat. In the beginning, each man did his best to impress at the weekly get-togethers. Andy brought vodka, chocolate, and flowers, while Igor's wife cooked all day. As soon as Andy had cleared an inch of food off his plate, it was refilled. There was also the customary ritual toasting, with the first round honoring the meeting, the second or third honoring the guest, and so forth. By June 2004, as Andy's Russian vocabulary had improved, he was using more words than he was absolutely sure of. At one dinner, when Sonia proposed the usual toast to their guest, Igor stunned them both by saying that Andy would never again be a guest in their house. Andy was sure he'd said something unforgivably offensive, and racked his brain for a blanket apology to salvage the deepest law-enforcement collaboration between their countries in a decade. As he began to splutter, Igor explained that Andy was no longer welcome as a guest because he was now part of the family. There were many dinners to come, but they were more what one might expect after stumbling into a buddy's dorm room. Igor would remain on the couch in a T-shirt and shorts, calling out what he wanted Andy to bring from the refrigerator.

Andy was beginning to feel better about Russia. Once he got past the habitual lying and the formality, these were some of the most warm and loyal people he had ever met. They would do anything for someone they trusted. (It didn't hurt that the women were lovely to look at, since Andy fancied himself a bit of a charmer.)

Being a high-ranking police officer in Russia had attractions that were nothing like being on the job in England, where Andy's superiors occasionally turned on the microphone in his police car to make sure nothing inappropriate was said. In Moscow Igor would go out for the evening and drive sloppily, making illegal turns. When the police pulled him over, all Igor had to do was flash his badge and tell the cop to piss off. No one could arrest him but a higher-ranking MVD officer, a judge, or the FSB. Still, the authoritarian structure had obvious downsides. There were many people Igor couldn't go after if he valued his position. When he asked whom Andy could arrest in England, Igor was shocked at the answer: any national officer could arrest anyone short of the Queen, since they were sworn to uphold the Queen's law.

As the men bonded, their investigation finally picked up speed. Within weeks of getting the case, Igor put an undercover man in Balakovo, watching Ivan Maksakov and monitoring his Internet use. That showed Maksakov in frequent contact over ICQ with an IP address in St. Petersburg that the Russians traced to one Denis Stepanov. And the Russians had identified three people who withdrew the money sent from Latvia to the Stran bank account in Pyatigorsk.

Andy and Igor began to rely on each other as deeply as longtime partners in Britain, at times in less conventional ways. One public holiday, after a riverside picnic that included several courses of vodka, the larger, stockier Russian colonel playfully tapped Andy's face with an open hand. Andy, the former competitive boxer, slapped back. Drunken momentum carried the contest into a gloveless fight that ended when Andy punched Igor hard in the eye. His pride wounded, the colonel immediately challenged Andy to a swimming race across the river, which Andy won as well.

The next day, sporting an enormous black eye, Igor went with Andy to visit a bank that had information on some money transfers. When a bank executive refused to hand it over without mounds of paperwork, Igor sat in silence and glared at him with his one good eye. Then he pointed to the other one and warned the executive truthfully: "If you don't help, the man who gave me this will interview you next."

When they had the evidence they needed in July 2004, the team organized what Andy called "a day of action," planning to arrest five prime suspects in one swoop before they had time to warn each other.

8

THE day
OF aCTION

ANDY CROCKER AND IGOR YAKOVLEV planned to make arrests in three cities on July 20, 2004. They scrambled fifteen officers and set their top target as Ivan Maksakov. The hacker lived in Balakovo, a small city on the Volga River. Target No. 2 was Denis Stepanov, to the northwest in St. Petersburg, whom they had seen in online contact with Maksakov. And third, they wanted to raid a house in Pyatigorsk, farther south than Balakovo and just seventy miles from the border with Georgia. The house belonged to a couple, Timur Arutchev and Maria Zarubina. Those two, and Timur's brother Yan Arutchev, were believed to have shared the online identity Stran, which received the extortion payoffs. Following the money-laundering arrests in Latvia, Andy and the investigators in that country and Russia had established that Stran was chatting online with the mules in Latvia while Timur Arutchev was also online on a forum devoted to Webmoney, the currency the mules were sending him. And the bank in Pyatigorsk had told the MVD investigators that all three had withdrawn Webmoney funds sent to an account there.

Since Andy could make it to only one of those far-flung places, he chose Maksakov's house in Balakovo. Andy flew with Igor and several national officers a few days beforehand to the regional capital, Saratov, and headed for the fanciest hotel in town, the Olympia. Andy was the only one with the budget to spring for a luxury room. What he got included a double bed with a single sheet and a bedspread covered with rockets. The stifling midsummer air was so hot that Andy asked about the air conditioning. The little old babushka who had unlocked the door laughed and opened the window. Andy tried washing his hands and then asked what time the hot water came on. The babushka laughed again and told him October 1.

Balakovo was worse. "A one-horse town," he complained to a colleague. "The horse is dead, and it may have been eaten." The detectives badly wanted Maksakov to be at his computer when they arrived to arrest him. If he were using any of his online aliases, that would be even better. He would then have a tough time complaining that someone else had been using his computer when the attacks had been launched and the conspiracy discussed. So Igor had an operative call the house where Maksakov lived with his parents and pretend to be an employee of Maksakov's Internet service provider. "There's a problem with your connection," the man told Maksakov. "Please go online to try it out, and don't turn the computer off. We'll send out a technician."

When the "technician" knocked at the door and Maksakov opened it in a shirt and shorts, the officers barged in. Two forced Maksakov back to his bedroom while the others raced through the house until they found the computer, where he was still logged in. "I'm from the National Hi-Tech Crime Unit in Britain," Andy said through a translator. "We've been following what you've been up to for a long time." Igor joined the double-team: "We know you've been running bots off your server," he said in Russian. "Did you think you could get away with it?"

Maksakov's thin shoulders slumped as he sat down on his bed, shaggy hair flopping over his pale face. Only twenty-one, he was no hard case. "No," Maksakov said quietly. "I knew one day this was coming." For three hours, the detectives let Maksakov tell them what he'd done. He showed real remorse, even writing down his passwords and the online handles he used, including eXe and x3m1st.

Igor tried to comfort Maksakov's parents before officers brought him to the local jail. That night, and for two days afterward, they brought him to the police station for questions, getting more and more detail from the man who until now had been their enemy. As Maksakov sketched out the operation, Andy realized he was taking part in the best interrogation to date of a Russian hacker.

Maksakov said he had been online only since 2000, when he bought his first computer. While he was just a semester shy of graduating from Balakovskova Institute of Technology and Management, like Barrett he had taught himself almost everything he knew about computers. In 2003 he started his own Internet Relay Chat channel, IRC.chatnet.org. To keep the channel active—and immune from takeover attempts—he wrote basic bot code. But he had no server to host the bot, so he read up on common vulnerabilities in Web servers. Then he broke into one and parked his bot command center there. Not long after Maksakov started up the bot, he heard from another man online who called himself Milsan and lived in Kazakhstan. Milsan introduced him to a third man, Zet, who lived in Astrakhan, a Russian city of 500,000 on the Volga an hour from its mouth on the Caspian Sea. Milsan and Zet were developing what Maksakov called a "self-breeding bot," one that would spread by itself among computers, enslaving them as it went. They invited him to join the effort. Asked who had been in charge of fbi.pp.ru, the server Andy had seized in Houston, Maksakov said it was yet another man, named Bra1n. Maksakov said he didn't know Bra1n's real name or where he lived, but that he was "into" DDoS attacks and extortion. After the Houston machine disappeared, Maksakov had to rent his own server, balakovo.cc.ru, and he also hosted an IRC channel called xakep.balakovo.pp.ru (*xakep* is Russian for hacker). That was the channel Maksakov used to infect new machines and attack websites. Maksakov said Milsan and Zet advertised "DDoS for hire" on websites central to the underground economy, including CarderPlanet. Maksakov said he was at least one and probably two people removed from those who did the hiring. Milsan and Zet handled inquiries drawn by the advertisement and then assigned Maksakov to conduct the attacks. He said that he thought Milsan had been hired by a Russian middleman for the DDoS attacks, and he remembered Milsan telling him that the original request came from American sportsbooks that were trying to take out the competition. He couldn't recall all the sites he had attacked, but he remembered that BetCRIS was one of them.

After a couple of months of attacking betting sites for hire, Milsan and Zet decided to start freelancing, Maksakov said. Without waiting for a job, they took it upon themselves to choose sportsbooks to attack, sending emails demanding $5,000 or $10,000 for "protection." Maksakov got paid $1,000 for each of two attacks and spent $500 of it on a new server. Milsan and Zet raised the price of protection to $15,000 or $20,000 and Maksakov got $2,000 for one attack, the only time a company in that round paid up.

Following three days of interviews, the MVD took Maksakov to a Moscow prison to await trial. But Igor decided Maksakov would be more useful if he weren't stuck behind bars. Igor suppressed news of the hacker's continuing time in custody and got him a day job at an Internet café. Andy promised he would ask the judge to spare Maksakov from a term in the harsh Russian penal system if he continued to help. Maksakov gave them still more information about the way the criminal rings worked, and he agreed to chat with his former associates as if nothing had happened.

The extortion system was more impressive than Andy and Barrett had realized. When Maksakov's ring struck out on its own, the hackers started by researching prospective targets. That included some online chats with members of the target's staff. They would pick an attack date just ahead of a major sporting event. Then they would investigate the technical infrastructure of the company. If it had its own domain name server, that would have to be attacked first, to stop the company from switching the numeric address behind the website. They also looked for parts of the website where bots could chew up the most resources, such as internal search pages, pages requiring authorization to use, and pages offering downloads.

To cover themselves during the reconnaissance effort, the ring's leaders would investigate potential targets with several hundred bots, confusing any search for the location of the real person. The spy would connect from his Internet service provider to an encrypted virtual private network (VPN), a kind of secure tunnel most common in large corporations with employees in the field. The VPN would take them to a bot, and only from there would the extortionists connect to the target. The eventual attacks would use "rooms" in IRC channels that had a thousand bots each.

One thing Maksakov said would make sense only years later when Andy ran it by Barrett. The ring had stopped attacking websites where the Internet Protocol address began with 140, because the bandwidth at those firms was so big that they were impossible to overwhelm. Maksakov thought the number 140 carried some special technological importance. In fact, Prolexic had simply been assigned a block of IP addresses that began with that number. Other IP addresses that began with 140 were owned by all manner of companies and individuals, but if a gambling website began that way, the odds were it had moved to Barrett's haven, where the attackers stood little chance.

To collect the extorted money, the rings went into the forums of CarderPlanet or a similar site aimed at English speakers, Shadowcrew, and advertised for an "executive" to coordinate "drops." These typically followed the pattern that Andy had seen with the Canbet payments to Latvia. In exchange for a cut of the proceeds, the executive would supply a list of locations and names to receive payments via Western Union. Those mules would then convert the cash into Webmoney, where it could be picked up in Russia and exchanged for rubles, usually by the hackers themselves, who could sign in at a franchise with little more than a first name.

Andy pressed Maksakov to tell him more about how attacks could be thwarted and how they were evolving. The overall picture wasn't a reassuring one. The best chance for discovering a hacker was when he was in reconnaissance mode. While many bots would be contacting the site at random for cover, they usually would look at only one page apiece. By examining the log file for the IP addresses of visitors and disregarding those that clicked just once, the target company might be able to pinpoint the IP of the computer that the attacker was using as a proxy for his probe. But that was still merely an ordinary zombie computer, and it would be quite a bit more work for the authorities to get control of that machine and then trace the VPN connection back to the attacker's real Internet service provider.

Killing off a botnet also would be much harder than Andy had thought. At first, the agent had thought that simply taking the controlling IRC server offline would do the trick. But since the attackers also had domain name servers to direct the bots to the right channel, they could just change the numeric address for the channel and start it up someplace new. Then Andy had thought that seizing the domain name server at the same time as the IRC server would be enough. But Maksakov pointed out that the attacker could just buy or capture another domain name server and once again change the IP address to which it referred connections. That meant that the authorities would have to persuade the domain registration company to cut off the domain name entirely—and there were any number of corrupt companies through which to register domain names.

The attack teams, meanwhile, were amassing more resources and adding new approaches. Among the more diabolical was a new assault on the legal British gambling site Blue Square. Instead of just overwhelming the site and extorting a payment in exchange for peace, a criminal crew had pilfered the email addresses of clients from the company's server. It then threatened to send child pornography to all of those addresses in such a way that the pictures would appear to be from Blue Square. That forced the company to make a public announcement of the threat in case the gang carried it out. The customers' displeasure at the insecurity of their contact information reinforced the decision of many other companies to pay quietly rather than fight.

• • •

ANDY HAD PICKED THE RIGHT RAID to go on. Denis Stepanov, arrested by another team in St. Petersburg, was surly and misleading from the first interview. The twenty-three-year-old, who worked as a computer system administrator, denied doing anything illegal. But after some time in prison, when confronted with his cell phone and Internet service provider records, he began offering some useful information. For starters, he admitted knowing Maksakov, Milsan, and Zet, and he said he knew that Stran had organized DDoS attacks for extortion.

Stepanov conceded he had connections with at least three more people in the DDoS business, nicknamed Faust, Pirog, and Red Hunter. Andy tracked down Faust from a phone number he had used to call Stepanov. He was identified as Vyacheslav Stepanov, no relation, a resident of Rostov-on-Don and the registered owner of a server called irc.jerry.pp.ru. He shared that machine with Pirog, another Stepanov contact. The server was physically hosted in Kissimmee,

Florida, and controlled a botnet that Andy watched attack Blue Square, William Hill, and others. Andy suspected the "jerry" ring of being behind the threat to email child pornography to customers of Blue Square and other targets. Faust evaded arrest but was believed to still be in Russia. Pirog, identified as Anton Valeryovich Slobodyanik, likewise went into hiding in St. Petersburg. Andy never got Red Hunter's real name.

Denis Stepanov also copped to dealing with one of the titans of the underground economy, a man known as King Arthur. The most respected figure on the carding fraud forums, and probably the most feared financial criminal of the era, King Arthur was best known for his mysterious ability to encode fake bankcards that would be accepted at ATMs.

He had run CarderPlanet, the most notorious of the cyberbazaars, and he settled disputes among participants there. He also advised up-and-comers on DDoS attacks and other crimes. But Andy's squad and other investigators had never gotten close to him. They didn't know his real identity or even his country. King Arthur was to them a real-life Keyser Soze from *The Usual Suspects*, a mythic persona they might have blamed for more things than one man could orchestrate.

Stepanov had gotten some Wells Fargo bank account numbers and online passwords, but he didn't know how best to extract the money from those accounts. On CarderPlanet, he asked King Arthur to help, and he offered an encryption program as payment. King Arthur instead wanted new exploits that could be used to hack into computers, and Stepanov either couldn't or wouldn't supply any. Later, King Arthur wanted to deploy a program for stealing bank account information on Stepanov's botnet, but Stepanov refused. He gave Andy two reasons. First, he was afraid that King Arthur might take control of the botnet. And second, he feared that if the two ever had a falling-out, King Arthur might have him killed.

Other names Stepanov gave would tantalize Andy. He said Stran's allies included a St. Petersburg hacker and former police officer named "02," after the phone number for a police emergency. More troubling, Stepanov said 02 might have worked for Dept. K, the national cybercrime squad, in St. Petersburg. A former cybercrime police officer in the national force would be a powerful man to have on board, someone who could pick up the phone and find out where an investigation was heading, along with what it might cost to make sure it never arrived. It was also the most likely conduit if something even worse existed. The local police chief or Dept. K division head or FSB man would be reluctant to be seen with crime lords. If the law enforcement leaders were involved in planning criminal activity, they would want to do business through an intermediary, and an ex-cop would be a prime candidate.

While corruption was a major problem everywhere in Russia, St. Petersburg was notorious. Igor had already warned Andy that he didn't trust the police there. The big western city was home to what was growing to be the single greatest nest of criminal activity online, the Russian Business Network. Two years down the road, the RBN would confound the West even more than King Arthur. The RBN wasn't a mob leader but an ongoing business, ownership unknown, with a headquarters address and a phone number. It was just that every single thing it did was wrong. Officially, the RBN was a service provider, with Web hosting and fast uplinks to the Internet. But it specialized in what the security trade called "bulletproof hosting" for the worst spammers, identity thieves, and child-porn businesses in the world. It charged more, but that meant that no amount of victim complaining could get the plug pulled on a customer. Complaints rolled in anyway, from Western law enforcement, security firms, legitimate service providers, and thousands of consumers whose computers were infected with spyware spewing pop-up ads. To operate as it did, the RBN needed powerful protection—most likely from local or national police as well as traditional organized crime. Andy would come to believe that 02 was part of the RBN.

The biggest disappointment in the day of action was in the raid in Pyatigorsk. Andy and Igor had hoped the police would find and arrest Maria Zarubina and Timur Arutchev, whom they believed to be two-thirds of Stran, the people on the receiving end of Canbet's payout. Timur was the presumed leader of the three: he had a ranking title on CarderPlanet, "Gabellotto," which is the Italian term for a tenant farmer who taxed peasants in a system that prefigured the mafia.

But when MVD officer Dmitri Bushman's team got to their apartment on Pestova Street, Zarubina and Timur Arutchev had fled. Then the agents learned that the couple had taken out $29,000 from a bank the previous day—the maximum allowed withdrawal. Even in their haste to flee, they had the presence of mind to take the hard drive from their computer. And the news got worse from there. In a single month the previous fall, at the peak of the attacks in Costa Rica, a staggering $1.2 million had passed through the couple's account. The day before they disappeared, phone records showed repeated calls to numbers in the Turks & Caicos Islands, an offshore banking haven.

Andy had thought Stran was just another mule, someone who passed along money to the big players. Now it looked like Stran was the kingpin—and one who had been tipped off by the authorities, to boot. The police did find Timur's brother, Yan Arutchev, believed to be the last part of Stran. Yan admitted to accepting money on his brother's behalf after electronic transfers, but said he didn't know what it was for. He said he had no idea where the couple had gone or why. Without more evidence, there was nothing the police could do to shake his story.

Two weeks after the fruitless raid, Maria Zarubina tried to cash $60,000 in American Express travelers checks at a Moscow bank. The Russian police had asked American Express to stop payments on those checks, and the bank clerk held on to them, asking Zarubina to wait. The clerk put Zarubina's passport down and walked away to call the MVD headquarters off Red Square. The call went to Misha Salenkov, a short, chubby detective who spoke almost no English. Salenkov ran down the hall, shouting "Zarubina bank! Zarubina bank!" Andy and Igor were just three miles from the scene. They ran out to the street and ordered a passing driver to stop his Russian-made Lada. Andy, Igor, Misha, and two other MVD men crammed in, joining the civilian driver in the tiny car as they raced across town. Unfortunately for Andy, Zarubina had grabbed her passport and fled. The team missed her by minutes. The next day a lawyer appeared at the bank and asked the manager why he had kept the American Express checks. Police, alerted when the lawyer asked for an appointment, trailed the man as he left the bank, hoping he would lead them to Zarubina. But they had no such luck. As technically proficient as Maksakov was, Zarubina and Timur Arutchev were clearly higher up in the food chain. And the Gabellotto had gotten away clean.

• • •

THE YEAR 2004 HAD BEGUN with Andy sitting in the office of the wrong Russian investigators, filling out paperwork and twiddling his thumbs. As the year drew to a close, he had the opposite problem: too many good leads to chase at once. And he had a strong hunch that local or national officials were protecting some of the people he wanted. Andy decided the best course was to go after the men Maksakov had fingered as his superiors in the extortion ring, since Maksakov was still cooperating. That meant Zet, Milsan, and Bra1n.

Milsan, and it would emerge Bra1n as well, lived in Kazakhstan, which made things much harder. The country was tied by economics and politics to its much larger neighbor Russia, without the rebelliousness of a Chechnya or Georgia. But it was still a wilder outpost with greater corruption, and Russian officials had to go through the same letter-of-request formalities that had proved such a burden earlier in the case. While requests for help in pursuing Milsan wended their way through the system, Andy found some Web pages that had been defaced in early 2003 by a group calling itself "RegoTeam," which left as Web graffiti the membership roster Milsan—Zet—Zerg. By May 2003, RegoTeam was bold enough to offer DDoS and other services in spam. "Do you want to get rid of your competitors? Or blackmail your boss because he didn't pay you? We can help!" one email read. The group also promised to assist those "looking for specific content for your web site (like child porn or anything weird)."

At the Internet café where Maksakov worked during the day, Andy and a detective from Moscow's Dept. R would join him for long sessions as he chatted with the suspects still at large. In ICQ chats with Milsan, Maksakov learned of several attacks as they were happening. Andy then had Maksakov log into the servers that Milsan was using. Digging around in those servers eventually produced Milsan's real name—Alexandr Milutin—and his Internet and physical addresses.

Maksakov also drew out the more arrestable, Russia-based Zet in online chats. Andy considered Zet to be the most central figure identified so far. Zet had hired Maksakov and knew Stepanov well. He also knew Faust, Pirog, and Milsan. And he was one step away from Bra1n, who continued to run DDoS servers, and Red Hunter, who was himself one step away from King Arthur.

Through Maksakov, Andy got Zet's real first name, Alexander, his Internet address, and finally his street address in Astrakhan. In December, Andy and one of Igor's deputies, Alexei Morning, flew to Astrakhan, an industrial and fishing city sixty miles from the Caspian Sea.

Out of concern for leaks, Igor's staff practiced the minimum disclosure allowed by their department's protocol for operations outside of the capital, notifying just the local chief of police, Alexander Petrov, and his No. 2. In Astrakhan, both top officers met Andy and Morning and drove them to a hotel to drop their bags. Then they invited the men to join them for dinner, as it was too late to arrest Zet that day. They went to a standard Russian-style restaurant, with meat salads and vodka. The police chief was a large, chubby man with short and spiky hair and the darker skin typical of the southern region. As the drinks flowed, Petrov was friendly and attentive. He asked Andy if he liked boar hunting. Andy did like hunting. Petrov suggested they go shooting together. Andy said he'd be delighted to, as soon as he'd made his arrest.

No, the police chief told him. We should go tonight, right after dinner. Andy began to get a bad feeling. He managed to get close to Morning, then whispered: "I don't like this. Pretend to go to the bathroom and then get out of here and flag down a car. Once you've got one, honk the horn. I'll go to the bathroom and out the back door." Now the grim Russian economy worked to Andy's advantage. While real taxis were scarce and expensive, most citizens outside of Moscow fortunate enough to own cars were happy to earn a few extra rubles by giving strangers a lift. Morning did his job, Andy made it out, and they drove back to the hotel.

They decided to hole up in Andy's room, doubling their numbers in case of trouble. They locked the door and did their best to sleep, knowing they would need to be up at 5 A.M. to make the arrest. But the phone rang at 2 A.M., jarring them both upright. "Andy, it's Igor," the colonel said. "The man you are going to arrest is the son of the police chief. I will get on the first plane to Astrakhan in the morning with some men. But don't open your door for anyone." Andy thought, *Oh shit*. He hung up, and the two men pushed chairs and whatever else they could find against the door. They had one gun between them, a cheap Russian pistol.

An hour later, at 3 A.M., came a pounding on the hotel room door. "Hotel security," a voice bellowed. "Open up!" Andy shouted back: "No. We are fine. Go away!" The pounding continued. "Hotel security!

You must open this door immediately!" Deciding to show that they were serious, and armed, Morning shouted that he had a gun. The men outside went away. Andy and Morning stayed on full alert, not budging until 9 A.M., when Igor and the cavalry arrived.

Andy wanted to go ahead with the arrest attempt. But when they arrived at the house where their target, like his father named Alexander Petrov, lived with his mother, the younger Petrov and his computer were gone. Igor called in the FSB, which arrested the police chief on suspicion of destroying the evidence on his son's PC. He was freed after a month and allowed to return to the police force in a lower position. Andy later learned that before his ascent to police chief, the elder Petrov had headed the cybercrime unit of the Astrakhan police department.

• • •

ANDY KEPT THE EVENTS of the previous night to himself. If he had spread the word that thugs had shown up at his hotel room, whatever their intent, the U.K. brass might have stopped the case in its tracks, and all his work would have gone for nothing. They might have gone further and complained to the Russian government, leaving relations worse than before he started.

With his father out of power, the younger Petrov had to decide between life on the run or coming in for questioning. He knew the physical evidence against him had been destroyed, so he decided to take his chances with the MVD. Petrov presented himself to Andy and Igor on his home turf, the Astrakhan police department, on Friday, January 28, 2005. Petrov was cocky, sporting a leather jacket and carrying himself as if he had no fear of anyone. *A classic gangster,* Igor thought. "We appreciate you coming in and being willing to tell the truth," Igor said. Petrov nodded. "You know a lot about computers," Andy began. "Not me," Petrov said. "I hardly know how to turn one on." Andy stared back at the man. Not only was he innocent of any crimes, Petrov insisted, he hadn't even had a computer since August 2004, when he sold it to someone. Sold it to whom? Petrov couldn't recall. Igor was not impressed. He arrested Petrov and had him taken to the local prison.

The next day, Igor and Andy went to the prison to try talking to Petrov again. On the ride over, the detectives agreed: Maksakov was the technical mind. Stepanov was the greedy mind, allying with any group that would have him. And Petrov was the criminal mind. Andy was certain a night in prison wouldn't have shaken him.

But then Andy got a look at Astrakhan's prison. It was straight out of a Dickens novel. They were greeted by a massive Kavkaz dog, looking like a wolf crossed with a lion, who lunged at them until a chain jerked it to a stop inches away from Andy's face. After waiting an hour, they were roughly frisked and ordered inside. They were still as freezing cold as they had been outside. It took Andy a moment to realize why: there were bars on the windows, but no glass. *Alcatraz was a luxury hotel,* Andy decided.

Andy crowded into the interrogation room with Igor, one of his deputies, and a translator. The room was bare save for a table, two chairs, and an underpowered radiator. Petrov was brought to the door of the chamber and kept his head down, staring at the ground in front of him. Only when the guards ordered him inside did he raise his eyes to move. Andy struggled to reconcile the man before him with the cocky suspect he had met the previous day.

Petrov continued to deny conducting the DDoS attacks or knowing Milsan. But after investigators showed him the chat logs of his discussions with Maksakov and Stepanov, Petrov admitted that he knew them and that he had monitored the servers and botnets. He feebly claimed that he didn't realize that they were attacking websites at the time. Despite all the conflicting information, a better picture began to emerge. Stran had been paid by someone to set up the initial wave of assaults, and that group had hired Bra1n to organize them. Bra1n had supervised not only the three Russian suspects under arrest but had also worked with, if not given orders to, Milsan. After Andy cut off the server in Houston, Bra1n went his own way, taking control of that botnet and setting up others. That forced Maksakov to establish a new server to keep doing business, while Milsan created a third. The thing was a Hydra, with heads that multiplied every time Andy made progress.

● ● ●

BETWEEN 2003 AND 2005, DDoS extortionists hit almost all the betting companies. But eventually all of those sites paid, beefed up their defenses, or went out of business. So the multiple gangs went in search of fresh hunting grounds. They attacked companies in all manner of industries. Only one sector got the constant pummeling that the gambling firms had received: the online payment industry, which came under fire about a year after BetCRIS. As before, sound logic led to the focus. The companies were usually small, since the industry had come into being only around the time PayPal was born in a 2000 merger. That meant they generally didn't have the massive infrastructure that could easily deflect DDoS attacks. Also like the gambling industry, the competition was intense. Every minute of downtime cost a company money and customer loyalty. So Bra1n went after StormPay, Protx Ltd., and other payment firms that were Prolexic customers.

The good news was that Bra1n had given Maksakov a user name and password to log onto Bra1n's server, and he had never disabled it. So much of what Bra1n did, including the StormPay and Protx attacks, Maksakov watched, either at the café where he was working or in the MVD offices. Usually Bra1n himself logged on through a virtual private network that disguised where he was dialing from. But once, as Maksakov watched, he logged on from his true Internet address, and Maksakov quickly printed it out. The authorities in Kazakhstan so far hadn't been of much use. But with the IP address, Andy and Igor finally managed to get Bra1n identified by his Internet service provider as Alexander Olegovich Grasman, a Kazakh national of German descent who was just eighteen years old.

Because Maksakov's fate had been kept a secret, he could also log into the exclusive carding forums that allowed hackers to communicate and buy and sell credit card numbers, hacking programs, and the addresses of compromised computers. From what Maksakov could see there and in his surreptitious monitoring, Bra1n was just getting bigger.

By the end of 2005, Bra1n was suspected of leading not only DDoS extortion rackets but carding and phishing scams as well. He was being sought by law enforcement in the U.K., U.S., Canada, and Germany. Bra1n had initially used the server fbi.pp.ru in Houston. When that was disconnected, he set up the same controlling software elsewhere. After the Houston shutdown, Andy tracked down the new host server for fbi.pp.ru, through a myriad of fake registrations, to a St. Petersburg company called Alfa Holdings. The same server had a wealth of child pornography. The Dept. K office in St. Petersburg reported that Alfa wasn't related to the Russian company Alfa Telecom but was owned by twenty-one-year-old Mikhail Valentinovich Romanov, alias Scope, who was already suspected of child porn and other illegal activities. The fact that so much of the world's child pornography traced back to St. Petersburg, they told Andy, wasn't necessarily because of mob power in the area. By dint of a local law that is unique in Russia, it is not illegal to possess child porn within the city's limits. It remains illegal to sell or distribute it, if such acts can be proved.

Andy already knew that corruption was a major problem in St. Petersburg. Now it seemed like the city was a center for a lot of the worst online criminal activity as well. That probably wasn't a coincidence, he thought. But he still hadn't heard of the Russian Business Network, and the local unit of Dept. K wasn't volunteering much in the way of lessons.

Andy and Igor flew from Moscow to St. Petersburg and raided the Alfa offices on May 30, 2005. The headquarters was in a ten-story building with so many back stairs and winding passages that Andy thought: *rabbit warren*. Inside the sprawling offices were three of Romanov's well-dressed young deputies. Andy spotted one ripping up slips of paper behind his desk and dropping the pieces into a trash can. Andy retrieved them and later reassembled the bits, which had numeric Internet addresses printed on them.

The Alfa employees weren't nervous in the least. They coolly said they couldn't discuss the company; only their boss Romanov could talk. They said they had no idea where he was, then clammed up. Remembering what an easy time he had interrogating Maksakov, Andy frowned. These were the professionals. They knew better than to admit a thing.

As Igor's men searched the office, they found a safe. There was a key, but it was buried in the gravel at the bottom of a fish tank, and in the tank was a large black scorpion. After some nervous trial and error, one of Igor's men got it out with a stick. Inside the safe was $120,000 in American $100 bills, which the team seized as evidence. The men also found several high-end personal computers. But the massive server they had been expecting was nowhere to be found. A Dept. K man went to the building administrator's office to ask where the major Internet connection came into the structure. Returning, the detective said it was two floors down.

The second office had a different name on the door, Alfa Soft. Behind that door was another door, this one made of metal as thick as those guarding bank vaults. There was no handle: it opened only from the other side. Igor banged on it and a man answered gruffly, telling Igor to go away. Igor mulled his options and then sent for a fire brigade with a circular saw. For an hour they seared noisily away at the stubborn door, their impatience and anticipation mounting.

When they at last broke through, they saw a dumbwaiter that was big enough to take a person and a computer—or many computers, one at a time—out through a hole in the floor. Then they looked up and saw an empty rack where servers would normally be. Andy looked closely at a thick cord that would have connected those servers to the Internet and the world outside. It was still swinging back and forth.

In a report to his superiors, Andy swallowed his rage that, as the MVD concluded, Romanov had been tipped off by a corrupt official. He also glossed over how close he had come to catching someone he later realized was allied with the despised Russian Business Network. "I'm not going to tell my fucking boss that it happened while I was on the other side of the door," he reasoned.

"It is suspected that the server in question was located at the office and had recently been removed," Andy wrote dryly. He declined to say who tipped off Romanov, but in St. Petersburg, only the local office of Dept. K had known what was about to happen.

• • •

THE EVIDENCE AGAINST BRA1N and his potentially more powerful ally Scope had been spirited away. But Andy was determined to at least cut Bra1n off from his botnet. Andy knew from Maksakov that he had to do more than physically knock a command server offline. At the same time, he had to get rid of the bad guy's domain name server, which might be thousands of miles away. And he had to persuade or force the bad guy's domain name registrar, which might well be crooked, to kill the domain name itself. It was like decapitating several of the Hydra's heads and burning all the necks except the main one, which had to be put under a heavy rock.

Andy had pulled off that trifecta with Milsan's server and the one named "jerry." Now he did it again on the day of the St. Petersburg raid. As they were cutting through the vault door, the U.S. Secret Service was at a hosting company called ZoneEdit Inc. on Broadway in New York, disabling Bra1n's domain name server, and the Moscow registrar Runet was removing fbi.pp.ru from the Internet, separating Bra1n from his botnet and leaving him no way to reconnect. So the raid was far from a total loss, at least as far as companies suffering from DDoS attacks were concerned. The instant that Alfa Soft's server disconnected, an ongoing assault on a major payment processor suddenly stopped.

The operation had its benefits for the MVD as well. Under Russian law, goods confiscated in an investigation can be turned over to the police for their own use, even if no charges are forthcoming. Within days, the flat-screen computer displays that had adorned the Alfa building in St. Petersburg had replaced the boxy monitors in the offices of Igor's squad.

Bra1n proved to be extremely resourceful. He launched a new botnet within two weeks of the raid, controlled from a server called zombies.zombies.name, which this time was physically based in the U.S. In June, Maksakov watched as that network attacked the domain name servers of Time Warner Inc. and others. At the end of the month, Andy pulled off another Russian MVD- and U.S. Secret Service–assisted triple play targeting Bra1n.

Then in July, Bra1n started over again with a server called syscab .biz. This time the domain name server was in the Russian city of Samara and the domain registration was through a company in Hong Kong. Maksakov watched as it attacked Bet365 and Prolexic, which had the gambling company as a client. It took a couple of weeks, but Andy shut that botnet down too.

After that, Bra1n switched strategies, stumping Andy and Maksakov for months. Eventually, though, they worked out what their worthy adversary was up to. Instead of relying on IRC servers, Bra1n had made the most of advances in the botnet world and moved to manage his zombie armies through websites. He created four new German-language sites to control the mechanical throng. Carefully tracking Bra1n's every move, Maksakov also saw how Bra1n was infecting new computers. He established two websites that appeared genuine, www.highconvert.com and www.installme.info, both porn pages hosted on machines at a major St. Petersburg service provider, Eltel. Those sites would infect Web surfers using an "exploit" that took advantage of a security hole in Internet Explorer. Andy and Igor set up a simultaneous takedown for December 30, 2005, and then retired to a sushi bar two blocks from MVD headquarters. Andy manned three cell phones and Igor two as they ordered the seizure of all four control sites and the two infectious pages. Andy thought about sending Bra1n a "Happy New Year!" email but decided against it.

After examining the computers operating the infectious sites, the forensics team finally worked out what made them so effective. For most visitors, including the sleuths, the sites appeared normal and harmless. But Bra1n had a friend in St. Petersburg who could hack into domain name servers and "poison" them, sending surfers seeking one site to a different one instead. If they agreed to pick Nike.com, for example, most people typing in that address would have gone to any of a large number of domain name servers and then to the right place. But if they happened to stumble on one of the poisoned servers, which were altered for just a half hour at a time, they would have been sent to highconvert.com or installme.info. Within ten seconds, the machines behind those websites would realize that the visitors were approved targets, check to see if they were running Internet Explorer as a Web browser, and if so use an exploit to install Trojan programs that would give control of the computers to Bra1n. Then they would dispatch the users to the real Nike.com.

Few consumers complained about a ten-second detour. If they did, and thought to check their browser history for where they had been, technical support people tended to assume that the user had clicked on the wrong thing and not noticed. In the worst-case scenario, they would navigate directly to the porn site, see that it wasn't trying to install anything malicious, and tell the user there was no problem. All in all, it was a damn good scheme, one that illustrated how the best criminal hackers were rapidly becoming more proficient.

That last takedown, one of the most complicated in history, finally got through to Bra1n. In an online chat watched by Maksakov, he complained that all of his bots were getting killed as soon as he started to use them. Maksakov felt a surge of triumph. Then he read the rest of the comment. From now on, Bra1n wrote, he would only use his bots to harvest the financial information that was stored in the computers or typed in by their oblivious owners.

Bra1n was through attacking big companies. Now he would be going after tens of thousands of consumers. On the underground forums where users bought and sold the most sensitive financial information in batches of millions, he bragged that he would never be caught. He lived in Kazakhstan, where the foreign law enforcement had no power and, he said, the local authorities would never arrest him.

9

THE
UNDERGROUND
ECONOMY

ANDY CROCKER HAD JUST CRASHED into the same epiphany as Barrett Lyon. If the worst criminals had improved their technology to the point that they could leave denial-of-service attacks behind, a whole new war was opening up. The previous one, he thought, had been at best a draw: most companies survived, but police caught only a handful out of the hundreds of thugs involved. Crossing the borders was one big challenge, and beheading the botnets another. But at least the DDoS schemes required central coordination, because all of the zombies had to ping the target site simultaneously. Siphoning off sensitive consumer information could happen slowly, over weeks and months, and the means to do it were already in hand. Bra1n and his ilk didn't need much more than a password-protected data center to hold the goodies until they crawled through the Net to collect them.

Andy pondered how to proceed. He would continue going up the food chain, trying to catch Bra1n and the other men above Ivan Maksakov, and he had to start thinking about the trial for the initial crew—Maksakov, Alexander Petrov, and Denis Stepanov. But beyond that, it looked like there was going to be a major problem for Internet commerce, and potentially an explosion in all manner of identity fraud. Andy saw just one weakness for the crime lords. No one could handle every part of a mass identity heist by himself. The ringleaders would have to coordinate with others; the underground markets were their lifeblood.

On such sites as CarderPlanet and the U.S.-based Shadow crew.com, Bra1n's denial-of-service ring advertised its services and King Arthur offered enormous quantities of credit card data. Also for sale: exploits for hacking into systems, versions of Bagle and other viruses for computer roundups, "phishing kits" for do-it-yourselfers to lure rubes with spurious emails, and rented time on the botnets. Website members could buy and sell banking particulars, passwords, and everything else a crook might want—together with professional services from "cashers" who turned bank account data into money, encoders who manufactured bogus credit cards with real numbers, and "executives" who provided networks of mules to pick up loot from Western Union, e-Gold, or Webmoney and deliver it to the guys in charge.

You could catch the masterminds if you could somehow tap those forums, the same way the feds used to watch restaurant hangouts as New York mobsters met and did business. The real question was whether the dark economy had evolved as quickly as the technological weapons in the criminal arsenals. If so, it might be too late to stop a hundred-year flood of sensitive financial data. Certainly the stealth markets were changing to stay ahead of law enforcement. Admittance was now granted only to those recommended by one or more trusted members. And the websites shunned sellers of financial information whose products were substandard due to age or overuse. They relied on electronic feedback like that used on eBay: no one would deal with a vendor who had more than one negative comment.

But those doing business over such sites still relied on people they weren't sitting down with and in many cases had never met. That gave committed law enforcement officers an opportunity to penetrate the rings. If detectives busted one member of a password-protected site, they could offer leniency in sentencing in exchange for the perpetrator's continuing to do deals under police supervision, as Andy was doing with Maksakov. Even if the suspect didn't cooperate, the detectives could send him to jail and assume his online identity, luring bigger targets into sting operations. Merely being a leading practitioner of identity theft didn't guarantee that one's own identity wouldn't be stolen.

Back before the launch of CarderPlanet and Shadowcrew, sites sold counterfeit documents as "novelties," and other entrepreneurs with good access through their workplaces offered detailed credit reports and supplemental information from the likes of Georgia-based ChoicePoint, delivering account numbers and asset listings. The successor sites were mega-malls, providing every tool in one place. CarderPlanet began first, in 2001. According to U.S. investigators, it grew out of a group of hackers based in Ukraine, although many leading members came from Russia. At the time, there was virtually no enforcement of computer intrusion laws in Ukraine. The group felt secure enough to publicize parties. At one such gathering, at an Odessa restaurant, the leading members decided to open the site for business.

The brazen group called itself the International Carders Alliance, and the top man went by Script, after the slang for a computer program. CarderPlanet.com had the gall to advertise on other Internet sites, boasting in slickly animated videos: "Looking for professional solution? Discover the power of technology. . . . The team you can rely on." Registered members could message each other in private or post publicly to forums dedicated to such topics as "Hacking," "Questions of beginners," and "Scammers/rippers activity," where the criminals complained about getting duped by fellow thieves. Practitioners who submitted their products or services to official reviewers, Script explained in a posting, could earn Reviewed Vendor status, allowing them to advertise counterfeit passports and other ID documents, U.S. addresses for receiving goods bought through fraud, and other vitals of the trade. Above the reviewers and the reviewed vendors sat site executives bearing Italian titles derived from mafia lore, like Gabellotto Timur Arutchev.

Script ruled as the godfather, at the very top. King Arthur and a man named Boa, who operated the site Boafactory.com, manufacturing new credit cards with the coded information provided by hackers, ranked near him. Beginning as a Russian-language site, CarderPlanet soon added sections in English, Chinese, Japanese, and Korean. By late 2003, more than 9,000 people had registered. Andy and his allies in law enforcement spent hours on the site, trying to learn as much as they could. They drafted crude portraits of the villains, ascribing specialties and business partners where they could. But with King Arthur and others, there were no pictures or true names to go with the organization charts. Instead, the investigators had to make do with the occasional capture of a lower-level operative in the West to round out their understanding of how the dark economy worked.

One of the more successful native English speakers was a young man from Texas named Douglas Havard. The child of a business executive, Havard went to a private high school and then Southern Methodist University. A smooth manipulator, Havard found that being captain of his high school football team wasn't enough. He made extra money by buying cheap electronics, switching their UPC barcodes, and returning them for a bigger refund. By seventeen, he was selling as much as $6,000 worth of Ecstasy in a month. Then one of his suppliers sold him some fake pills. Havard and two other young men barged into the man's apartment with guns drawn. As they demanded their money back, the upstream dealer's brother hid in a closet, dialing 911 on his cell phone. Police charged Havard with aggravated robbery in 2001. Out on bond, he entered college, set his dormmates to work turning out fake driver's licenses, and preyed on a girl with the date-rape drug GHB. An undercover cop finally bought gallons of the drug from Havard and arrested him in mid-sale.

Havard skipped bail and traipsed through several countries before settling in England. There he answered an ad on CarderPlanet and went to work as a casher for King Arthur and others running the site. Havard also coordinated groups in America who were doing the same thing. They all re-encoded Citibank ATM cards with a special program and jotted down the numeric passcodes King Arthur had cracked. Havard was in awe of King Arthur, writing to a sidekick named On-The-Fringe: "He can transfer money between cards and see how much we take out. At one point he was making $1 million a week lol."

The Americans hit multiple banks daily, splitting their 40 percent with Havard and sending 60 percent to the Russian. In online chats with his accomplices, Havard estimated that he had made millionaires of several Eastern Europeans, including Script, who were sharing the wealth among themselves. No wonder, he said, that he was getting promoted to "Capo di Capi," or Boss of Bosses, one step below the ruling clique. Then twenty-four, Havard kept enough for himself—as much as $100,000 a month—to enjoy a champagne lifestyle in the nightclubs. "Mercedes don't buy themselves," he wrote to one associate. "I can't rap and my jump shot sucks, so I really can't think of another way to make this kind of money."

U.S. agents caught one of Havard's U.S. accomplices trying to board a plane in Austin, Texas, with $32,000 in cash. After he talked, the FBI called the NHTCU, which assigned Trevor Dickey to arrest Havard in Leeds in June 2004. Dickey surprised Havard in his room, finding him with guns, forged passports, and fake drivers' licenses. Havard's computer still contained chats with Script and with his U.S. team. In 2005 an English judge sent Havard to prison for six years.

• • •

SINCE CARDERPLANET OPERATED so openly and attracted so many, it quickly became a top target for the FBI and other law enforcement agencies. The U.S. Postal Service, like the Secret Service, proved more nimble than the larger force. It had long tracked credit cards that were stolen from the mail and the use of false addresses to receive plundered goods. A team of postal inspectors stuck with the mission as the criminals moved online, and they allied with FBI agents working out of Los Angeles. The FBI recruited a Russian-speaking informant who joined CarderPlanet in 2002. That fall the informant chatted with Script over ICQ and bought two collections of 110 stolen credit card numbers for $400 per batch, sending the money through Western Union to mules in Estonia and Ukraine. In his instant messages, Script said he had created CarderPlanet and lived in Odessa. Script worried so little about exposure that he granted interviews. Explaining his embrace of the underground market, he told a Ukrainian website: "There are no universal carders. Sooner or later, this carder will need services of another person."

He emailed the website that his real name was Dmitry Golubov, providing his passport, phone numbers, and date of birth for good measure. Golubov obviously enjoyed special protection, investigators said. "There was always information that said there were cops involved," said then FBI agent E. J. Hilbert, who helped lead the probe. Indeed, investigators at the Ukrainian MVD would conclude that Golubov's co-conspirators included Andrey Gerashenko, identified as a police captain by a researcher for antivirus firm McAfee.

A break in the CarderPlanet case came with the February 2003 arrest in Cyprus of Boa, whose real name was Roman Stepanenko and was also known as Roman Vega. Following an alert from a payment processor, police in the island country showed up at a Nicosia store that was submitting a suspiciously large number of credit card transactions. The local police officer found Stepanenko swiping through card after card. The authorities charged Stepanenko with fraud, won a conviction, and sent him off for a stint in jail. Near the end of his term, U.S. authorities who had heard about Boa's remanufactured cards got Stepanenko extradited. They also got a better look at the largely encrypted Sony Vaio computer from his hotel room. It contained logs of his ICQ chats, which included negotiations to sell credit card data to Script, among others. The Justice Department announced Stepanenko's transfer to the United States along with a slew of unrelated cybercrime busts, not realizing how big a fish it had. Prosecutors in San Francisco charged Stepanenko with making the bogus credit cards and defrauding some forty merchants. After he struck a secret deal to cooperate, he pleaded guilty to twenty counts and received a sentence of just a few years. But the cooperation was far short of what agents should have been able to wrest if they had known who they had, according to someone who worked the case. They could have gotten Stepanenko to help them break into the inner circle ruling CarderPlanet.

That's because Stepanenko's logs indicated that he did far more than try to sell thousands of credit card numbers and the supporting data, as the Justice Department had announced. In fact, they showed him bragging that his "guys" had pulled off one of the worst identity hacks of all time—albeit one that had gotten no press attention, because back then no laws required notification of those who lost sensitive financial information. The target was Data Processors International, later bought by another firm. The company handled millions of transactions for credit card issuers, and after some banks complained of mass fraud, it admitted that hackers had obtained 8 million card numbers in early 2003. Stepanenko told another hacker that the correct number was 14 million. No officials ever announced Stepanenko's role, or that of any other hacker, in the DPI break-in. It was buried in a second indictment against him in New York, filed in 2007. Those charges suggested that prosecutors had initially missed how bad Stepanenko was, that he had fallen short of the promised help, and that agents hadn't been eager to advertise either fact. "We thought he hadn't cooperated," a federal agent acknowledged.

Stepanenko's chat logs as Boa did get U.S. officials closer to Script. They showed the founder of CarderPlanet identifying himself as Dmitry Golubov. A picture on Boa's hard drive labeled "Scriptek" showed Golubov too. Postal Inspector Greg Crabb and FBI Agent Hilbert flew to Ukraine repeatedly to lobby the government there to help them. They got nowhere. "First they said 'No, no, no, he's clean,'" Hilbert recalled. "Then it became: 'We know he's bad, but we've been told we can't go after him.'" Until fall 2003, hacking outside of the country's borders wasn't a crime. When the law changed, the ban carried a penalty of five years in jail or a mere $1,000 fine—the sort of money a carder could earn in a day.

Like Andy Crocker, Hilbert tried to ingratiate himself with his host country. Once he gave a cybercrime training class at the Ukraine national police academy. Over three and a half hours, he felt that he connected with the earnest but unskilled group. He got them on the Internet, showed them Internet Relay Chat, and covered the basic lingo. Then the staff brought in a young technical expert to modify the computer settings and enable an instant-messaging session. Hilbert looked down and saw that the expert was using the same handle as a carder he had been monitoring, Dracul. "Good to meet you," Hilbert told the youth. Then Hilbert asked whether he had been involved in a particular scam. The kid said he had. When Hilbert reported this fact to his audience, they saw no problem at all.

It had been the same story with Russia. Numerous cases there fizzled, increasing the distrust on both sides. There were legitimate concerns about corruption among Russian officers. But the FBI took those concerns too far. With its insular culture, the FBI didn't even care to share details about its cases with law enforcement peers in the

U.S. and England, let alone rival powers. Besides, the agency gained clout in parallel with the rise of Red-obsessed leader J. Edgar Hoover. Working with the Russians, which necessitated sharing data with them, went against something very deep in the FBI's fabric. "There was reluctance to send information on suspects to Russia," Hilbert said. "There was concern they [the authorities] would go out and hire them for hacking."

That attitude backfired. The Russians were offended and thought the FBI arrogant. In 2000, FBI Agent Michael Schuler posed as a private company executive to induce two Russian hackers to fly to Seattle, where they were arrested. After Schuler used Bureau machines to search the suspects' computers back home, angry Russian police began investigating Schuler. Andy was lucky to be working for an agency that believed deeply in international cooperation, and he was lucky to be working in a country with less historical antipathy to Russia.

In 2004, the divided Ukraine populace elected a Western-oriented leader in what was dubbed the Orange Revolution. In mid-2005, the new authorities changed direction and arrested Golubov. Hilbert interviewed the young man in jail. Golubov barely managed to keep a straight face as he denied that he was Script. Hilbert left the country convinced that one of the most dangerous and effective cyber-criminals on the planet had been put away. Ukraine declined to extradite Golubov, saying it would try him in local court. He spent six months in jail.

Then two members of the Ukraine parliament vouched for Golubov, and the judge released him to howls from the Postal Service and FBI. "When you can call in some favors and get some politician in the Ukraine [to] vouch for your upstandedness, there's not much the U.S. can do after that," Postal Inspector Crabb told Wired.com.

In an online chat, Script told Doug Havard that legal pressure spurred his retirement. But he had an unorthodox way of showing any new circumspection. Golubov formed a political party, the Internet Party of Ukraine, which said it would push for greater national investment in technology. Security experts called the party a gag that didn't exist beyond its website. Few in U.S. law enforcement thought it funny.

After Golubov's arrest, control of CarderPlanet, its Web address, and its physical location shifted among King Arthur and others before the leadership shut it down in the summer of 2004, shortly after Havard's arrest and not long before Andy's first moves in Russia. By then CarderPlanet had facilitated fraud worth tens of millions of dollars or more, trained a generation of scammers, and established a model for black Internet commerce. Many more sites sprang up to succeed it, most with tighter internal security.

• • •

WHILE CARDERPLANET WAS WREAKING havoc on a global scale, Shadowcrew was doing major damage in the U.S. Shadowcrew grew out of the collaboration of two very different men, a Scottsdale (Arizona) Community College business student in his early twenties named Andrew Mantovani and a former mortgage broker in New Jersey nearly twice his age, David Appleyard. From 2002 until late 2004, "ThnkYouPleaseDie" and "BlackOps" ran the Shadowcrew site, setting the rules for the 4,000 users who registered, those who reviewed the offerings of others, the vendors themselves, and the moderators of discussions. It convened buyers and sellers who collectively swapped in the low millions of credit card numbers along with card-making machinery and other identity-theft goodies. The group rang up at least $4 million in fake credit card charges. In a single transaction in May 2004, a Shadowcrew member sold 110,000 card numbers. Another vendor, Omar Dhanani, promised to turn cash into e-Gold for a 10 percent cut. Mantovani and Appleyard threatened "rippers" who didn't carry through on their promises, once publishing the real name, address, and photo of a bad supplier.

While Shadowcrew wasn't especially secretive, the feds still needed to get lucky in order to make their big case. The FBI picked up a high-ranking member named CumbaJohnny, whose real name was Albert Gonzalez, on a low-level fraud rap. Bargaining for his freedom, Gonzalez told them that he was a third administrator of Shadowcrew, along with Mantovani and Appleyard, and that the feds could watch whatever he did. A fourth administrator, Anatoly "Vox" Tyukanov, was in Moscow. The Secret Service took over the case. Having learned that the bad guys favored virtual private networks to disguise their location, the agents came up with an innovative idea. They had Gonzalez tell his cohorts that he had access to an ultra-secure network, and that henceforth they should log in through that. The move gave the agents carte blanche to monitor everything that transpired on the network and made it much easier for them to figure out the real Internet addresses of the villains, which led in turn to their real identities and street addresses.

At 9 P.M. Tuesday, October 26, 2004, most of the Shadowcrew leaders assembled for a mandatory online meeting that Gonzalez orchestrated. Agents with semiautomatic weapons simultaneously raided houses across the country and a few locations overseas. Brandon Monchamp, a moderator who lived with Mantovani in Scottsdale, jumped out of a second-floor window and fled on foot, leaving a loaded assault rifle behind. Officers racing after Monchamp caught him from behind. Also arrested was Nicolas Jacobsen, who used the online handle Ethics. He had offered to crack any T-Mobile voicemail and email accounts. Jacobsen himself had already scoured four hundred accounts, including those of heiress Paris Hilton and Peter Cavicchia, a Secret Service agent investigating Shadowcrew.

The Cavicchia breach embarrassed the agency. Cavicchia broke internal rules by forwarding work email to his personal address and by accessing both those messages and his office computer via his T-Mobile Sidekick. For that reason, Jacobsen could read some of

Cavicchia's emails, including those listing the ICQ numbers monitored in the Shadowcrew probe. Luckily, the emails didn't expose Gonzalez as an informant. Gonzalez pursued the anonymous offer for T-Mobile account access and wound up in chats with Jacobsen, who showed him excerpts of the Secret Service emails.

Two days after the Shadowcrew raid, the Justice Department trumpeted twenty-eight arrests in the largest-ever cybercrime roundup. "The Department of Justice is committed to taking on those who deal in identity theft or fraud, whether they act online or off," Attorney General John Ashcroft said in a press release. Everyone who was both arrested and indicted pleaded guilty, though some just got probation.

But for all the manpower devoted to the case and the enormously positive press accounts of the operation, few top criminals suffered. Two of the four administrators got way clean, including Gonzalez, who would later admit to committing crimes an order of magnitude greater than those he helped solve.

Despite the indictment, nothing ever happened to Tyukanov, the fourth key administrator. He remained free in Moscow, reportedly protected by a Russian general. According to an agent on the case, a lure to get Tyukanov to another, friendlier country for arrest had been set, with the target ready to travel. But Secret Service headquarters nixed the plan, deciding that capturing even one of the heads of Shadowcrew wasn't worth angering the Russians while the agency was negotiating to reestablish a Moscow office. So Tyukanov was never brought to justice.

Shadowcrew would have been small potatoes without the presence of Tyukanov and other Russians and East Europeans. Those men provided the bulk of the identifying information contained in credit cards' magnetic stripes, which those in the U.S. resold in smaller quantities. Others in the U.S. acted as cashers, pillaging ATMs or using their U.S. addresses to receive goods purchased with fake credit card information. Then they resold the goods and shipped most of the profit overseas.

"All [the Americans] had back then was just making novelty identification things, dumpster diving, a few small-time hacks here and there, and then a lot of shit-talking," said fraudster turned FBI informant David R. Thomas, who went by El Mariachi on the boards. "On the Russian side it was more effective, businesslike. They were workaholics. They could pile up millions of dollars and they would still be pounding away at the keyboard 14 hours a day." Thomas echoed Doug Havard's amazement that King Arthur could see what was happening with the bank accounts in near–real time. If you said that you had just withdrawn $2,000 from an ATM, he could tell if it was true.

The Russians were essential to Shadowcrew. One law enforcement source explained, "Almost none of what I would describe as downstream wholesaling of track information would have been possible without the hacking by Russian and Eastern European rings."

The American wing of the Shadowcrew gang constituted organized crime in its own right, though nothing tied the members to more traditional mobs. They practiced ad hoc organized crime, meaning that they got together for a specific purpose instead of starting out as a criminal group and then looking for ways to score. The same went for many other cybercrime groups that coalesced around websites.

In Russia, the Ukraine, and elsewhere, by contrast, the key conspirators in mass cybercrime had at least one major element typically found in traditional organized crime—the ability to metastasize. Many of these mobs started out in cyberspace. But they branched out in at least one significant new direction in an effort to continue their enterprises. That direction was the corruption of government officials, either well-placed individuals in major law-enforcement roles or, in some instances, effectively of the governments themselves.

• • •

THE FAILURE TO REACH THE TOP wasn't the only drawback to the U.S. attacks on Shadowcrew and CarderPlanet. Those sites operated relatively openly, and the agents had one shot at them. Afterward, the vast majority of the users who didn't face prosecution scattered and formed dozens of smaller, more secretive sites that were far harder to penetrate.

There would be more isolated successes. But sitting in his Moscow hotel, Andy saw that the window he and his colleagues could have used to take on the underground economy was closing.

Looking back on the big cases years later, the Justice Department's head of cybercrime efforts said the busts were still a success, in part because they shook up the underworld wheeler-dealers. "They were very, very confident that it would be impossible to catch them," said the department's Kimberly Kiefer Peretti. "What the Shadowcrew case did was all of a sudden disturb their trust" in making arrangements with people they hadn't met. "They didn't know anymore who they were dealing with." Peretti said the experience also taught agents who the big sellers and hackers were and how they operated, even if they weren't nabbed at the time.

But it's also true that the limited prosecutions allowed even small-timers at the major sites to build up enough cash to hire new people, like drug dealers who get a stake and then work their way up. "What is so important about CarderPlanet is that just about every major player in today's world got started on that website," a federal agent said. "Individuals that were low-level players back then are some of the biggest players today, from hackers to cashers to ID makers to the money launderers. They all got started on CarderPlanet."

Many other forums for carders and phishers continued to flourish. One such site, again protected behind passwords, featured a free and detailed fraud tutorial and an offer to share the use of a program for checking whether credit card numbers were still valid. A Bulgarian poster, under the nickname Zeus, gave his email address for anyone willing to sell "fresh cc's" with the associated data for identifying the cardholder. "I am serious buyer," he wrote. "Will pay with Western Union." Breaches at ATM networks, at least those that were disclosed, also got bigger. On one day in November 2008, cashers hit more than a hundred automated tellers from Atlanta to Hong Kong and sucked out $9 million with data stolen from a payment processor owned by the Royal Bank of Scotland.

There were also the matters of how the authorities handled their informants, the crimes they knowingly allowed to continue, and the crimes they unknowingly allowed to continue.

David Thomas, for one, was arrested in November 2002 as he tried to collect $30,000 in merchandise that a CarderPlanet guru named BigBuyer had ordered from Outpost.com. The Russians did arrest and imprison BigBuyer, identified in U.S. documents as A. N. Lyashenko, in what probably remains that country's most significant capture to date. After a few months in jail, Thomas began working as a full-time informant for the FBI, which gave him a computer. As El Mariachi, he was active on the CarderPlanet site and also ran his own identity theft clearinghouse, TheGrifters.net. There he helped King Arthur with major phishing and cashing operations. But his collaboration with the FBI didn't lead to King Arthur's arrest. Instead, all manner of real identity crimes came together on TheGrifters as the FBI gathered intelligence.

The FBI was clearly happy with the tradeoff. In 2006, the agency went further. An undercover agent, Keith Mularski, invented an Eastern European spammer named Pavel Kaminski, alias Master Splynter, with the assistance of Spamhaus, the private research group. Spamhaus announced that Splyntr was linked to phishing scams, botnets, and carder forums. With that reputation, Mularski infiltrated the leadership of one of CarderPlanet's many children, a site called DarkMarket. In 2006 he managed to become the site's top administrator, banishing rippers who stole from other thieves and boosting his credibility in the process. He built the user base to 2,500.

Mularski didn't fool everyone. Before he ascended to the top spot at DarkMarket, Max Ray "Iceman" Butler, who ran the rival forum CardersMarket, hacked into a DarkMarket server and grabbed logs showing that Master Splynter was logging in not from Eastern Europe but from the Pittsburgh home of an FBI task force. As Butler posted the logs for other scammers to read, Mularski rapidly sanitized his connection and succeeded in convincing many that Butler had fabricated the logs in a power play. Butler was an unusual talent, and his undoing was hastened because he had an ego to match. Not content with running his own underground forum, Butler hacked into his competition. He harvested all their user information, then crashed the sites. When he sent out an email to the users announcing a "merger," they had little choice but to come to him. Bragging of his ability to keep a site secure, Mularski used the opening to take full control of Dark Market. In September 2008, the FBI and Secret Service worked together and caught Butler, who was suspected of personally hacking Citibank, the Pentagon Federal Credit Union, and other institutions. A recently passed law treating unused credit numbers as stolen goods worth $500 meant that Butler faced as long as decades in prison, the most ever for a cybercrime case. He pleaded guilty in June 2009.

Mularski did good work. As Splynter, he tracked the Internet locations of DarkMarket users and compared some transactions on the board to e-Gold transfers the government won access to in its money-laundering investigation at that Prolexic customer. The combination often gave investigators what they needed to get real names and addresses. Among the biggest busts was that of Cha0, a DarkMarket vendor from Turkey who sold software programs known as "skimmers" to siphon off bank customers' ATM codes as they were entered. After Cha0 kidnapped and tortured a police informant, Mularski helped get him arrested, along with more than fifty others in multiple countries. "What's worked for us in taking down spy rings and entire mob families over the years—embedding an undercover agent deep within a criminal organization—worked beautifully in taking down DarkMarket," said FBI Assistant Director Shawn Henry. After pulling the plug in September 2008, the FBI claimed that Mularski's team had succeeded in stopping more than $70 million in illegal commerce. When users did post stolen account information on the general discussion boards, Mularski warned the financial institutions. But Mularski conceded that real crimes were committed by board users over ICQ, where Mularski couldn't see them.

Andy thought Mularski's operation was a success overall, but one tainted by the collateral damage it caused. "Whenever I met up with Keith, I asked him: 'How much information do you need?'" Andy said. "Two years facilitating crime on a forum is too long. I cannot see what extra could be achieved by running that for two years rather than running it for six months, once you know the identities of the main players."

That, sadly, is not the worst of it. Hacker CumbaJohnny had been helping run Shadowcrew, while his real-life alter ego, Albert Gonzalez, was helping the Secret Service track what happened there. But the same man had a third identity, "Segvec." Federal agents knew Segvec was bad, they just didn't know he was one of their own. In filings against e-Gold, they described customer Segvec as a known Ukrainian carder. In reality, the Secret Service later admitted, Segvec was the young Cuban American who had been aiding their Shadowcrew probe since 2003. All the while, Gonzalez and two young men in Miami had been "wardriving"—driving up and down outside major businesses seeking wireless vulnerabilities to tap into. They hacked into OfficeMax, BJ's Wholesale Club, and Barnes & Noble.

They hit the mother lode in July 2005, when they got into the network at a Marshall's department store and installed a "sniffer" on the computers of parent company TJX, which also owned the T.J. Maxx chain. All told, they sucked down as many as 45 million credit and debit card numbers, about twenty times what Shadowcrew members were accused of trafficking. TJX racked up more than $100 million in expenses to settle litigation and belatedly improve its security. In terms of the hundreds of breaches publicly reported since ChoicePoint, "T.J. Maxx is kind of the grand-daddy of them all," said an executive of a top encryption firm.

The investigation began in the U.S., went overseas, and boomeranged back. From their work on Shadowcrew and CarderPlanet, federal agents knew that one of the biggest wholesalers of purloined financial data was a Ukrainian named Maksym Yastremskiy, who went by Maksik. The Orange Revolution notwithstanding, they didn't have any more luck apprehending him than they had nabbing Golubov. But when Yastremskiy made the mistake of going on vacation to Turkey, the U.S. persuaded authorities there to make an arrest. They caught him outside a Kemer nightclub in July 2007. Yastremskiy had thoughtfully brought his laptop on the trip. It contained millions of credit card numbers, a sniffer program, and records of ICQ chats with someone calling himself Segvec. Segvec's ICQ address was tied elsewhere to an email address, soupnazi@efnet.ru, styled after a *Seinfeld* character.

Their U.S. informants and other records led the Secret Service, once again, to Albert Gonzalez. He had gone by both Soupnazi and Segvec. Agents busted the former star informant at a luxury hotel in Miami, where he had $20,000 in cash and a Glock pistol. Indictments ultimately named Gonzalez, his two Miami cohorts, Yastremskiy, and an Estonian hacker who blundered by traveling to Germany. They made up five of the eleven charged for the T.J. Maxx breach. The majority of those named—two more in Ukraine, one in Belarus, and three in China—appeared in no imminent danger of arrest. Attorney General Michael Mukasey, in announcing another in a series of largest-ever cyberbusts, didn't mention that.

Now that they realized they had been duped, the feds went after Gonzalez with a vengeance. In August 2009, they would charge him with the largest identity theft of all time, one three times bigger than T.J. Maxx. No. 5 card-processing firm Heartland Payment Systems alone coughed up records from 130 million transactions, and Gonzalez was also charged with a successful attack on Citibank ATMs. But the pattern from Shadowcrew and T.J. Maxx repeated itself. The indictment named three people: Gonzalez, and "Hacker 1" and "Hacker 2," both of Russia. A prosecution source described those two as the leaders of the ring.

The Justice Department's Peretti said getting duped by cybercrime informants who pull off unauthorized crimes was "a professional hazard. They all think that they are smarter than law enforcement." She compared identity thieves to junkies who are always at risk of relapsing: "Everywhere you walk in society, you have access to a computer," Peretti said. "It is so tempting to computer criminals. They are used to spending their entire lives in front of a computer screen, and they have many identities they've created."

If the informants were addicted to misusing computers, though, the FBI and Secret Service appeared addicted to using poorly controlled informants.

At least Andy didn't have that problem. Already jailed, Maksakov did most of his online chatting while Andy watched, and he was eager to please. After he had spent a few months in a Moscow jail, Andy and Igor arranged for him to stay in the same apartment complex as the MVD's Alexei Morning, knowing he was too frightened to run. Once, the detectives granted Maksakov a weekend away from his online duties, and the young man sadly observed that he didn't have the train fare to see his girlfriend back home. Andy gave him the money out of his own pocket.

Even more important than his handling of Maksakov, Andy had used every trick in the book, along with several he made up on the spot, to burrow deeper into the Russian criminal justice system than perhaps any Westerner since the Cold War ended. If anyone could get to the top of criminal hacking society—or at least learn how far it was possible to get—it was Andy.

10

TRIAL

AS ANDY CROCKER AND THE MVD officers continued to track pay-master Stran, denial-of-service gang leaders Bra1n and Milsan, and Bra1n's partners in St. Petersburg, they also prepared for a trial sched-uled to begin in January 2006 and run most of the year. Late in 2005, Andy learned prosecutor Anton Pohamov had been assigned to the case. Igor Yakovlev checked Pohamov out and told Andy they were lucky to get him. The prosecutor had worked his way up over many years and knew the Volga River region well. In a country where the morality of those with power was always shaded in gray, Pohamov had gone after a cop involved in illegal gun sales, as well as the usual complement of drug dealers and multiple murderers. It helped that his office was one of the braver outposts. Pohamov's boss, the chief prosecutor in the region, pursued charges against a number of high-ranking officials in the area. Pohamov was friendly, tall, and hand-some, and his English was excellent. He had enough years under his belt to know the court system well, but not so many that he was no longer interested in learning new types of cases. At their first meeting, he told Andy he had asked around, and there had never been an international denial-of-service attack prosecuted in Russia. Pohamov had tried a case against minor-league hackers who had swiped some financial passwords, which was better than nothing. He said he would be happy to add a few denial-of-service and extortion convictions to his résumé.

Andy and Igor spent weeks going over the file with Pohamov, taking long detours to explain the technology issues. Because they might have to spend months working through that material with the judge, they quickly decided to try all three defendants at once. That way, they would only have to roll out the conspiracy and technology backdrops a single time. Ivan Maksakov had been cooperating extensively, so they would use his testimony against the other two—Denis Stepanov, the greedy joiner, and Alexander Petrov, the menacing police chief's son who had worked most closely with Andy's remaining targets. Pohamov asked questions as they went, usually honing in on what evidence the trio had left in their wake. Barrett's logged chats with Maksakov and the others helped, but Pohamov warned Andy that the contents of the conversations themselves wouldn't be admitted in court because of the informal way Barrett had passed them on. They could only use the fact that someone with the right nickname had been online in the chat channel at the specified time and that he had connected using the IP addresses Barrett recorded.

Maksakov's hard drive and confession, and the logs of his monitored chats with others in the ring, would be a major plus. But with an unprecedented and complicated trial, it would hurt that Petrov's machine was gone. Petrov's father's remaining influence in the region was a wild card.

All in all, Pohamov said, they had a better than even chance. "I'll do my best," he said. "But I'm not promising you anything." Andy pledged to stay through the whole trial, providing testimony whenever it was needed. Igor had other cases to work back in Moscow, so he would show up when he could.

Pohamov saw that Maksakov's cooperation had been critical. Andy told the prosecutor that he had grown fond of the remorseful hacker. Andy had even spent time with his parents, a sweet woman in her sixties and her mechanic husband, a guileless soul who had volunteered to fix a local police van while he was waiting to see his son in jail. Andy asked if Pohamov would stand behind the offer they had given Maksakov and request that the judge not sentence him to additional jail time. Pohamov said he had no problem with that. If Maksakov testified to everything he and the others had done, the case would be far stronger, and Petrov and Stepanov could get as much as a decade in prison.

Because Maksakov's server had been located in the town of Balakovo, Russian law called for the trial to be held there as well. Pohamov said he could argue that it be moved somewhere else, such as the larger city nearby where he normally worked, Saratov. Since the trial would probably last for months at least, Saratov would provide many more pleasant distractions. But the safety issues would be trickier to navigate. If some friend of Petrov's wanted to, he could keep an eye on the courthouse door, then follow Andy back to wherever he was spending his nights. The prosecutor's office appreciated Andy's assistance and bravery, but it wasn't going to spring for a rotating shift of bodyguards.

"Maybe Balakovo is a better idea," Andy admitted. Even there, Andy and Pohamov weren't foolish enough to risk staying in town. They picked out a convalescent home four miles away, taking care to keep the choice a secret.

• • •

THE PALE BRICK COURTHOUSE sat in the middle of the town square, an uninspiring but clean and functional building with wood furniture from the 1960s. Pohamov had worked for days on his opening statement, which laid out an overview of the case and the evidence that would be presented. Andy jotted some notes himself, because Pohamov said he might call on him to speak early on through a courtroom translator.

When the trial opened, Maksakov stunned them all. He reversed himself and pleaded not guilty, claiming that he had confessed falsely under threats of violence. Andy's jaw dropped as he took in the betrayal. He had been at the interrogation himself, and he would never have permitted abuse. Maksakov's family had sent a lawyer to the interviews as well, and he too had never complained. During a smoking break, Andy asked the judge, Igor Grigoriev, if the prosecution could summon that first lawyer to testify about Maksakov's fair treatment. "If I believed his story, you could do that," Grigoriev told him. "But I don't, so it's not important."

At the next opportunity, Andy and Pohamov cornered Maksakov's new lawyer outside of court and warned that his client would lose if he fought. They ran down some of the evidence against him and assured him that the judge wouldn't believe the confession had been forced.

But the lawyer pointed out that Russian prosecutors had never won a conviction in a denial-of-service case, and they could claim precious few hacking convictions of any sort. Andy was disappointed. He thought the attorney really felt he could get his client acquitted despite Maksakov's statements. But Pohamov looked hard at the lawyer and stopped arguing. *Petrov is a dangerous man*, he thought. Pohamov was convinced that Petrov had scared Maksakov into denying wrongdoing, knowing that his testimony otherwise would have ruined Petrov's defense.

Either way, Maksakov's about-face raised the stakes dramatically for the young hacker. Under the law, there could be no leniency in sentencing for anyone who refused a plea deal and was subsequently found guilty. With the risk of tuberculosis and other harsh conditions, ten years in a Russian prison could easily turn into a death sentence.

Pohamov's opening statement ran for a couple of hours. Then he turned to Andy and asked him to take over. Andy felt badly unprepared, but he glanced at his notes and stood. Reliving everything from the past two years, Andy spoke for the rest of the session and all of the next day's. The three defendants sat near the front of the section that would have been reserved for the audience, if the trial had been open to the public. On most days they were accompanied by family members or girlfriends. Maksakov followed what was happening most closely, through his hangdog eyes. Stepanov's attention wandered more. And Petrov would glower at one witness or another, then make a show of being bored by the whole affair, as if refusing to believe the next decade of his life was at issue.

The courtroom procedure baffled Andy. The two sides didn't take turns presenting their case, as they would in Britain or America. Instead, witnesses from one side prompted the other to call counterwitnesses on the spot. Anyone could ask questions at any time.

After a full day in court, Andy and Pohamov would drive off together, and they quickly developed a routine. When their translator was with them and had his gun, they would chance a local restaurant as a group. Otherwise, they would head out of town, and because their car usually was the only one on the road, they could make sure they weren't followed. They had no stove where they were staying. So they bought cold food in the supermarket, then returned to the convalescent home. They would eat, drink vodka, and plan the next day's testimony until midnight. Weekends presented the comparative luxury of a road trip to Saratov. The journey was just eighty miles each way, but it took two and a half hours to negotiate the potholes. The summer rains that filled the cracks and holes in the highway froze in winter and expanded, making the gaps even bigger.

The case broke so much new ground that the defense lawyers had a field day challenging different types of evidence. Once Andy used a PowerPoint slide show to illustrate that while the extortion emails went out from different names and used a variety of phrasing, each message had something in common with at least one other email. Most logically, they had come from the same gang. The only problem: no one had ever presented a PowerPoint in a Russian court. Arguments and appeals over the admissibility of the slides ate up a week of the trial.

Maksakov's lawyer began presenting his evidence a month into the proceedings. He admitted that Maksakov had viruses for assembling bot networks on his computer, but argued that the youth was only studying them. Records from Stepanov's computer likewise damaged the St. Petersburg man's defense, which was that he had done bad things, but not DDoS attacks.

Petrov didn't have that problem, since his father had illegally disposed of his machine. Petrov testified that he didn't even own a computer at the crucial time and never went online. But Pohamov figured that records from Petrov's Internet service provider could get the job done. Normally, that sort of request for evidence might have involved the Astrakhan police department, led until recently by Petrov's father. "If that happens, the papers will disappear," Pohamov told Andy. "But don't worry, I have a friend." He routed the request through a man he knew in the prosecutor's office in Astrakhan. Sure enough, the records came back, and the evidence showed that someone on Petrov's account was online during all of the attacks and chats, with the times corresponding to the minute. Petrov was left claiming that a friend had been using a laptop from his house on each of those occasions.

Nevertheless, during a smoking break in the judge's chambers, Petrov's lawyer told the judge stiffly that Petrov's father "would not allow" a guilty verdict. Andy stared at the man, who had otherwise seemed a reasonable sort. From the way the lawyer averted his eyes,

Andy guessed that he had been ordered by the police chief to say what he did. He never said anything of the kind again.

Andy had developed a good rapport with the judge and others who were in the courtroom every day, including the defense lawyers. But Petrov was another matter. Once, while Andy was speaking with Pohamov, he heard a faint clicking sound. Andy wheeled around and thought he saw Petrov sliding a cell phone into his pocket. Andy bolted upright and waved for the judge's attention. Any picture of him circulating on the Internet or in the Russian underground would mean he might not see England again. The judge, who had banned cameras from the trial at the outset, immediately ordered the defendants' phones turned over. When they complied, Andy saw that Petrov had indeed managed to get a pretty fair shot of him. The hair stood up on his neck.

Pohamov and Andy thought they had a good chance of winning from the start. But Judge Grigoriev was no pushover. When it came time that summer to present the expert analysis of the programs found inside Maksakov's and Stepanov's machines, Grigoriev asked good, reasonable questions. So many of them, in fact, that the prosecution team realized that the analysis it had commissioned was hopelessly weak. They pleaded for the weekend to get a new study done. Friday afternoon, they raced from the courthouse to Saratov and an MVD training site. A small crew there taught computer forensics, and Pohamov begged for help. The two instructors available were glad to be useful. As the Russian lawyer and the British detective returned with more and more food and cold drinks to keep them going without air conditioning, the teachers teased apart more than a hundred programs and wrote up their functioning in plain language.

They worked all Saturday, all Sunday, and all Sunday night until Pohamov and Andy had to leave early Monday morning. Later that day, nearly dead on his feet in court, Pohamov went through the new analysis with the judge. He turned back and saw the defeated looks on the three defendants. Now he was sure the case was his, barring some sort of back-channel deal.

• • •

IN LATE SUMMER, three weeks before the end of the ten-month trial, Igor told Andy that Timur Arutchev, the main part of Stran, had returned from abroad to his hometown of Pyatigorsk. Andy was exuberant. He immediately asked Pohamov if he could add Arutchev to the case. Pohamov asked Grigoriev, who answered that it was up to them. If they did so, though, they would have to start the trial all over—and they might have to move it to Pyatigorsk. There was no way it was worth it, all agreed, not after they'd come this far.

Arutchev's return also triggered an intense and hurried conversation between the attorneys for Maksakov and Petrov. If they could bring Arutchev to testify, they figured, he would certainly deny knowing either of their clients, throwing serious doubt on the case. The defense lawyers asked Grigoriev if they could summon Arutchev, and the judge agreed. Andy fumed again. Not only was the moneyman behind the trio confident enough that he could return to Russia unmolested, he had a good chance of blowing up the case against them.

There was one complication. If Arutchev did try to come, he probably wouldn't make it, because he was still officially a wanted man in Russia, and he would have to go through numerous checkpoints. When the defense lawyers made that point, Grigoriev declared that he would grant the paymaster safe passage. Pohamov tried to cheer Andy up, pointing out that they would at least get Arutchev testifying on the record. While it's expected that defendants will lie in Russian courts to protect themselves, witnesses who lie face severe penalties.

Grigoriev issued the guarantee of safe passage and ordered Arutchev to appear. He and his brother Yan arrived together. They were clean-cut, sporting fancy T-shirts and smart trousers, looking like many others who were well off in southern Russia. When the judge wouldn't notice, they glared at Pohamov and Andy. Timur Arutchev testified that he didn't know the defendants and never used the nickname Stran. He admitted that he had received $1.2 million from the Latvians. But Arutchev said the money was from American friends investing with him in a new business venture. When the police came after him, he said, he couldn't get the business going. Now they were poor. "If we were criminals," Arutchev said, "we would drive big cars."

At this, the judge smiled. He had guaranteed safe passage to Balakovo, but he had also made sure that the brothers' car would be stopped at least once before the witnesses arrived at court, and he had arranged for a full report of the traffic stop. So he knew that they had been driving a $150,000 BMW, even though they had been careful to park it far from the courthouse. He also noted that while he had promised that they wouldn't be arrested on the way to testify, he had never pledged that they wouldn't get picked up on the way home.

"You are not serious people," Grigoriev told the Arutchev brothers. "You are liars. I know you have a great deal of money. You are dressed in designer clothes, and you drive to court in a car that you could not afford if you were honest men." The judge had told Igor to be ready, and MVD officers surrounded the courthouse. They arrested Timur Arutchev as he left and jailed him overnight. A different judge heard his case in the morning. He allowed Arutchev to post bail and return to Pyatigorsk but ordered him to report to the local police daily and stay in Russia.

Andy asked Igor whether he thought they would ever get a conviction and real jail time for Arutchev. Igor shrugged. "It depends on how much he pays," he said. But it was definitely not a good sign that he had come home. No way would he have returned without assuring himself that he would be protected.

While Grigoriev worked on his verdict, a friend of his got in touch and asked if he would be willing to accept a bribe of about

$1 million to find Petrov not guilty. The judge reported it to Andy and the prosecutor, who wanted to outfit the judge with a hidden microphone and record a follow-up to the bribe attempt. But it was the weekend, and they couldn't get the equipment together in time. Instead, the judge handled it solo. Grigoriev agreed to a meeting, then bluffed by informing the tempters that the FSB was recording everything. They drove away in a hurry. Not long after, the judge reported that his life had been threatened.

In early October 2006, after more than a week working on his decision, Grigoriev rendered a 120-page verdict. As all in the courtroom stood, he read from the ruling for five hours. Near the end, police entered the courthouse. Grigoriev found that all three men were guilty of the key charges, having orchestrated DDoS attacks with as many as 600,000 simultaneous Web connections to Canbet, Blue Square, and many others. "Having analyzed all the obtained and investigated evidence, the court reaches the decision that the guilt of Maksakov, Petrov and Stepanov, in extorting money by threatening to destroy and damage one's property committed by the organized group, is confirmed."

With regard to Timur Arutchev's version of events, Grigoriev wrote that he "did not accept it as evidence for this criminal case." The judge said he was not in a position to rule whether Arutchev was guilty of the investigators' accusation "of extorting money from foreign companies by using harmful computer programs." But he suggested that Arutchev was already on the hook for perjury. "For giving false evidence to the court as a witness, Arutchev can be considered to be criminally responsible." Grigoriev sentenced the original trio to eight years in prison with hard labor.

Pohamov was named trial prosecutor of the year for his region. He told Andy he wanted him as the godfather for his first child, who was due early the next year. With the MVD happy to brag about a rare jail term for computer crimes, the verdict featured prominently on Russian television news and in the papers.

Andy's boss had come for the ruling, and they went out to a restaurant to celebrate. The next day, Andy went to his room and did something he'd been looking forward to for a long time. During all his years on the case, he had never spoken to Barrett Lyon, in part because his cell phones didn't work in Balakovo and in part because of the eleven-hour time difference. There had been just a few direct emails; otherwise he had fed his questions to his colleagues in London, who typically relayed them via email to Barrett. But Andy had kept Barrett's phone number handy, and at last he dug it out.

Barrett was at home in Pacifica, groggily getting ready for a day at BitGravity. Besides worrying about his start-up, Barrett was in the middle of his traumatic final departure from Prolexic. Congress had passed the bill banning online gambling the previous week, and he would resign from the company's board within the month. He hadn't gotten an update from the British in ages, and Ivan Maksakov was far from his mind.

"Hello, is that Barrett?" Andy began. "This is Detective Constable Andy Crocker. I thought you might like to know that a Russian court yesterday convicted Ivan Maksakov, Denis Stepanov, and Alexander Petrov, sentencing each of them to eight years in prison. And I wanted to thank you for all your help."

"Holy shit," Barrett said, and sat down. He had a million questions. Why had the trial taken so long? Had Andy been there the whole time? Who else had been involved? What was it like?

Andy loosened up, telling Barrett whatever he wanted to know and explaining how they had gotten the rest of the evidence they needed. They were still going after Bra1n, he said, and he would like to come to California to interview Barrett properly. "Absolutely," Barrett said. Barrett certainly hoped they got whoever had been in charge.

He felt a pang of remorse that Maksakov had drawn such a long sentence after cooperating.

Barrett hadn't worked at Prolexic for the past half year. He had never even met some of the company's newer employees. But he sent out a message to the entire company anyway with the news. "Hi Prolexic, A lot of you have no idea who I am, I am the founder of Prolexic," he wrote. "We worked harder than I could imagine to get the company on its feet. We also spent a large effort tracking down some of these idiot DDoS people, and our efforts finally resulted in the imprisonment of three people. . . .

"I find it important for everyone in this company to understand why you do what you do: It's not about money, when I started Prolexic, I never thought I would get rich from it. I thought I could make a nice living, but a greed machine was never something I envisioned. What I envisioned was a company that saved companies. A company that would stand up and do scary and difficult work when everyone said it was impossible. . . . So when you come to work and you wonder why you may be there, try to think about what the company should represent. The more positive work the company does the higher chances it has to become what I wish it would be. It's in your hands. Barrett."

• • •

ANDY ASSUMED THE BRITISH GOVERNMENT would crow about the victory. That had been the plan all along, to get convictions in the most unlikely of places, then trumpet the story to make sure every underground hacker got the message to stay away from the U.K. But in the middle of Maksakov's trial, five years after the NHTCU's creation, it was dissolved and replaced by the new Serious Organised Crime Agency, which took up so many other responsibilities that its first website didn't even mention the NHTCU. SOCA's mission was to go after all manner of mob crime, and its leaders felt there was nothing special about computer-assisted thuggery. Drugs were the top target, consuming 40 percent of the 4,000-person agency's resources. The idea was to use intelligence-agency and anti-terrorism techniques to go after the most successful criminals in the country. But the management ranks were thick, the experience of the street-level operatives was modest, and the arrests were few. From the first, several members of Parliament and tech security experts warned that cybercrime would get far less attention than it deserved. Their pleas brought no changes.

The head of SOCA was a British intelligence veteran who believed in keeping things quiet. SOCA was exempted from freedom-of-information laws on disclosure. And it issued no press releases on the Russian case. In fact, it didn't issue a press release about anything until January 2008, when complaints about its poor performance left it fighting to prove its usefulness. A year after that, conservatives began calling for its abolition.

Andy felt like he was living the ending of *Raiders of the Lost Ark:* he brought home one of the wonders of the criminal justice world, and they stuck it in a numbered crate in some anonymous government warehouse.

11

bEYONd CRIME

BARRETT LYON AND ANDY CROCKER had done what no one thought possible, catching and jailing Russian hackers who were attacking Western targets for financial gain. Now Andy wanted to see how much further they could go. He didn't see any way to cut off the cybercrime forums. But he had worked with good men at all levels of the MVD, and he had been impressed with the prosecutor and judge. Together, could they go after the kingpins? The only way to find out was to try. There were plenty of targets, including Stran, King Arthur, Bra1n, Milsan, and the leaders of the Russian Business Network. But Andy's new bosses at the Serious Organised Crime Agency didn't want an employee essentially stationed full time in Russia. SOCA recalled Andy to the U.K., and it sent no one to take his place.

Local corruption rendered Stran a lost cause, frustrating England and the MVD. Police in Pyatigorsk said they found nothing to charge the Arutchevs with, and one even wrote to the MVD in Moscow, asking for the return of Zarubina's travelers checks. Steaming, Igor

Yakovlev released them. Before he left the country, Andy thought he would aim as high as possible, at King Arthur.

Through dogged but until now secret work on the CarderPlanet case, the U.S. Postal Service's Greg Crabb had succeeded in identifying King Arthur as Artur Galegov, a man in his early twenties living in the Russian republic of Dagestan. Galegov was taking in millions of dollars from Citibank phishing and other scams with the aid of numerous U.S. accomplices, according to Postal Service documents.

In a meeting with two MVD men to discuss other business, Andy pressed his luck. "This case is going well. Let's keep it going, follow this thing upstream," he told the others. "Let's go after King Arthur. He's as bad as they get, and he's gotten millions of dollars. If we get him, that will show everyone how serious the Russian government is. It could change everything." There was an awkward pause. "He's in Dagestan," one of the MVD men said. The tone reminded Andy of the famous line from Roman Polanski's great corruption movie: "Forget about it, Jake, it's Chinatown."

"So, he's in Dagestan, great, you know where he is!" Andy persisted, feigning ignorance. "It's different there, very rough," the other man put in, as if talking to a child. "That's not a problem," Andy said. "I'm not afraid; I can go anywhere." The MVD men exchanged looks. The first cleared his throat. "The FSB is dealing with him. They know who he is," he said, trying to sound reassuring. "Well, then, the FSB can go to Dagestan," Andy said. But he sensed this wasn't going to work out. "They aren't interested in him right now," the MVD agent shrugged, signaling an end to the subject.

What they didn't tell Andy was that Dept. K operatives had already tried to get King Arthur. They had prepared a report and sent it to the MVD Investigative Committee, asking the elite squad to conduct interviews and make an arrest. The committee never pursued the case. Andy also brought up the issue with Igor. "Why won't anyone arrest King Arthur?" he asked. The politically savvy Igor shrugged, said he didn't know, and gave the all-purpose explanation Andy had heard most of the days he had been in the country. "Eta Rossiya." It is Russia.

It made an unfortunate amount of sense to Andy. *They've got him with the threat of ten years in prison,* he thought. *They said, "Either come work for us, or go to prison." Why would he not, especially if they let him continue making money?* Knowing how things worked in Russia, it was possible that King Arthur was just bribing his way to continued freedom. But that was unlikely. In the ordinary course of events, a suspect would be arrested first, giving officials the most leverage to negotiate payment. Not only had King Arthur been arrested, but no one had come close to arresting him. Besides, too many countries had been demanding King Arthur's head for too long for a simple bribe to work. "It would be too sensitive to just take money to not arrest him," Andy told a friend. "So the only reason it goes nowhere is, he's protected by someone."

Andy's colleague Trevor Dickey, who investigated King Arthur as part of the Doug Havard case, said that when he first pressed for action on King Arthur, Russian detectives had passed back the word through Andy that the mastermind "was a nobody, living in a run-down part of Dagestan and clearing perhaps $200 a month." That answer was so ridiculous that Dickey also decided the Russian government was either using King Arthur extensively or protecting him for another reason. "My educated guess is, he has some connection to something like the Russian Business Network," Dickey said.

Andy told colleagues he believed King Arthur was specializing in electronic warfare, including DDoS attacks. But he would also be invaluable to any organization seeking the power to disrupt Western economy or to monitor, and perhaps divert, bank transfers. "I think it's a combination," Dickey said. "With his expertise, he's probably an asset the FSB could put to good use." In 2009, King Arthur was still dispensing advice on carder forums, serving as a mentor to the next generation.

• • •

THE MOST LOGICAL REMAINING TARGET was Bra1n, who had been identified as Alexander Olegovich Grasman. Andy, Barrett, and the MVD had compiled a mountain of evidence against him. Andy flew to San Francisco in January 2007 to take a formal statement from Barrett for the Bra1n investigation. Barrett organized a barbecue in honor of Andy, other British agents who made the trip, and British-born Secret Service agent Trevor Fenwick, who had helped in the U.S. botnet takedowns. Fenwick would officiate at the handoff of evidence from a U.S. citizen to a British officer, just as the FBI had more than three years before.

It was the first time Barrett and Andy had met in person. As far as Barrett was concerned, it was as if James Bond had just stopped by. Andy regaled Barrett and the others with tales of bravery, corruption, and drunken foolishness. Barrett grew so engrossed in the conversation that the hamburgers he was in charge of grilling shriveled to the size of dollar coins. Barrett was forced to call for a pizza delivery, much to Andy's amusement.

Barrett took the crew sightseeing that week, and they spent a few hours each day in the BitGravity offices, going over Barrett's logs and talking about the case against Bra1n. As they spoke, it struck Barrett that Bra1n's bots might still exist, faithfully checking in on the Internet Relay Chat channel for instructions from the gang whose members had been jailed or moved on. With Andy watching over his shoulder, Barrett got back into the channel. Sure enough, the bots were still there. "Could we hijack them?" Andy asked. Barrett said he thought they probably could. They began to sketch out a plan to submit to SOCA that would call for seizing control of Bra1n's botnet and others, then directing the computers to warn their true owners about what had been happening. The plan was never adopted.

Andy also asked the Kazakhstan government for help, to little avail. Britain passed along a formal letter of request asking for a joint operation, but because SOCA didn't want to invest in another long-term deployment, it didn't insist on having an investigator along when the Kazakhstan authorities interviewed Bra1n.

Andy eventually got a report from the police in Kazakhstan. According to the document, detectives had gone to Bra1n's house. They had started with the relatives, then interviewed the suspect himself. Apparently they had left plenty of time for Bra1n to square his story with those of his far less technology-savvy parents and sister. All of them said they didn't use the Internet from the home. All of them said there was a switch at the end of the road where someone else might have tapped into the line and masqueraded as one of them.

Unfathomably, the police let Bra1n keep his computer after he promised not to delete any files. They didn't even make a digital copy of the hard drive. Andy showed the report to Igor, who read it and burst out laughing. Both complained to MVD General Boris Miroshnikov that the Kazakhs were hopelessly corrupt. "You can't interview four people and have all four say the same thing," said prosecutor Anton Pohamov. "If it had been me and Andy and an investigator from Moscow, it would have been totally different."

At an electronic-crimes conference held later in Moscow, Andy saw a chance to revive the effort. The prosecutor general for Kazakhstan was there, and so was Miroshnikov. Andy and Miroshnikov orchestrated a cigarette break where they had the prosecutor general outnumbered, Andy later told Pohamov. When both men complained about the shoddy investigation of Bra1n, the Kazakhstan prosecutor asked them to give his country another chance.

Back in England, Andy spent months compiling the evidence against Bra1n. He thought he had enough for a denial-of-service prosecution, even with everything in Bra1n's home computer long gone. Andy took another three months preparing the paperwork in the Russian style, which would also work in Kazakhstan. He had to drill four holes on the left margin by hand. String had to be woven through the holes in just the right way, with the ends on the last page held in place with sticky paper. Every one of the hundreds of pages had to be numbered by hand. In November 2008, the volume was delivered to Kazakhstan, along with boxes of exhibits from the U.K., Russia, and America.

In addition to digesting Andy's work, Kazakhstan promised to infiltrate Bra1n's new forum of choice for carding activities, Vendorsname. That forum required two references and a native's use of Russian to join. The FBI was on Vendorsname as well, and it was chasing others left over from Andy's case, including Milsan. Months passed with no arrest, but Andy didn't give up hope.

Andy was still angry that SOCA had dropped the ball, as he saw it. The case he'd led in Russia was supposed to open a new era of co-operation that would make the Internet much safer for everyone. That was certainly how Andy justified the enormous amount of time and money his government had devoted to a single set of criminals. Perhaps Bra1n still would be brought to justice, but it didn't seem likely. King Arthur and Stran were nonstarters. And then, in all likelihood, the crusade was over. SOCA's retreat meant that Andy was never able to pave the way for dozens of similar joint investigations, as he had hoped. In the end, Andy wasn't a pathfinder: he was an outlier. The Russian mob went on as before.

Andy caught up with what had transpired in his absence. During the three years he had been locked in on the Maksakov ring and its allies, identity theft and related crimes had gotten much worse. Broad phishing attacks rose and then declined. In their place came wider distribution, often through legitimate websites that had been hacked, of the worst kind of spyware—the type that logged users when they enter passwords to brokerage or bank accounts. Some variants built on the success of the extortion racket, locking consumers' computer files and demanding ransom.

The sheer volume of new viruses and other "malware" grew so vast—being reported at clips as rapid as two a minute—that security firms could no longer analyze each one by hand. Instead, they relied on machines to identify the most pernicious. The number that could evade antivirus software and firewalls soared as well. Hackers even trained viruses to mutate on their own, making them harder to block systematically: one called Storm spawned 5,000 variants within days of its release. Facebook, Twitter, and other social networks soon made it easy to take one stolen identity and then induce the victims' friends to click on poisoned links.

A Gartner survey found that 30 percent of Americans had been victimized by identity fraud by 2009. They got back an average of 86 percent of the money drained from credit cards and 77 percent of the money stolen from ATM and debit cards. Victims of bogus account transfers, though, recovered only 54 percent of their losses. Small businesses were increasingly targeted in account transfers, and the banks often refused to make up the losses. As for the banking industry's red ink, that was anyone's guess. Convictions remained an extreme rarity, striking far less than half of 1 percent of the perpetrators.

While the U.S. got better at domestic arrests, taking down the likes of Max Butler and Albert Gonzalez, it still struggled to get anywhere near as much assistance from the former Eastern Bloc as Andy managed. The most notable success was in Romania, which arrested dozens in mostly small-time identity theft cases. According to many, that was money talking. "The European Union brought down the hammer on Romania. They said there's no funding for technology assistance unless they cracked down, and they did," said VeriSign security analyst Kimberly Zenz. FBI Assistant Director Shawn Henry said it helped that Romania was looking to join NATO. Still, in mid-2009 Andy's initial interview with Ivan Maksakov remained the most fruitful interrogation to date of any hacker in the top country for hacking.

While Andy had advanced against cybercrime on one front, the situation on every other front had deteriorated. It was now a full-blown geopolitical struggle, and neither the U.K. nor the U.S. wanted to fight it.

• • •

THOSE WHO ESCAPED ANDY'S GRASP were just a sampling of the dangerous men protected by superior political force. The most likely authors of two of the worst viruses of all time, SoBig and Bagle, were identified to no avail. Top Ukrainian carder Script, aka Dmitry Golubov, walked out of prison on no less authority than the good word of two members of that country's parliament.

For every entry-level crook picked up overseas in cooperation with U.S. or U.K. investigators, a known modern-day mob boss thumbed his nose, certain of safety. In 2005, the FBI and Secret Service worked with other U.S. officials to try to bust one notorious Russian gang, the HangUp Team. Their officials met with Russian authorities multiple times, identified the members behind the crew, and even provided their locations. The Russians did nothing. "Same goes for King Arthur," said one agent involved. "American authorities couldn't even get a picture of the guy."

Worst of all was the Russian Business Network, Andy learned. By following the trail from the denial-of-service hackers, he realized, he had come as near to the infamous RBN as anyone in the West, perhaps within a steel door's thickness of a close affiliate. Now Andy began to doubt that anyone would ever get that close again.

Bra1n's St. Petersburg crew had been tipped off, it had been tied to child porn, and it ran a slick operation that could make evidence disappear down a dumbwaiter at short notice. That sounded a lot like the way the RBN did business. Researchers who spent much of their time tracking the RBN said the group enjoyed some kind of special protection. A key figure in the group called himself Flyman and might have been the world's largest supplier of child pornography. But he was off-limits to police, according to reports from several investigators, including Zenz, who spent many months in Russia. Zenz reported that a senior MVD investigator told her in Moscow in 2006 that his efforts to arrest Flyman "met forceful, official resistance. Flyman's father is an influential St. Petersburg politician who used his leverage and money to persuade law enforcement authorities to prevent do-gooders from pursuing the case." She elaborated: "Flyman is a very rare type, in that he has both mafia protection and political protection at a very strong level."

Without some cover from above, no organization could have been so deeply involved in everything from DDoS attacks to spyware—and so public that it advertised "bulletproof hosting" and other services and gave out staffers' names—while escaping prosecution. The RBN gave off an astonishing combination of mystery and openness that made it all the more menacing: it hid in plain sight. The group dated back as far as 1998, according to Zenz and another of the most influential experts on the gang, a security professional using the pseudonym Jart Armin. Armin believes that the RBN started out as a conventional, if proficient, circle of hackers. Then it had a merger with one of the most powerful traditional organized crime groups in Russia, the Tambov gang of St. Petersburg.

If this reading is accurate, the combination became a model for other cybercrime groups throughout the country. Although most hackers started on their own, as they got bigger they developed a need for protection by old-school mobsters, who were better connected politically. Even if they didn't see such a need, the mobsters might point it out to them in a very persuasive manner. It's not so much that the hackers feared getting arrested: it's more that they feared that any police who identified them would demand a bribe. The typical way to avoid paying an exorbitant bribe in Russia is to have one's own mob ally, or "roof," negotiate for you, according to Joe Serio, an American who worked in the Soviet government's anti–organized crime bureau.

It remains a challenge to figure out who does what at the Russian Business Network, and not everyone agrees even what functions the group carries out as a whole. But tremendous work has gone into the effort by such researchers as Zenz; Armin; David Bizeul, a security expert for French banks; Paul Ferguson, of the big security firm Trend Micro; Don Jackson of SecureWorks; and the people at Team Cymru. Independently and teamed up, such researchers have written a number of analyses, posting some of them on the Web for criticism and refinement.

It is worth noting why experts are willing to work with people like Armin, who masks his real identity. It's because they understand the personal risk he is taking in trying to expose the RBN. The threats Andy faced in Russia are not unheard of. The name of the author of "Who Wrote SoBig" is known to a very few individuals, mainly in government. Ferguson and security firm F-Secure's Mikko Hypponen take steps to obscure where they live. The group Cymru, which helped Barrett track botnets, names its top executives but never takes credit for any of its activities. Zenz said she knows Flyman's real name but wouldn't be the first to make it public. "If he's not going to get picked up, I'm not going to pick a fight with him personally," she said. "He's a nasty piece of work."

A former colleague of Armin's once went to St. Petersburg to investigate some thefts of material worth millions of dollars. As Armin put it later, his colleague made the mistake of trusting the police there, working with them, and using his real identity. Shortly afterward, the man's teenage daughter permanently disappeared from their home in a Western country. He was told that if he forgot about the matter in St. Petersburg, his other children would be left alone.

What's already known is that the Russian Business Network offers hosting and connections to the Internet, and probably much more. This gives it a layer of deniability: it can always say that someone else bought technology services and used them to criminal ends without the company's knowledge. That is an obvious smoke screen, because with the exception of a small number of porn sites, no one has ever found legitimate content hosted by RBN. French expert Bizeul probed thousands of servers bearing Internet addresses under the control of RBN and its close affiliates. He found 555 addresses that tried to infect visitors' Web browsers, 47 containing child porn, 15 with conventional porn, 8 providing command-and-control functions that managed botnets, 5 selling scareware (the fake anti-spyware programs that trick users into thinking a download will scan and secure their computers), 4 used in financial fraud, 3 offering to pay outsiders to install malicious programs on PCs, 2 holding masses of pirated software, and 1 recruiting mules to move money around the planet. Until 2007, when the RBN got too much attention and dropped its public website, it had an official responsible for handling abuse complaints. The official generally demanded a Russian court order before cutting anyone off. But that's not to say the company didn't take note of such complaints—according to Zenz, it warned customers that if there was too much heat from what they were doing, it would have to charge them more.

Describing everything bad that happened on RBN computers would fill a separate book. In its early days the outfit hosted Cool-WebSearch, a piece of nefarious, ad-spewing spyware that was so hard to disentangle from infected PCs that many consumers threw their machines away. More recently, RBN provided the home for the first major marketplace for automated hacking as a service. On those computers, an outfit called 76service, successor to the HangUp Team, sold subscriptions for access to machines infected by a Trojan called

Gozi. Would-be criminals could purchase a freshly infected machine most likely to provide new and valuable financial data for $1,000 a month. "Used" computers were cheaper, according to one researcher who was able to log onto the home site.

A leading figure at the group that ran Gozi was in all likelihood one of the two critical allies for Albert Gonzalez, the biggest American identity thief ever accused. A source close to the 2009 prosecution of Gonzalez in the 130 million–card Heartland Payment Systems breach said that Gonzalez's indicted but unnamed Russian co-conspirators, "Hacker 1" and "Hacker 2," used the online nicknames Anex and Grig, and the source said Grig had used that alias in posting to Shadowcrew. Don Jackson, the SecureWorks analyst who logged into Gozi's customer interface and chatted with Russians involved there, said that only one major Shadowcrew poster went by Grig. That was the hacker who refashioned himself as a major figure in the HangUp Team and as "76," co-leader of 76Service. As Gonzalez pleaded guilty in August 2009, the FBI asked the FSB to go after Grig and Anex. But Jackson said that Grig's longtime prominence made it plain that the FSB already knew who he was and had decided not to arrest him. "If they wanted to do it, they would have," Jackson said. "They have had many opportunities."

RBN was also involved in the 2007 attack that took control of the Bank of India's main website. A piece of bad software measuring just one pixel by one pixel—and therefore essentially invisible to the naked eye—was placed on BankofIndia.com. When people visited the site, the bug connected to an RBN page that tried to install twenty-two different pieces of malicious code, including identity-theft tools. And RBN was the largest host for pages taking advantage of MPack, an innovative crime kit that sold for $1,500 in the Russian underground. MPack used the same technique as that in the Bank of India attack, known as an iFrame exploit, to corrupt thousands of legitimate Web pages, including many related to Italian tourism, and then breach the systems of as many as half of those sites' visitors. The bugs succeeded so often because they tried to find holes in many different pieces of software a visitor's computer might be running, including Windows, Internet Explorer, and Apple's QuickTime.

Theoretically, a constantly updated PC would have few holes. But more than 98 percent of computers run at least one piece of code with a serious, well-publicized security hole that has not been fixed with an available patch, according to an analysis of 20,000 machines scanned by security firm Secunia. MPack installed a variety of payloads. Among the worst, delivered again by RBN machines, was a 2006 keylogger called Torpig. It waited for computer users to log onto one of a list of sites including eBay, PayPal, and Bank of America. Then it flashed a realistic error message indicating that the log-on was incorrect and asking for bona fides, including social security numbers and bankcard codes. Anything typed in was whisked off to St. Petersburg—more than half a million bank credentials. "Primarily, the RBN's objective is to use any and many alternative means to infect your PC and then gain or extort personal information, and if possible hijack and enslave the PC as a zombie," said Armin.

Using public domain name registration filings and other sources, Bizeul identified several names apparently at the center of RBN activity, including Vladimir Kuznetsov and the unnameable Flyman. Armin added more, including Nikolae Shishkin, listed as a director of the U.K. company that registered many of RBN's Internet addresses. Some security researchers have theorized that one of RBN's biggest clients has been Rock Phish, an operation blamed by security firm RSA for half of the world's phishing attacks. What the researchers don't know is that law enforcement believes it made the definitive link, showing that an RBN leader controlled Rock Phish directly. In a secret report in 2006, the FBI, Britain's NHTCU, and others, working with a wide number of banks whose sites had been mimicked, identified a leader of the Rock Phish attacks as one Igor

Vladimirovich Kuznetsov. The report noted that in some registration forms Kuznetsov used the pseudonym Vladimir Igor Kuznetsov. While the law enforcement report didn't mention the Russian Business Network, Vladimir Kuznetsov was named as a central figure at RBN by both Bizeul and Armin, who relied on other sources.

Kuznetsov's most legitimate work appeared to be running a St. Petersburg retail outlet at www.lefthandshop.ru, which customized products for left-handed people. But he also advertised spamming services. Rock Phish targeted customers of Barclays, Chase, Wells Fargo, and many other financial institutions—an average of eighteen brands every day. Industry researchers assisting law enforcement agencies hacked into the administrative console for the Rock Phish program. It showed twelve administrators permitted access, including one named Russell. By tracking the websites under Russell's control, the investigators established that he was really Kuznetsov. Whoever received that international police report didn't do much to dismantle Rock Phish. Two years later, the group allied itself with a cutting-edge botnet known as Asprox, which used a new technology to constantly shift Internet addresses and evade blocking.

• • •

AS A WHOLE, ANDY SAW THAT admitted criminals and obvious suspects were committing fraud worth hundreds of millions of dollars, enslaving tens of millions of computers, and enjoying the power to severely damage electronic commerce. It was as if a dozen Al Capones were allowed complete freedom. How did they operate with such impunity?

The answer to that crucial question lies in the economics and politics of the countries where they based themselves. Many countries in Eastern Europe had fairly strong technical education programs, but much less in the way of solid career opportunities in computing fields. Most of the worst extortionists, identity thieves, and other cybercriminals, meanwhile, were naturally inclined to pick victims far from home, because credit cards had yet to deeply penetrate the middle classes where they lived. Combine that with a general resentment of American power, and few of those in government cared much about curbing cybercrime. Such forums as Russia's *Hacker* magazine ran ads from the likes of Microsoft and Hewlett-Packard but openly celebrated a criminal techno-culture—depicting attractive women hanging on moneyed new mobsters—and distributed CDs enabling subscribers to hack their own Internet service providers without any technical skills. Added to that was the significant predisposition toward corruption in countries where police officials, even the top brass at the Russian equivalent of the FBI, earned just a few hundred dollars a month. According to one watchdog group, the portion of Russians engaging in corruption rose from 50 percent in 2001 to 55 percent in 2005. Another survey identified police officials as the most corrupt.

All of that would be bad enough. It would show how far the world has to go in confronting a problem that is already dire and poised to get far worse—potentially wiping out faith in electronic transactions and rendering the Internet unfit for more than entertainment and informal, quasi-public communication.

Unfortunately, the full truth is much worse than that. The full truth is that a number of enormously powerful national governments, especially those of Russia and China, have picked the blossoming of the Internet age as the time to ally with organized crime.

What reason would they have to do so? Simply put, the benefits outweigh the costs. As for the price, such alliances are easier in countries without deep democratic traditions—but even the United States, for a prize deemed as important as the elimination of Fidel Castro, has dallied with the mafia. Neither the China nor the Russia of 2009 is accountable to its people. And organized crime is so endemic in Russia that some argue the government itself is an ongoing criminal enterprise. Joe Serio, who probed organized crime for the old Soviet government and then headed the Moscow office of private security firm Kroll Associates, describes organized crime, business, and government as so intertwined as to make unraveling the strands impossible. Just as the powerful English nobility during the long-ago Wars of the Roses picked figurehead contenders for the throne who suited their needs, the richest mobs in Russia championed candidates for federal office. The big difference between the Russian Federation's first president, Boris Yeltsin, and his successor, Vladimir Putin, is that the outside plutocrats were in charge of Yeltsin, while Putin is in charge of the plutocrats, centralizing corruption.

Preoccupied with terrorism, wars in Iraq, Afghanistan, and Georgia, and Russian oil production, the West has done very little to press Russia for action on cybercrime. As a result, the government faces few consequences for its sordid alliances.

• • •

THE BENEFITS TO STATE-SPONSORED CYBERCRIME, on the other hand, are vast. Starting with the theoretical and moving toward absolute certainty: primarily Eastern European gangs possess about half of the world's credit card numbers, according to the head of the Justice Department's computer crime section, though they haven't used most of them. Justice's Kimberly Kiefer Peretti said the greater danger would come if they cracked debit and ATM cards en masse as well. The more precise statement would be not if, but when. King Arthur could do it, and so could Albert Gonzalez's Russian partners. The Russian government, and possibly the Chinese government, has access to minds capable not only of stealing millions upon millions of dollars, but potentially disrupting the Western economy. Why wouldn't they encourage additional research to nurture such a weapon?

Next, the anonymous author of "Who Wrote SoBig" said that the most important beneficiary of the SoBig virus was not the Send-Safe spamming company but one particular customer of that company, which was not an ordinary spammer. More afraid for his life than unsure of his findings, he never directly stated whom he believed that customer to be, but he advised "looking behind" the RBN, which he called a front. Given the rest of the conversation, the most reasonable interpretation of what he was saying was that the customer is the FSB, though he could have meant another spying operation. There is no obvious reason that such an agency would want access to controllable computers scattered across the globe. But there are some intriguing possibilities. One, again put forward by the white paper's author, is that Send-Safe's customer could be sending spam containing coded messages. That might sound far-fetched. But the author pointed to an article in a computer security publication, *CompSec Online*, which said unnamed U.S. intelligence sources had found codes in the ubiquitous Nigerian advance-fees spam that held instructions for the assassinations of two officials in the Ivory Coast and an attempted coup there. Sending the same message from co-opted machines to thousands or millions of people makes it impossible for investigators to trace the plotters' chain of command. Another explanation could be that the FSB wants to keep a network of machines in reserve for offensive acts, such as denial-of-service attacks, or to cover the origins of clandestine spying through technical breaches.

The Russians have not been publicly exposed for using hacking to spy in the U.S. But officials told the *Los Angeles Times* in late 2008 that they suspected that a recent Trojan attack on Defense Department networks, including U.S. Central Command and classified systems, was directed from Russian computers. The attacks spread in large part through ultra-portable flash drives, where the stealth program could overcome most network security policies. It was so severe that Pentagon leaders briefed President George W. Bush on the matter and banned the use of flash drives, until then in heavy use by U.S. forces in Iraq and Afghanistan. Some outside security experts, including those at Team Cymru, cautioned that the Russian computers could have been commandeered by hackers from another country. "None of these things are definitive," said Howard Schmidt, who served as head of cybersecurity in the early years of Bush's White House. "If people are as good as they are purported to be, it wouldn't be leading right to them. I worry more about the stuff where we have no clue it's even happening." But Bruce McConnell, who was briefed on the attacks during his time on a cyberthreat commission at the Center for Strategic and International Studies, said, "I think they know who it was, and it was state sponsored."

The Russian government also might have used Russian Business Network machines to spy on the country of Georgia's networks, which were penetrated during the land war in late 2008. That hasn't been proved. But it is clear that those computers assaulted official websites in Estonia and Georgia with denial-of-service attacks. When Barrett walked away from Prolexic, DDoS attacks were becoming routine, and the mob was beginning to use botnets for more profitable mass identity theft instead. But Russia's cyber military campaigns of 2007 and 2008 demonstrated that DDoS assaults, far from disappearing, had reemerged as a geopolitical weapon.

In April 2007, after Estonian officials removed a major statue of a Soviet soldier from a park in Tallinn, street riots by those of Russian descent were joined by an unprecedented and sustained denial-of-service attack on Estonian government websites. Sites for banks, media, and infrastructure companies fell as well in the first all-out cyber-attack on an entire country. More than a million computers from all over the world inundated the sites at once, generating two hundred times the normal traffic. A simultaneous spam flood shut down the parliament's email service for days. The only thing the government could do to keep functioning, said Estonian President Toomas Ilves, was cut itself off from the outside world, blocking all foreign Internet traffic.

Technologists traced some of the DDoS packets to Internet addresses within Putin's administration. A Russian government spokesman pointed out that the IP addresses could have been faked or the machines hijacked. Analysts disagreed over whether the Russian government directed the assaults, which nevertheless prompted a call for stronger cyberdefense from NATO. Russian blogs were full of instructions for how to join in the DDoS campaign, and certainly some citizens volunteered for the cause. But the major part of the assault suddenly stopped a month after it began, suggesting that a botnet had been leased for that period. "It was a new form of public-private partnership," Estonia's Ilves said drily. "This was clearly paid for, but I think it was a policy decision." Even if the Russian government wasn't calling the shots, it clearly could have acted to stop the flow, and it did not. "In Estonia," said National Security Agency chief General Keith Alexander, "all of a sudden we went from cybercrime to cyberwarfare." Andy Crocker's theory is that the Estonia attack was "a proof of concept," in which the RBN picked a target to show the Russian authorities how valuable it could be.

In Georgia, the plausible deniability wore even thinner. The massive digital attacks began against government sites before the Russians tanks rolled in August 2008, eventually driving the prime minister's site to safe haven in the U.S. Armin and others who spoke with network administrators in Georgia found that a lot of the malicious traffic came from servers controlled by the Russian Business Network. James McQuaid, who collaborated with Armin, traced much of the early attack to a swath of Internet addresses controlled by RBN operatives Alexander Boykov and Sergey Smirnov, whose previous schemes included a fake antivirus program and a faux Canadian pharmacy outlet, respectively. More intriguingly, some better-hidden machines directing the attack resided on Internet addresses belonging to state-owned telecommunications companies in Russia, according to Don

Jackson of SecureWorks. The choice of targets is also telling. Denial-of-service attacks shut down official sites in the smaller Georgian city of Gori, along with local news sites, before the Russian planes got there. "How did they know that they were going to drop bombs on Gori and not the capital?" Jackson asked, adding that Boykov's associates said he was a retired FSB agent. "From what I've seen first-hand, there was at some level actual coordination and/or direction [by the Russian government], especially in regard to the timing and the targets of some of the attacks." This time it wasn't just denial-of-service attacks: people also infiltrated Georgia's government networks to steal information and deface websites, replacing the content with pro-Russia propaganda.

Theoretically, free-spending and spontaneously patriotic hackers could have done much of the damage to Georgia. But other, less-noticed attacks have mysteriously silenced critics of the Kremlin, and it's hard to see why even patriotic hackers would have cared to help. Take Compramat.ru, a scandal site similar to The Smoking Gun in the U.S. It publishes dossiers on politicians and other prominent people. In mid-2006, it evidently offended the wrong people, and a denial-of-service attack downed it, Zenz said. Other scandal sites failed as well, and so have those belonging to opposition politicians including Garry Kasparov. DDoS assaults also pummeled mainstream news outlets, including the daily *Kommersant*, which was apparently hit for printing an interview with the exiled tycoon Boris Berezovsky.

The denial-of-service retributions finally came to Western attention in the summer of 2009, when one knocked the popular messaging site Twitter offline and slowed down Facebook on the anniversary of the Georgian war. Facebook discovered that it had been crippled by requests to view the page of a single user, a Georgian professor and Russia critic who blogged under the name Cyxymu. The attack was "directed at an individual who has a presence on a number of sites, rather than the sites themselves," Facebook said.

The fate of Ingushetia.ru, an opposition news site in the strife-torn Caucusus region, was more serious. Moscow blocked access to the site for a time, and the local government sued to have it taken down. Then owner Magomed Evloev was arrested and "accidentally" shot in the head.

"Every time there are elections, we see DDoS attacks against political dissidents or independent media," said Rafal Rohozinski, who worked in the Caucusus and co-founded the OpenNet Initiative, which tracks Web restrictions. He said the attacks formed a more subtle part of a broader Kremlin crackdown on media that includes the unsolved murders of many journalists. "With a DDoS attack, how do you actually prove that it's happening, as opposed to the network failing? The plausible deniability becomes much more of a gray area, and for average users, the bottom line is the site is unavailable."

Rohozinski concluded that the government has spared many criminal hackers on condition that they do some work for the country. "From the knowledge we have, it's clear there's a nod and wink that goes on: 'We won't prosecute you as long as you make yourself available for things like Estonia and Georgia.'" Zenz agreed. Cyber-attacks "were better and more organized in Georgia, and that's only going to continue," she said. "It used to be people thought crime is one thing, politics and diplomacy are a second thing, but I think it's going to continue to merge."

Patriotic individuals do some damage by themselves. They helped go after Estonia and Georgia, and in January 2009 a group called Help Israel Win persuaded ordinary Israelis to volunteer their computers for a botnet launching DDoS attacks on Palestinian sites. Years before, patriotic Chinese defaced U.S. military sites and probably released the costly Code Red worm after a U.S. spy plane crashed into a Chinese jet and killed the pilot. U.S. hackers retaliated with their own defacements and may have launched the Code Blue worm, which reinfected Code Red machines and used them for denial-of-service attacks on Chinese sites.

But in Russia, the current model appears similar to the one the government uses with Nashi, a government-supported patriotic youth group that protests internal and external "fascists" and other Kremlin enemies. The authorities officially disapprove of any extralegal actions. But there is no way they would happen without guidance from above. Indeed, the FSB has implicitly drawn the parallel. The Moscow investigative journalist Andrei Soldatov reported in 2007 that the government's National Antiterrorist Committee appeared to be taking the lead in coordinating citizen hacking attacks. Soldatov traced such attacks as far back as 2002, after hackers broke into the Sweden-based pro-Chechen rebel site Kavkaz-Tsentr. In a highly unusual move, the FSB issued a press release saying that no laws had been broken in the attacks and that the hackers were acting in a patriotic manner worthy of respect.

Three years later, Russian officials complained publicly that Sweden had refused to pull the plug on the site. The next day, the Russian site Mediactivist.ru coordinated another attack on the Chechen pages. The hackers have returned frequently, defacing the site and temporarily redirecting traffic to anti-Chechen sites. Since other governments have declined to shut down objectionable sites and will continue to do so, Moscow will continue to rely on such hackers, Soldatov said. A member of the Russian legislature went so far as to issue a proclamation thanking a hacking group for attacking sites in Israel. "A small force of hackers is stronger than multiple thousands of the current armed forces," Duma deputy Nikolai Kuryanovich's certificate read. "I hope that from now on your work will not become any less productive."

Another ultra-nationalist member of the Duma was the source of a startling admission at a forum on cyber issues in 2009, when he said an assistant in his office dreamed up the attack on Estonia and said such "spontaneous" responses would likely continue. He was referring to Konstantin Goloshkov, a commissar of Nashi, who confirmed the story to the *Financial Times*. "It was cyber defense," he said. "We taught the Estonian regime a lesson that if they act illegally, we will respond in an adequate way." He denied Kremlin direction, saying: "We did everything based on our own initiative." Even if that were true, such public statements show what little hold international norms of cyber behavior have on Russia.

The Russians are not alone in seeing cyberwarfare as a golden opportunity to catch up to the U.S. in military strength. The convicted Bali nightclub bomber used his autobiography to praise computer-assisted credit card fraud as a means of raising funds. And three British jihadists convicted in 2007 for inciting murder used access to a database with 37,000 stolen credit cards to buy 250 airline tickets, night-vision goggles, hundreds of prepaid cell phones, GPS devices, and more—some $3.5 million in total purchases—to assist others in the movement. Investigators said one of the men, Tariq al-Daour, was a regular on CarderPlanet and phished eBay customers. In one trick for laundering the proceeds, al-Daour set up more than a hundred gambling accounts at AbsolutePoker.com, Canbet.com, and other sites, bet often, and cashed out the winnings.

• • •

THE CHINESE, MEANWHILE, have been comparatively open about their cyber military aspirations. Chinese military analyst Wang Huacheng, in a 2000 paper, described U.S. reliance on information technology and space as "soft ribs and strategic weaknesses." And the country's efforts in the area have been extremely successful. For several years beginning in 2002, Chinese forces penetrated Sandia National Laboratories, the U.S. Army Information Systems Engineering Command, and other sites in an operation known as Titan Rain. Air Force Major General William Lord said the Chinese downloaded at least ten terabytes of data, the same amount contained in the Library of Congress. The Chinese also have accessed the Defense Department's Internet-connected system for distributing unclassified information, including schedules for top commanders and troop movements.

A bipartisan commission on U.S.-China issues that reports to Congress annually said in November 2008 that major Chinese cyberspace and space initiatives could provide "capability enabling it to prevail in a conflict with U.S. forces." The report concluded that "since China's current cyber operations capability is so advanced, it can engage in forms of cyberwarfare so sophisticated that the United States may be unable to counteract or even detect the efforts." Major targets might include Internet-linked financial networks and systems for controlling aircraft and distributing electrical power. The electric grid is so poorly defended, said one expert, that an enemy could knock it offline for months.

In a parallel with the situation in Russia, Western authorities can trace many cyberattacks only as far back as known hacker groups, while China denies spying. U.S. military experts said that one of the key attractions of cyber operations for the Chinese is that the difficulty proving responsibility hamstrings any reaction. In addition, Chinese authorities work so hard to monitor use of the Internet that it's impossible to imagine a major international data-stealing operation being carried out without government support. The U.S.-China Economic and Security Review Commission reported that as many as 250 hacking groups "are tolerated and may even be encouraged by the government to enter and disrupt computer networks." In contrast to the Russian experience, where profit predated patriotism, almost all of the early cyberattacks from within China expressed nationalistic sentiments. Numerous assaults on sites in Taiwan, Indonesia, and Japan followed some perceived insult against China. Such groups as the Red Hacker Alliance said they put patriotism first. Only after several years of pro-China activities did a profit motive emerge to such an extent that it splintered some of the most important organizations.

Again like the Russians, the Chinese have used cyberattacks to harass and silence civilian foes based outside the country's borders. Proponents of the Falun Gang and Tibetan independence movements have been targeted, and at least one small Tibetan alliance disbanded rather than risk further electronic communications. Chinese hackers have hit virtually all the groups with "zero-day exploits," those that use a vulnerability that has not been openly identified and patched. One especially clever email used a previously unknown flaw in Microsoft Word to try to infiltrate a pro-Taiwan group. Two weeks later, the same gambit was used against a big defense contractor in the U.K., according to Finnish expert Mikko Hypponen, strongly suggesting the hand of Chinese government.

Groups such as Students for a Free Tibet long ago switched to Macs, which are less vulnerable to viruses, stopped opening attachments, and barred sensitive topics from email. "The place where it got really disturbing was during the March 2008 uprising, when information was really hard to get out of Tibet and it was an awful time for people," said Lhadon Tethong, director of the organization. Penetration attempts appeared in "messages coming in saying 'Please help me, I'm in Tibet, I saw everything, I have photos,'" Tethong said. "It was really awful manipulation of emotions." Despite precautions, the breaches have been constant and possibly deadly for some who have disappeared within Tibet. In one case, Tethong said, a virus sent data back to a machine in the mainland's railway ministry. In another incident, everyone in Tethon's inner circle got infected, and the only common link was emails from her. Security experts found that her machine had been compromised through the wireless network at the exiled Tibetan leadership's main offices in India.

Similar email attacks penetrated dozens of U.S. defense contractors. A typical attempt came in an attachment to a credible 2007 email apparently from Air Force military sales official Stephen Moree to Booz Allen Hamilton military consultant Jack Mulhern. If Mulhern had opened the purported enumeration of India's desired Pentagon gear, which echoed a recently released wish list, his every subsequent keystroke would have been sent off to someone relying on an infamous Chinese domain name registrar, 3322.org. Another target of a Chinese Trojan was a client of security firm iDefense. That company, looking for the originating hacker, scanned Chinese-language sites and found that a man going by Wicked Rose (or, as translated by others, Withered Rose) claimed to have written the previously unknown remote-control technology installed by the Trojans. He also claimed responsibility for targeted email attacks using vulnerabilities in Word, which was the way the Trojans got in. A university student in Chengdu, Wicked Rose won two hacking competitions sponsored by the military and led what he called the Network Crack Program Hacker group, earning enough to leave school. His real name was Tan Dailin, according to *Time* magazine, which tracked him down for an interview in which he nervously denied hacking the Pentagon.

IDefense concluded that "there is little doubt left as to his involvement in attacks to date." Like other worldwide security firms, iDefense hesitated to finger the Chinese government. But Tan Dailin did not come across as a freelancer. In 2008 and 2009, a team that included Rafal Rohozinski and experts at the University of Toronto tracked stolen documents flowing out from Tibetan groups to Chinese command-and-control servers and then hacked into those machines and saw the other sites that had been compromised. The vast network, which the group dubbed GhostNet in a report, had infected 1,295 machines, 397 of which were "either significant to the relationship between China and Tibet, Taiwan or India, or were identified as computers at foreign embassies, diplomatic missions, government ministries or international organizations."

• • •

DURING THE BUSH ADMINISTRATION, the White House response to the cyberwar threat was abysmal—far worse than its tepid reaction to the rising power of cybercriminal gangs. As far back as 2002, before the rise of the botnets, a broad and distinguished group was so concerned about cyberattacks on the country's infrastructure that it asked Bush to invest an initial $500 million in a new Manhattan Project for Internet defense. Signatories to the letter included former directors of the CIA, NSA, and Defense Intelligence Agency. Organizer Sami Saydjari, himself a highly ranked veteran of the NSA and DARPA, the agency that gave birth to the Internet, politely described the reaction as "mixed," although Congress did authorize hundreds of millions of dollars in research.

Cyber issues got such short shrift in the Department of Homeland Security that four successive heads of technology safety resigned in less than two years, starting with Howard Schmidt, who left in 2003. "I recall at a White House meeting, we had a section in our [national cybersecurity] plan related to end users, and how with the power of broadband, how they could be used as a potential weapon as part of botnets, such as with distributed denial-of-service attacks," Schmidt said in 2009. "They had someone fighting against us, an economist, who said 'I took a semester of computer science in college, and when we look at impact on vital infrastructure, they have nothing to do with it.'" Schmidt said plans such as giving Internet service providers more power to cut off malicious machines and block access to bad sites were dismissed. "The actions that could have been taken were not. Which is why we're sitting here almost six years down the road trying to figure it all out."

The Homeland Security Department routinely issued calls for the private sector to do more, observing that most of the Internet infrastructure is in private hands. Officials published countless strategy documents stressing the need for public-private cooperation. Yet the private sector had long before grasped the enormity of the problem, put aside its traditional libertarian posture, and called for increased regulation. In February 2005, a group of chief information officers from both hardware and software companies traveled to the White House together for the first time. Executives from Microsoft, Dell, IBM, Hewlett-Packard, and security giant Symantec, among others, carried a three-item wish list. No. 1 was the creation of a government commission on organized cybercrime. They didn't get it. Cybercrime had risen to the level where it constituted a threat to national security by mid-2007, according to Congress's Government Accountability Office.

The Homeland Security Department was itself compromised electronically or infected with viruses hundreds of times. Hackers even read the Secretary of Defense's unclassified email. The State Department was so riddled with intrusions that it had to cut off all Internet access for a time. While CIA officials said that a cyberwar had been going on for years, top Bush appointees didn't focus on the issue until 2006, when Director of National Intelligence Mike McConnell told Bush that if the 9/11 hijackers had instead carried out a successful cyber assault on a U.S. bank, the damage to the economy would have been ten times worse. In January 2008, Bush finally issued a classified directive in response that called for the National Security Agency to keep an eye on U.S. government networks and for investments in the billions of dollars to that end.

The disconnect was still on show at the Black Hat computer security convention in Las Vegas in July 2008. One evening, members of an all-star commission convened by the Center for Strategic and International Studies to make recommendations for the next president said that cybersecurity should be a high priority—but acknowledged that it probably wouldn't be. "How many of you think that IP is broken?" one panelist asked those assembled, referring to the Internet protocol that provides the fundamental functioning of the Internet. Almost everyone in the audience raised their hands. "Nothing is happening," said commission member Jerry Dixon, a former director of the National Cyber Security Division at Homeland Security who joined Team Cymru. The CSIS panel was chaired by the two leaders of the U.S. House committee on cybersecurity, a retired Air Force general, and the head of Microsoft's Trustworthy Computing effort. When it issued its report in the fall of 2008, the group called for a White House–led strategy that would use diplomatic, intelligence, military, and economic policy to protect U.S. cyber infrastructure "using all elements of national power." Hearings and briefings that informed the report "made it clear we are in a long-term struggle with criminals, foreign intelligence agencies, militaries, and others . . . and this struggle does more real damage every day to the economic health and national security of the United States than any other threat," the panel wrote, putting cybersecurity on "a strategic issue on par with weapons of mass destructions and global jihad."

• • •

SHORTLY AFTER BARACK OBAMA took office as president, he asked cybersecurity industry veteran Melissa Hathaway to conduct a complete sixty-day review of the country's policies. When the White House released the report in late May 2009, it echoed the findings of the CSIS study. "The architecture of the nation's digital infrastructure, based largely upon the Internet, is not secure or resilient," Hathaway wrote. "Without major advances in the security of these systems or significant change in how they are constructed or operated, it is doubtful that the United States can protect itself from the growing threat of cybercrime and state-sponsored intrusions and operations."

On the same day, Obama gave the first presidential speech in history devoted to cybersecurity. He pledged to invest more in research and public education and to appoint a White House czar, though not one that would report directly to him, as Obama had promised during his campaign. "Our defense and military networks are under constant attack," Obama said. Beginning immediately, "the networks and computers we depend on every day will be treated as they should be: as a strategic national asset."

For weeks after the speech, private and government experts felt surprised gratitude that the leader of the free world, beset as he was with economic and military problems, would begin to tackle the cybercrime crisis. They expected Obama to name the czar, now officially called a coordinator, within two weeks. But the position as advertised would have reported to both the National Economic Council and the National Security Council, and it would have wielded an uncertain authority and budget. The top Microsoft security official from the CSIS panel and the former head of Symantec both declined overtures to serve. As five months passed without a nomination to the Senate, and even Hathaway resigned from her caretaker role, the sense of hopelessness returned.

12

FIXING
WHAT'S
FIXABLE

BARRETT LYON DID AS MUCH AS anyone in the private sector could
do to fight denial-of-service attacks, the leading edge of a tsunami
of organized cybercrime. Yet by 2009, every new day brought more
than 1,000 DDoS attacks—not just against companies, but against
governments and activists as well. It was so easy to orchestrate a
DDoS that a Canadian teenager who disliked tech commentator
Kevin Rose took aim and wiped out Rose's Digg.com, one of the
most popular news sites in the world. Unfortunately for the teen,
Digg CEO Jay Adelson previously founded Web hosting giant
Equinix and was a good friend of Barrett's. In exchange for a pizza,
Barrett got Digg back up in five minutes. Within days, Barrett had
the teen's nickname, while his mysterious allies at Team Cymru used
their undisclosed methods to produce a log of the assailant boasting
of the attack on an IRC channel. For those less connected, however,
things were very much worse than before Barrett started.

Andy Crocker did the most that an individual in government could do to punish some of the worst of the cyber mafia. At a minimum, Andy's shoe-leather investigation and the prosecutions he championed set a new standard for cooperation on criminal cases between the West and Russia, home to some of the most heinous crooks anywhere. Yet because of internal bureaucratic shifts and deteriorating relations with Moscow, the U.K. abandoned the claim that Andy staked. It had no one in Russia or Kazakhstan working with the honest members of the MVD to pursue Bra1n, Milsan, and others high up in the criminal hierarchy. Andy saw that he couldn't accomplish much more in what was now a matter of geopolitics, albeit one unrecognized as such by Western government. He followed Barrett's lead and walked away, retiring from public service in 2009.

Three things would help mitigate the enormous overall problem: catching the bad guys, who are growing more numerous; disabling the tools they use, which are growing more powerful; and separating them from their chief prey—governments, consumers, and businesses trusting the Internet with more sensitive information while using less effective protection software. There is cause for hope in each of those areas and good ideas about what more could be done.

Without much help from abroad, it's still possible to nab the occasional kingpin—even when they aren't on vacation. With an impressive effort, a group including the Secret Service, the Manhattan district attorney's office, and the New York Police Department showed they could lure prey all the way to the U.S. The target was Igor Klopov of Moscow, who law enforcement sources said pioneered selling counterfeit credit cards along with the ability to change the billing address assigned to those cards. Perfecting a system for address changes was a key innovation, because it meant that the victims would never see the bills that would give away bogus purchases. Klopov sold his card numbers on Shadowcrew and CarderPlanet, then Mazafaka, for much more than card numbers tethered to real addresses.

Klopov might have remained safe in the Russian shadows, but greed took hold of him. Only twenty-four, he came up with another innovation: targeting home-equity lines of credit. He picked out victims from sources including the Forbes 400 list of the richest Americans, then narrowed his focus to those in states with extensive online information about properties and deeds. With that data, he could click on "I forgot my password" at financial sites and often answer the challenge questions to "prove" he was the target. Klopov recruited assistants through Monster.com and CareerBuilder.com, giving them all fake identity documents and arranging their travel to five-star hotels. He gave the accomplices dossiers on the targets, then dispatched them to banks and brokerages to arrange money transfers. Klopov and his crew took in $1.5 million. But they aimed too high when they went after Texas investor Charles Wyly Jr.

Posing as Wyly, Klopov asked that a checkbook for his home-equity account be sent to a new address. An accomplice then used one of the checks to arrange to buy $7 million in gold from a Westchester, New York, bullion dealer. But the dealer called the bank, J.P. Morgan, which contacted Wyly, who said he didn't send the check. The bank notified authorities, who had begun tracking Klopov after an earlier suspicious transaction. An ex–homicide detective then assumed the online identity of an arrested Klopov ally, said the gold deal had been pulled off, and even sent a picture of himself posing with the bars. That persuaded Klopov to travel as close as the Dominican Republic for a rendezvous. The undercover cop got Klopov to join him on a private plane to sneak into the U.S. and collect the loot, and he was arrested soon after arrival.

Men who worked on the Klopov case called his capture a miracle. Cracking such cases is ten times more difficult than a few years ago, they said, because as the biggest underground forums have collapsed, the leaders of such criminal cells have restricted themselves to dealing with a dozen or so associates apiece, all online, with heavy encryption.

The only way in is through a turned informant or the takeover of an accomplice's identity. "Right now, online criminals have very little risk," said Steve Santorelli of Team Cymru.

Many more criminals could be brought in with the cooperation of other governments, especially those in former Soviet states. And Andy proved that's possible to get. "You need to have those personal relationships, and the only way that happens is by spending a lot of time with them and not calling them just when you need something. The U.S. misplayed that pretty good," said one senior U.S. agent amazed by Andy's work. "We failed to understand the Russian mentality and work in and around their system." When Andy brought Igor Yakovlev to conferences in the U.S. and other countries, Western investigators beseeched him for help with their cases. But when Igor told them about the formal procedure, most gave up.

FBI Assistant Director Shawn Henry said that the FBI and FSB began cooperating on multiple cases in 2008, and he said the Russians made a number of undisclosed arrests in St. Petersburg based on U.S. information. In early 2009, Henry sent an agent to work for two weeks at the MVD. That almost caught the feds up to where Andy had been five years earlier. "We're still kind of in the infant stages of this relationship," Henry said. "It's going to take some time to show evidence, but I think the foundation is there."

What it will take going forward is a commitment to deal with other powers as they are, with respect and openness: "working with the Russians, not against them," Andy said. There has to be a carrot, in the form of sharing information and techniques, and a stick, in the form of diplomatic penalties. Above all, the harboring and sponsorship of arch criminals must be elevated to the levels that Andy required to get his Russian peers moving, the U.K. equivalent of the U.S. secretary of state. The integrity of corporate, consumer, and government technology and the online financial system has to be recognized as a top priority. It deserves to be an issue at head-of-state summits. If the U.S. is going to wheel and deal with others on the world stage about matters ranging from invasions to crop subsidies, their treatment of cybercriminals has to be on the agenda too. A good place to start would be with pressure on Russia and others to ratify something like the European Convention on Cyber Crime, which sets out a framework for what constitutes criminal activity.

The Obama administration initially appeared to be getting some of the picture. The president said online crime was costing the world $1 trillion every year, and Melissa Hathaway's report called on the White House to stop passing the buck and to lead. While giving Obama credit for his May speech, Andy said much of what he and Hathaway said was old news. He said nothing in it would get Russia or China to change their ways. He said the world's Net authorities, from the Internet Corporation for Assigned Names and Numbers (ICANN) to the major service providers, needed to be given more power.

The U.S. was just taking the first steps toward sharing information on new attack modes with the electric utilities and other private industries. Government officials said they felt more urgency in developing offensive cyberweapons, which in theory could retaliate in kind for acts against U.S. assets or allies—that is, if the initial attackers could be identified. Most of the other key actions called for in Obama's speech remained on hold.

In February 2009 Senate testimony, two weeks after he was named director of national intelligence, Admiral Dennis Blair had warned that Russia and China had the capability to break parts of the U.S. information infrastructure and collect intelligence. "We expect disruptive cyber activities to be the norm in future political or military conflicts," he testified. Using some of the most direct language to date from such a high official, Blair continued, "powerful, high-profile Eurasian criminal groups often form strategic alliances with senior political leaders and business tycoons and operate from a relative safe-haven status with little to no fear of international arrest and prosecution. . . . The change in the structure and types of activities conducted by transnational criminal groups is making it increasingly hard to identify and attack them." He said 15 percent of all online computers were expected to become bots by the end of 2009, and that spam-related fraud alone cost $140 billion the previous year.

Senate Intelligence Chair and California Senator Dianne Feinstein tried to coax Blair still further, into exposing the connections between the Russian mob and the Kremlin, but Blair wasn't ready for that step. "Do you see any nexus between Russian organized crime, cybernetworks, and the government?" she asked. "I'd rather not answer that in this session, Madame Chairman," Blair replied.

As Obama's first summit with Prime Minister Putin and President Dmitry Medvedev approached in July 2009, experts briefed Obama on cybercrime, suggesting he press for greater law enforcement cooperation. They warned him that the Russian preference for subjecting cyberweapons to arms control treaties would leave the Kremlin too much freedom to keep outsourcing to organized crime without detection. But Obama was ill-equipped to deal seriously because he still had no cybersecurity czar, and sources said the issue never came up. It was a missed opportunity.

• • •

THE U.S. CAN'T RELY ON DIPLOMACY ALONE. That's why it must also try harder to disable or blunt the major weapons in the criminals' arsenal, including their botnets and access to bulletproof server hosting and high-speed access in the West. As for the botnets themselves, the landscape is bleak. By 2009, there were perhaps 1,000 of the old-fashioned zombie armies controlled by Internet Relay Channels, another 100 directed with greater stealth from websites like those Bra1n switched to, and 10 run like the more recent Conficker worm in peer-to-peer fashion, with drones updating each other and no head to cut off, according to Team Cymru. Experts said the fight against the bots is now unwinnable. What's worse, "we're losing at an accelerating rate," said Alan Paller, director of the SANS Institute, a nonprofit security training outfit.

Except for the peer-to-peer setups, though, the bad guys still need places from which to control the botnets. They also need spots to store their digital treasure and process transactions. The Russian Business Network provided those things. But when people like Jart Armin, David Bizeul, and others started tracking RBN and its vendors and customers, then shared their findings with others and the media, even the RBN felt the heat. It dropped its main Internet connections in St. Petersburg in summer 2007 and began operating through other links.

Some crowed that the RBN was dead. Others complained that it should have been left alone, since it was now harder to track. But Armin and his allies learned about the operation by following how it reconnected. One of the things they realized was that the RBN and its ilk want hosting outside of Russia, ideally in the United States. That way the power never goes out, the links to the Internet backbone are fastest, and the outgoing traffic eludes security systems that bar entire countries from protected networks.

For years the Eastern European mobsters got that. They found service providers based in the U.S. or with operations in the country that were either crooked themselves or very willing to take the money and ask no questions. But researchers obsessed with tracking where new viruses, phishing attacks, and Trojans were coming from spent months following the threads and comparing notes. Many were volunteers like James McQuaid, a Michigan programmer in the health care industry. McQuaid had been running some servers for a hospital group in the year 2000 that kept getting hacked by someone who used the machines to sell pirated DVDs. McQuaid traced the Internet address back to St. Petersburg, then kicked the pirates off and locked the machines down. Four years later, McQuaid bought a new PC for his teenage son. McQuaid kept the computer fully patched and behind a firewall. But when he switched antivirus programs, the new software picked up a remote-access Trojan that had been there almost from the beginning, when it got in through an anime site and a Microsoft flaw that hadn't been fixed yet. McQuaid read up on the Trojan, which SANS attributed to the RBN.

After that, McQuaid said, "I pretty much concluded that you couldn't avoid the RBN, and the best defense was to find where they were at and apply that knowledge to your defensive mechanism." McQuaid began assembling a blacklist of RBN IP addresses and domain names, and he has been updating it ever since. Companies that adopted his list have reported a major drop in intrusions and malware.

In the second half of 2008, Armin edited and published two reports with contributions from McQuaid, Bizeul, and others, some of them unnamed. The effort brought together experts at tracking criminal groups, at analyzing how code works, and at tracing Internet connections. They produced work largely aimed at Internet service professionals like those Barrett had spoken to years before at the Peering Forum. The first report targeted Atrivo, a notorious service provider that was hosting many RBN-affiliated scam pages. Among the findings: of the 100 most widespread fake anti-spyware programs, 66 were distributed through Atrivo machines. Atrivo also hosted child porn, more than 1,000 botnet control servers, and an array of other malware. More than 3 percent of the Atrivo sites tested were dangerous, compared with 0.1 percent at an average hosting company. After the report's publication, some of Atrivo's service providers stopped giving it connections to the rest of the Net. The world volume of spam dropped by 10 percent.

The second Armin report exposed McColo Corporation, which had gained some Atrivo customers in addition to its previous clientele.

McColo's upstream providers Global Crossing Ltd. and Hurricane Electric Internet Services dropped it as a customer, slashing spam by an astonishing two-thirds, independent mail filtering companies said. The FBI also began investigating whether McColo knowingly hosted child porn and scam artists.

Under Obama's new chairman, the Federal Trade Commission tried to catch up. Acting with help from private experts, it took unprecedented federal action against a third provider, Pricewert, convincing a judge to shut it down without giving notice to the owners, who might have destroyed evidence. "Almost anything that you can find that harms consumers on the Internet, this ISP was involved in," said new FTC Chair Jon Leibowitz, noting that it hosted seventeen botnet command servers and advertised on Russian-language criminal forums. All of the Pricewert employees investigators could track worked from Ukraine or Estonia, though the company was incorporated in Oregon and gave Belize as its base. Perhaps more significant was the private pressure on registrar EST Domains, which sold domain names and hosted many fraudulent sites out of Estonia, especially through Atrivo. U.S. investigators and others had run into walls at the company for years. In one case, a Secret Service agent was working with Andy to track one of Bra1n's botnets. He disabled a server hosted at an Atrivo data center in Silicon Valley and was told that the server had been leased to EST Domains. To his surprise, an EST executive called and asked what the problem was. The agent flew to meet him in Estonia, where the executive told him that he had re-leased the server to a customer in Moscow whom he only dealt with over ICQ.

Armin and his allies got better results when they provided information on EST to Brian Krebs, a *Washington Post* tech security writer who gave the Atrivo and McColo studies the broadest exposure. Krebs reported on hundreds of malicious sites at EST Domains, then followed up with a report that EST Chief Executive Vladimir Tsastsin had recently been convicted of credit card fraud and forgery. ICANN, which for years had allowed companies to sell domain names with almost total secrecy to whomever they wanted, took the historic step of revoking EST's right to peddle website addresses. ICANN, the slow-moving governance body run by consensus, had all of four people assigned to police registrars. If it had more power and money, Andy said, the world would be a safer place. Failing that, the volunteer efforts aren't going to do much more than force the criminals to go farther afield for hosting and connections. But other service providers might feel compelled to ask for documentation before cutting deals, or even check what is happening on their machines.

The potential for bad publicity reached Eastern Europe again in mid-2009, when Armin and his allies found that a provider called Real Host housed botnet command sites and served up malware through a Latvian hosting firm, Junik, which used the major Nordic telecommunications company TeliaSonera for bandwidth. Armin contacted the *Financial Times*, which called TeliaSonera, which told Junik to drop Real Host or get dropped itself. Junik pulled the plug, briefly sending world spam volume down 38 percent.

Peer pressure could help the demand for accountability, possibly setting the stage for new legal requirements. "Embarrassing these guys is the future," said a longtime Secret Service agent. "There has to be more due diligence from Internet service providers, some verification of information from their customers. We have the technology."

• • •

In some ways, the easiest part of the puzzle is how to best protect the victims, especially once everyone realizes what is possible and what is not. There is no point wasting resources fighting things that the Internet has changed forever. That includes poker. People have shown that they will continue to gamble on the Internet, even if they must entrust their money to obvious crooks operating in shady jurisdictions, and even if they have to transfer money from PayPal to some shadier company and then to an offshore account. At a time when industry after industry is coming to Washington seeking bailout money, the gambling industry could offer billions of dollars in new tax revenue. The market could be closely regulated, protecting players from cheating. And more money would stay in the U.S., increasing employment. Even if the professional sports leagues manage to block legalized sports betting, many American mobsters would have to move from poker companies to a new line of work. In May 2009, U.S. Representative Barney Frank, head of the House Financial Services Committee, introduced a bill to legalize and regulate the market. A Senate equivalent was introduced over the summer, though top poker company executives didn't expect action before 2010.

Next, consumers need to do a much better job of educating themselves. The people who won't let their lawns go uncut out of respect for the neighbors need to realize that turning on a home PC without a strong firewall and without an operating system and antivirus software that each update automatically is like leaving a loaded shotgun on the front porch for passersby; it almost guarantees that their computers will be compromised and used for nefarious activities. The population must change what it does online and develop a habit of checking credit reports and guarding personal information more closely on social networks. Another major effort should educate children about safer online practices. If they are going to be taught in public schools how to drive a car, they should most certainly be taught how to operate a computer responsibly. Furthermore, the government should heed the desperate pleas of the National Academy of Sciences for a vast increase in U.S.-funded computer security research.

Poorly designed software carries a great deal of the blame for the disintegration of network security. Commercially, large software buyers, including the federal government, should use their leverage to demand fewer flaws in their goods and greater disclosure when flaws are discovered. They must implement rapid patching procedures. The threat of litigation over poor security must be increased, both against the banks and retailers that hold personal information and against the software producers. As it stands, the latter companies are all but immune from product liability suits. That's because courts have adopted the technology industry's argument that software is "licensed," not sold, so the usual rules regarding shoddy merchandise do not apply. The combination of such a lopsided legal construction and what is in some cases monopoly market power is disastrous for quality. If the courts remain sluggish in allowing lawsuit threats to be consummated, they should be encouraged with new legislation.

A modest step toward establishing minimal standards of responsibility came in 2009 from SANS, the nonprofit security training institute. Working with the National Security Agency, the Department of Homeland Security, and others, SANS published a list of the twenty-five most serious types of programming errors, along with guidelines for how to avoid making them. Just two of the errors were responsible for 1.5 million breaches of websites, many of which in turn infected thousands of site visitors. Some state governments immediately pledged to write into their purchase agreements a requirement that software be certified free of the top twenty-five mistakes. Other big buyers, including the federal government, should follow suit.

Other new laws would certainly help, as long as they are the right ones. The Cyber-Security Enhancement Act of 2008 was a start. Among other things, the law made it a crime to access a computer without permission and remove personal information, and it eliminated a requirement that prosecutors establish $5,000 in damages before charging someone with a computer attack. Mandated national disclosure by companies that lose personal financial information should be enacted as well. So should requirements for encryption of such sensitive data.

Beyond that, banks should demand greater proof of identity before approving transactions and before granting credit to people in the first place. They haven't to date because they don't bear the brunt of the fraud: the retailers do, and they have nowhere near the financial industry's clout in Washington. Both the banks and the merchants that operate online should stop relying on credit and debit card numbers alone, instead making phone calls and taking other steps to confirm customer identities, such as issuing tokens with passwords that automatically change every minute. And banks should be forced to admit the depth of the problem. Hathaway told the CSIS panel that the amount of online fraud had quadrupled in the previous six months. But the public was never told. The banks should be required to separate fraud losses from credit losses on their balance sheets, so investors and others could see what is happening and the banks would have to focus on it.

More important, the executive branch has to get its act together. Starting with the FBI, law enforcement agencies need to learn that they don't have all the answers and that cooperation is better than secrecy. The Department of Homeland Security needs to follow through on its professed commitment to cybersecurity, encouraging the development of email authentication standards and perhaps an equivalent to verify that websites are actually hosted by the people who claim to be hosting them. The department needs to end the bickering among agencies and spend what it takes to hire talented technology specialists and start catching criminals. It needs to communicate better with the public, with companies, and with Congress. The Defense Department and NSA need to protect federal networks and offer assistance to commercial operators without compromising customer privacy.

This last is no small concern. As the gravity of the threats posed by Internet attackers becomes increasingly stark, pressure is growing for more inspection of traffic before it reaches its destination. Private network operators should continue such efforts to thwart denials of service, but they should disclose what they are doing, and any government involvement must come with oversight. Anything more intrusive, secretive, or uncontrolled puts us on the road to the destruction of Internet privacy, the consequences of which are on view in such places as China and Iran.

• • •

THE AREA WITH THE MOST COMPLEXITY—and the greatest short-term potential—lies in the nascent communities of private sleuths like Barrett, the team that identified the suspected author of the SoBig virus, and those tracking the RBN. There should be more of a coordinated movement to save the Net, which should set out credos with the moral force that has driven the development of Linux, the Firefox Web browser, and other open-source projects. Those efforts attracted thousands of volunteer programmers to help develop alternatives to commercial products that were riddled with flaws. Certainly protecting the public is a higher calling still.

Such campaigns could simultaneously aid law enforcement and shame them into action. And they should be opened up as much as possible, allowing more people to contribute their time and expertise. If a loose collection of bloggers could together find fraud in documents about Bush's military service that misled CBS News, surely the world's several thousand cybersleuths can identify those behind the code that comprises the greatest engine for mob-driven fraud in the world today.

Joe Stewart, the researcher who fingered the Bagle suspect, thinks dedicated clusters of paid specialists in and out of law enforcement should work together on specific gangs or new types of malware. Like Andy, he thinks that every country should have a Computer Emergency Response Team (CERT) that can order service providers to shut down rogue websites. As of now, South Korea's CERT is the largest with that authority.

In the longer term, the chances for serious improvement in Internet security depend on an initial hard look at where things are and how they got there. Not only is the system broken, but it was never supposed to be particularly secure in the first place. "We didn't design the network to defend against these things," said Vint Cerf, who was co-author of one of the core Internet protocols before chairing ICANN. "My thought at the time, thirty-five years ago, was not to build an ultra-secure system, because I couldn't even tell if the basic ideas would work." Cerf, who has a generally upbeat tone about most things, gives the impression that he remains pleasantly surprised that the Internet has continued to function and thrive—even though, as he put it, "We never got to do the production engineering," the version ready for prime time.

Even after his years on the front line, Barrett found such statements amazing. "It's incredibly disturbing," he said. "The engine of the world economy is based on this really cool experiment that is not designed for security, it's designed for fault-tolerance," which is a system's ability to withstand some failures. "You can reduce your risks, but the naughty truth is that the Net is just not a secure place for business or society."

Cerf listed a dozen things that could be done to make the Internet safer. Among them: encouraging research into "hardware-assisted security mechanisms," limiting the enormous damage that Web browsers can wreak on operating systems, and hiring more and better trained federal cybercrime agents while pursuing international legal frameworks. But he conceded that those steps wouldn't constitute a cure. "Multilateral agreements depend on the goodwill of the parties," Cerf said. "If the parties lack goodwill, one wonders if the situation will become so severe that the benefits of being connected will be sufficiently eroded that the international community will say it's not worth it to be connected anymore."

That's pretty much Cerf's biggest fear: that networks in America, for example, will stop accepting traffic from Russia or Kazakhstan, the way some companies won't accept credit cards from fraud-riddled countries. But the truth is that even such an amputation wouldn't work. If the Russians can continue to shepherd hundreds of thousands of computers inside the U.S., they can fool the networks into thinking they are locals. "There is no light at the end of the tunnel. There isn't a secret team working in a bunker that knows the answer," said one top security expert who ought to know, since he's on a secret team that's been looking for one.

One possibility, treated with caution by Cerf, by the Center for Strategic and International Studies' Commission on Cybersecurity for the 44th Presidency, and by virtually everyone else who has studied the idea seriously, is for a mandatory identification system for Internet users. "If everything you did had public scrutiny, we would probably have a safer country," Cerf said. "On the other hand, you probably wouldn't want to live in that country." The CSIS commission called for a government-supported ID that companies would adopt. "You need to have a government-issued ID of some sort that gets you onto critical infrastructures," said Bruce McConnell, a commission member who went on to join Obama's Department of Homeland Security. "Without that, I don't see how we're going to make real progress."

Barrett said he found the notion of an Internet ID card "terrifying," both for privacy reasons and the false sense of security it might engender. The bad guys would still be able to impersonate others, and with a fake Internet ID they would be farther inside the trusted network, able to do more damage.

Barrett has reluctantly come to the same conclusion as Cymru's Steve Santorelli, SANS's Paller, McConnell, and others: that the only way to create a secure Internet is to start over. The fiber optics can stay and the same chips can be used. But there needs to be a new protocol. It could be privately financed, as banks and others give up on making transactions secure in the current framework, or publicly financed, as the initial Internet research was.

In the meantime, Paller uses some of the same language as Harvard scholar Jonathan Zittrain, author of *The Future of the Internet— And How to Stop It*. While calling for a "latter-day Manhattan Project," Zittrain advocates temporarily putting two operating systems on every personal computer, which isn't as daunting as it sounds. One would be free to explore the Web but would be barred from making changes to the machine. The other would be walled off and secure. Paller said the same approach could work for the broader network. "One part of it that absolutely has to happen is the 'red' and 'green' Internet," Paller said. "The red Internet is what we have now, where nobody knows you're a dog, and with green you have absolute knowledge of who you're dealing with."

An increasing number of authorities are sounding the same theme. "Do we need to develop an enhanced Net, with two-factor authentication [such as passwords and tokens] and secure fingerprints? These are the things we should be working toward, including changing TCP," the basic protocol Cerf co-wrote, said former cybersecurity czar Schmidt. "I support that. We need to make a good investment in looking toward that direction, instead of fixing it for this week."

The investments to date have been miniscule, one hundredth of what is needed. In 2007 the National Science Foundation granted just $2.5 million a year to the Global Environment for Network Innovations, a platform for experiments that could lead to a new Internet. The next year, Deutsche Telekom and Japanese computer maker NEC said they would each give $750,000 annually for similar work at a new Clean Slate Lab at Stanford University.

In the longer term, Barrett said, "If we could build ships to put people on a separate planet, we should be able to articulate a specification for a protocol that would make society flourish digitally. We need an Apollo Project, with Vint Cerf and others. That would be pretty exciting. A new protocol could solve network neutrality, security, other flaws, DDoS attacks, and all kinds of scaling issues. Am I sure it's doable? Absolutely."

EPILOGUE

ANDY CROCKER RETIRED FROM THE Serious Organised Crime Agency, the squad that absorbed the United Kingdom's National Hi-Tech Crime Unit, in 2009. He was rewarded with a pension and a commendation at a ceremony led by Britain's home secretary. The certificate praised Andy's "outstanding commitment, investigative ability, fortitude and professionalism" in "a complex investigation into a Russian organized criminal enterprise." The ceremony was conducted behind closed doors, befitting an agency that was as opaque as the FBI and even less effective. Andy began working with Barrett Lyon's help to set up a private company, Cyber Security Shield, to defend against botnets, aiming at financial companies and government agencies as clients.

The careers of Andy's key allies inside Russia, including Igor Yakovlev and Anton Pohamov, failed to flourish after their most famous case concluded. Similar trials were not forthcoming. Kazakhstan, meanwhile, reported that it found insufficient evidence to proceed against the man accused of being Bra1n, prompting SOCA to close the case. Pohamov's boss, the chief prosecutor in Saratov, announced another in a series of corruption probes against high regional officials and was assassinated by a gunman.

Barrett's BitGravity did well in Silicon Valley as companies continued to invest in Internet video through the economic downturn. By 2009, BitGravity's customers included the largest Web video company on the planet, YouTube, and it had been named one of the ten best start-ups at DEMO, the famed technology conference. Private investments valued the company at more than $10 million, with Barrett owning close to 50 percent.

But Barrett himself ran into problems. Always outspoken and skeptical about authority, he clashed with BitGravity co-founder and chief executive Perry Wu over how a few customers had been treated. The battle escalated until the young company's board had to choose between the two men. Some directors had been close to the CEO for years, and the group as a whole was more accustomed to hearing from Wu than from Barrett. Barrett lost the fight and had to leave the company.

It didn't take Barrett long to come up with a new idea, combining what he knew about content-delivery networks with the lessons from his war with the botnets. The existing content networks relied on massive company-owned storage and bandwidth, while the botnets had demonstrated that millions of PCs could together form a sort of supercomputer. Barrett thought he might be able to harness the unused bandwidth and processing on idle PCs and networks, letting the owners sell their excess capacity to those who needed it. By fall 2009, Barrett was negotiating with venture capital firms interested in investing millions.

Barrett also grew tired of the FBI as he kept answering agents' questions without seeing any arrests of members of the group from Costa Rica. Things with Miami agent Paul Betancourt came to a head after Barrett, Andy, and I traveled together to Moscow for research. Betancourt told Barrett he knew about the trip, and he started asking Barrett what he knew about the Russian Business Network. Then Betancourt asked Barrett to fly east and take a polygraph. Barrett declined. He told Betancourt that he didn't want to hear from him again unless Barrett needed to testify in court.

Other parts of the government, however, grew increasingly interested in Barrett. In June 2009, the Defense Department announced a new Cyber Command under the head of the National Security Agency. At about the same time, Barrett and Andy spoke on a panel at a secret Washington conference, dominated by intelligence officials, on fighting terrorism. Andy talked about how Al Qaeda and other terrorists could easily use the Russian Business Network or other criminal service providers to attack the U.S. Barrett explained why the Internet was being held together with duct tape and needed to be rebuilt.

The spies didn't seem very interested in launching that kind of effort. But the director of a Pentagon office flush with new money for fighting terrorism online asked Barrett to deliver a menu of offensive weapons he might be willing to provide for hacking into or destroying enemy networks. Barrett did no such thing, instead devoting himself to his new content-delivery company, called 3Crowd Technologies. It would, he mused, put him at the helm of the world's biggest botnet.

AUTHOR'S NOTE

REPORTING THE RUSSIAN SIDE of the events in this book presented considerable challenges. Despite the fact that the prosecution of the three hackers was a success, the FSB instructed the MVD not to cooperate during my trip to that country, informing the agency that I was "probably" a spy. Inside the hotels where I stayed, muscled security guards kept track of whom I met and spoke into wireless mouthpieces when I moved. I did manage to meet safely with people involved in the case, from the MVD and elsewhere, but most spoke on the condition they not be named. My efforts to contact the men accused of being King Arthur, Bra1n, the head of Rock Phish, and the author of Bagle, among others, were unsuccessful.

I want to give some flavor from reporting on the ground in Moscow, if for no other reason than to suggest the hurdles before solid technical research and law enforcement. As one example of an on-the-record session, I had been looking forward to an appointment with Kaspersky Labs, which I figured would have a unique perspective. The company is one of the best antivirus outfits in the world. Yet it's based in the belly of the beast, routinely analyzing malicious programs for Russian police investigations and judges overseeing trials.

I told Chief Executive Eugene Kaspersky, research chief Alexander Gostev, and senior researcher Vitaliy Kamlyuk that I was writing about the hunt for the world's worst cyber criminals, and that a decent proportion of that group appeared to live nearby. Kaspersky jumped to control the discussion from the outset, writing down possible definitions of "worst." The greatest financial damage, he said, was in the £229 million cyber heist of a Sumitomo bank branch in London in 2005. Of those arrested, one was Israeli, one was Swedish, and four were from the U.K. Kaspersky appeared pleased. Actually, that attack failed. In terms of damage to the Net, he continued, the worst attacks were the viruses Sasser, Blaster, and Slammer. None of those involved making money. "With hundreds of arrests," Kaspersky asserted, "we have never had a connection to traditional organized crime."

The conversation was confusing because the three analysts had different approaches for warding off what one termed "the myth of the evil Russian hacker taking over the world." Despite the lack of prosecutions, the police have been intent on catching the leaders of the Russian Business Network for two years. Yet at the same time, what the RBN does is legal. The RBN is just a hosting provider. Yet it is close enough to the world of credit card fraudsters that when the founder of McColo, which Gostev called an RBN subsidiary, died as a passenger in a St. Petersburg street-racing accident, the driver fleeing the scene was a well-known carder. The RBN leaders have escaped thus far because they are master criminals—but master criminals who mysteriously have no need of government sponsors.

I asked about politically motivated attacks, such as that against Georgia. "There was no need to attack Georgia," Kaspersky said, because the fight on the ground went so well for Russia. Gostev reported that a major DDoS attack on Kyrgyzstan was currently under way and that "there are allegations that it's from the Russian special services." Kaspersky shook his head. "I don't think Russia has any reason to attack them," he said. In fact, Russia had an excellent reason.

Days after the electronic assault on its main Internet service providers all but wiped out local Web access, Kyrgyzstan would stun the U.S. by announcing that it would stop letting it use the Manas air base—which was playing a major role in the American war effort in Afghanistan—and join a new regional military alliance led by Russia.

I WANT TO ESPECIALLY THANK the Russians who took considerable risks to speak more forthrightly. Barrett Lyon and Andy Crocker are obviously brave and unusually talented men: they were also exceedingly generous with their time and patience. I am also indebted to other law enforcement officers in the U.S. and England, especially those who dared to speak unofficially.

Cybersecurity is one of the most complex topics in the world today, and no one can hope to understand all aspects of it. Some of the premier experts in government are cited in the text, while others asked not to be exposed. I was fortunate to be aided by many of the most able private researchers, not all of whom are paid for their work, including Joe Stewart, Rafal Rohozinski, Don Jackson, Jart Armin, Paul Ferguson, Avivah Litan, and Dmitri Alperovich. My fellow journalistic specialists also do an important service for followers like me and for the world at large. Among the very best are Brian Krebs, John Markoff, Jon Swartz, Byron Acohido, Kevin Poulsen, Kim Zetter, John Leyden, and Robert McMillan.

I am grateful to my former colleagues at the *Los Angeles Times*, who supported my early reporting and allowed me a leave to write; my new friends at the *Financial Times*, who gave me time to finish; Lindsay Jones and others at PublicAffairs; my agent Jill Marsal; Chris Gaither, who served as an unpaid manuscript editor; and those close to me who dealt with my prolonged distraction and repeated absences.

This book is for all those who face dire consequences for telling the truth but do so anyway.

Los Angeles—Las Vegas—San Francisco—London—Moscow

NOTES

WEBSITE ADDRESSES LISTED HERE were live as of July 2009. If they no longer work, search-engine caches and www.archive.org preserve many old copies. Some are duplicated at www.josephmenn.com/FatalSystemError. That site also contains many of the original source documents cited in the body of the book.

Under SOCA's strict policies, Andy Crocker is not allowed to speak to outsiders about his work at that agency. The account of his activities after SOCA replaced the NHTCU is pieced together from interviews with his allies in law enforcement in Russia, England, and the U.S., as well as with Anton Pohamov and Barrett Lyon.

INTRODUCTION

x **gave a panoramic view of organized crime's brazen new initiative:** The story is at www.josephmenn.com/other_delete_online_extortion.php.

x **30 percent of Americans had become identity theft victims:** According to analyst Avivah Litan of Gartner Research.

x **$1 trillion a year to Internet criminals:** According to a McAfee analysis cited by President Barack Obama in May 2009.

xi **catching less than 1 percent of the bad guys:** Litan.

CHAPTER 1

4 **as much as $5 million:** BetCRIS has given out conflicting estimates of its revenue and has tended to exaggerate. This number is based on internal figures.

5 **Glenn had no idea:** Major sources for this section include Richardson, Lebumfacil, Turner, other BetCRIS employees, competitors, and Lyon.

6 **"Your site is under attack":** All emails quoted in this book are from the original material.

8 **whatever else the underworld marketplace found profitable:** Sources for this section include numerous security experts and law enforcement officials interviewed over the course of a decade.

11 **said nothing to Rachelle:** Major sources for this section include Lyon, Sterling, Turner, Lebumfacil, and Richardson.

14 **a relief to die:** Major sources for this section include Lyon, Bruce Lyon, Pat Lyon, and Andy Lyon.

20 **Museum of Modern Art in New York:** www.moma.org/collection/object.php?object_id=110263.

23 **"Big Dumb Kid":** http://drennick.blogspot.com/. Rennick declined an interview request.

CHAPTER 2

29 **taking out its enemies:** Major sources for this section include Lyon and Turner.

30 **"yes, im here":** Sources here and later in this chapter include the chat transcripts, Lyon, Turner, Andy Crocker, and others in law enforcement.

32 **growth of the world economy:** Interview with Deats.

32 **"the best environment in the world for e-commerce":** A copy of Blair's report is at www.josephmenn.com/FatalSystemError.

34 **"DDoS Terrorism Report":** Lyon's report, available at www.josephmenn.com/FatalSystemError.

35 **press the Russians for action:** Crocker and other law enforcement sources.

CHAPTER 3

38 **More than $1 million in wagers every month:** Pittsburgh papers covered the arrest in articles such as www.pittsburghlive.com/x/pittsburghtrib/news/cityregion/s_453831.html.

38 **Brian thought that was hilarious:** Major sources on Brian Green's background include an author interview with him, Lyon, others who did business with him, bookie Steve Budin, and Budin's book *Bets, Drugs, and Rock & Roll*. Green said he has been off drugs for a dozen years.

39 **gloomily complaining that he had lost as much:** Green's poker wins are recounted on such sites as www.pokerpages.com/tournament/result1708.htm.

41 **"our client's financial and personal affairs strictly private":** www.betcris.com/about-us.aspx.

42 **IQ-Ladorum's code for running casino games:** Rennick's personal Web pages and press releases about him usually omit IQ-Ladorum, but he told Lyon about his time there.

44 **one of the 9 million U.S. residents victimized by identity theft:** According to Federal Trade Commission estimates.

47 **what Barrett wanted him to on staff and equipment:** Major sources for Prolexic's time in Florida include Lyon, Rachelle Lyon, Joe Daly, Terry Rodery, Lebumfacil, and Bruce Lyon.

48 **who had multiple ties to the Gambinos back east:** Sources for Sacco's mob connections include former FBI organized crime squad chief Jim Moody, then lead FBI agent Joe Davidson, private detective Dan Hanks, coverage in the *San Francisco Examiner* and *Los Angeles Times*, numerous court documents, and the *60 Minutes* transcript.

51 **at times even answering Mickey's private phone number:** Sources include Lyon and others in the BetCRIS building.

51 **Annual online poker revenue soared from $90 million in 2002 to $2.4 billion in 2005:** Christiansen Capital Advisors.

52 **businesses with names unrelated to the sites:** Major sources for the Martino scams include the FTC lawsuit, both indictments, Doug Wolfe, Gary Kremen, Charles Carreon, Russell Lownie, and several other employees at the interrelated companies. Habari declined interview requests.

53 **said the FTC's lead attorney on the case:** Interview with the FTC's Wolfe.

54 **who went on to front a goth-rock band:** Sources for Parasol's career include Ricarda Parasol, Kremen, Nelson Rose, Bryan Bailey, Bradley Keller, Jon Mendelsohn, Michael Shackleford, former PartyGaming employees, papers from the FTC lawsuit against Eisenberg, the Parasols' suit against Eisenberg, and the state lawsuits against a Parasol-backed 900-number company.

56 **"moved on down the road":** Interview with attorney Keller.

58 **regularly hosted 70,000 at a time:** Company filings and PokerPulse.

59 **to end the threat of federal legal action:** The Justice Department seizure was reported in a PartyGaming securities filing, while the advertising settlements were covered in the media.

60 **a detective from Scotland Yard:** www.combatingcybercrime.co.uk/2009/index.cfm?page=speakers.

CHAPTER 4

63 **"scammer," and "CC fraud":** E-Gold case documents including http://docs.justia.com/cases/federal/district-courts/district ofcolumbia/dcdce/1:2007cv01316/126695/1/1.pdf.

64 **just before Christmas 2005:** Sources for the Proliflik battle include Lyon, Rodery, and emails from the time.

65 **asked the Secret Service to come instead:** Sources for the rivalry between the Secret Service and the FBI include current and former agents for both, current and former federal prosecutors, and victim companies.

66 **made available to those who needed access:** Cymru charged for many of its services. Sources include Cymru's website, Steve Santorelli, and Jay Adelson, who reviewed IRC transcripts obtained by the company.

68   **there often didn't seem to be enough money:** Revenue and profit figures are from internal documents.

68   **"corrupt organization" with multiple bookies:** Coverage at www.post-gazette.com/neigh_washington/20030817wacover2.asp.

69   **"You tell me somebody who'll do that today":** The *Inquirer* article was available at www.nrn.com/offthewire.aspx?id=338600.

76   **could save the Net from a host of ills:** Contemporaneous interviews with Blue Security executives and others.

77   **"and make them ddos you":** Chat transcript provided at the time by Blue Security.

77   **"Adios bluefreaks":** This comment was reposted to the CastleCops bulletin board.

77   **associated with the popular TypePad blogging software:** The crash got wide coverage. One article is at http://news.cnet.com/Blue-Security-attack-linked-to-blog-crashes/2100–7349_3-6068607.html.

78   **never gave any interviews about why he quit:** He declined requests again during research for this book.

78   **proclaimed the *Washington Post*:** www.washingtonpost.com/wp-dyn/content/article/2006/05/16/AR2006051601873.html.

78   **"Let's hope that is enough":** CastleCops itself was later put out of operation by a DDoS onslaught.

79   **"Blue Security will be missed":** The page is gone from Prolexic's site, but a copy of Rennick's statement is at www.josephmenn.com/FatalSystem Error.

79   **that had been Prolexic's early customer base:** Interview with a former UltraDNS executive and others.

81   **Strause had succeeded Darren in running Digital Gaming:** Strause declined an interview request.

CHAPTER 5

85   **Pelican Sports, a Costa Rican book, in 2000 and 2001:** The 2002 indictment was announced at www.oag.state.ny.us/media_center/2002/jun/jun04a_02.html.

85   **Police busted four Mobile Promotions staffers:** Reported in local media at the time and picked up by some of the online gambling news sites, including www.winneronline.com/articles/october2002/betonsports.htm.

85   **a total of $31.5 million in cash and public-service warnings:** www.reuters.com/article/companyNewsAndPR/idUSN196259052007121.

85   **en route to the company's Costa Rica headquarters:** Carruthers's indictment is at www.usdoj.gov/usao/moe/press_releases/archived_press_releases/2006_press_releases/july/betonsports_indictment.pdf, and his guilty plea was reported atwww.usdoj.gov/usao/moe/press_releases/archived_press_releases/2009_press_releases/april/carruthers_david.html.

86   **more than most casinos:** Kelly's quote appeared in the *New York Daily News*. The indictment was in Queens County Supreme Court, *People v. Arnold Fuchs et al.*

87   **"Shut up and sit down!":** Interviews with Daly and those he told about the raid as it was happening.

88   **were controlled by BetonSports:** See, for example, the Carruthers indictment cited above.

88   **Even Brian Green said he wouldn't play for serious money:** Green interview.

89   **"bots are better than the average person":** Interviews with Ken Mages, Hilton Givens, Phil Laak, and others. One of the author's articles on the subject is at www.josephmenn.com/other_poker_faced.php.

89   **"a one-in-a-million jackpot six consecutive times":** Sources for this section include people close to Absolute Poker employees, the *60 Minutes* episode, and articles in the *New York Times* and *Washington Post*, such as http://freakonomics.blogs.nytimes.com/2007/10/17/the-absolute-poker-cheating-scandal-blown-wide-open/.

90   **an early advisor of Ruth Parasol:** Interview with Rose.

90   **"prohibited by federal law," Barankin said:** Interviews with Barankin and others.

91   **how online betting could be regulated best:** Interviews with casino executives and lobbyists. Lanni's quote appeared in *Forbes*.

91   **also barred the betting companies themselves from accepting U.S. wagers:** The history of the bill is given in various news accounts.

92   **to pay off a $5,000 online poker debt:** "Ex-Class President Pleads Guilty in Bank Robbery," www.msnbc.msn.com/id/13834272/.

93   **both pleaded guilty:** *U.S. v. Lefebvre*, U.S. District Court in Manhattan.

93   **targets appeared to be Parasol and her three co-founders:** Interviews with people familiar with the investigation and news accounts including those in London's *Daily Telegraph*.

93   **He quit lobbying:** http://abcnews.go.com/Politics/wireStory?id=5792792.

94   **an astonishing $300 million fine:** http://business.timesonline.co.uk/tol/business/industry_sectors/leisure/article5403301.ece.

94   **would be ruled out forever:** Interviews with PartyGaming sources.

95   **IPVG, the Philippines Web company:** According to company documents.

95   **into a lawsuit in which he wasn't a defendant:** *A. Farber & Partners Inc. v. Maynard Hal Garber*, U.S. District Court in Los Angeles.

98   **who had quietly been indicted by a state grand jury in Arizona**: Betancourt declined an interview request. As of late 2009, Sacco's name appeared only in a related forfeiture case. That complaint said that "between approximately March 29, 2005 and April 23, 2007, DEFENDANT SACCO engaged in the following activity: Created, owned, maintained, managed and controlled an offshore based website known as BETCRIS that was designed to accept, record and process gambling transactions." Under state

law, an indictment itself does not become public record if the defendant has not been served with the papers.

CHAPTER 6

100 **exactly the same thing two years before:** The author's *LA Times* article "Fraud Ring Taps Into Credit Data," on the California-only disclosure, at http://articles.latimes.com/2005/feb/16/business/fi-hacker16 prompted the fuller admission. The *Times* then reported the prior infiltration, despite denials, and that's available at http://attrition.org/dataloss/2005/09/choice point04.html.

101 **first appeared in an email group in 1993:** Net pioneer Brad Templeton, now chair of the Electronic Frontier Foundation, gives a brief history of the term "spam" on his personal page, www.templetons.com/brad/spam term.html.

101 **get-rich-quick schemes, and counterfeit pharmaceuticals:** The best account of the trade's titans is in Brian McWilliams's book *Spam Kings*.

103 **disguising the initial source of the mailing:** There was extensive press coverage of SoBig. The paper "Who Wrote SoBig" is available at www.joseph menn.com/FatalSystemError.

104 **shut down CSX passenger trains:** "SoBig Worm Not Slowing Down Yet," http://money.cnn.com/2003/08/21/technology/sobig/index.htm.

104 **hated to imagine what the next step would be:** A colorful account of the hunt for the twentieth machine is in a January 2004 *Vanity Fair* article, "The Code Warrior."

105 **according to Russia's Kaspersky Labs:** Interview in Moscow with Kaspersky analysts.

106 **all traces of the infections:** Interviews with Hypponen and other researchers, law enforcement on the case, and media reports on the charges against Jaschen.

108 **directly benefited the makers of Send-Safe:** Sources include "Who Wrote SoBig," that document's author, and other researchers. The "bullshit" quote is from a story by Brian McWilliams at www.oreillynet.com/pub/a/network/2004/11/02/sobig.html.

108 **"I'm very impressed . . . ," he wrote:** According to a copy of the email.

109 **the Bagle family of viruses.** Joe Stewart's "Who Wrote Bagle."

112 **as they became available:** Sources include Frank Eissmann, U.S. agents, and court filings against Gembe, Walker, Ashley, and Echouafni.

114 **with more than 35 million identities at risk just that year:** Identity Theft Resource Center report, www.idtheftcenter.org/artman2/publish/m_press/2008_Data_Breach_Totals_Soar.shtml.

115 **actually earned money from many instances of fraud:** Interviews with banking and retailing executives, among others. See the author's *LA Times* article "Industry at Odds Over ID Theft Liability," available at http://articles.latimes.com/2005/mar/07/business/fi-idtheft7. The most compre-

hensive analysis of the culpability of the financial industry in identity theft is by *USA Today* reporters Byron Acohido and Jon Swartz, in their insightful book *Zero Day Threat*.

115 **harassed by debt collectors after such fraud:** According to the 2003 FTC report, available at www.josephmenn.com/FatalSystemError.

116 **advisors on the 2005 report:** The author covered the Javelin report's problems in "Data Brokers Press for U.S. Law" at http://articles.latimes.com/2005/dec/26/business/fi-idlobby26.

117 **the *Wall Street Journal*, and elsewhere:** See, for example, "Net Fraud Study," http://query.nytimes.com/gst/fullpage.html?res=9A00E6DD173BF934A1 5752C0A9639C8B63.

117 **one would expect most theft to occur there:** Interviews with Van Dyke, Greisman, and others.

118 **thousands of CheckFree clients:** The hack of CheckFree was reported at http://voices.washingtonpost.com/securityfix/2008/12/hackers_hijacked_ large_e-bill.html and elsewhere.

CHAPTER 7

122 **pushed to bring him aboard:** Sources include Crocker, his CV, and his colleagues.

123 **accomplices in Latvia:** Sources for this section include Crocker, Trevor Dickey, and Lyon.

127 **when everything was working:** Sources for this section include Ross, Smith, Crocker, Lyon, and a visit to SportingIndex.

129 **grumpily sent them back:** Sources for this include Crocker and his former colleagues.

131 **those were orchestrated by the FSB:** The bombings leveled four buildings in the middle of the night between September 4 and September 16, 1999, killing 295 a few months ahead of what would be President Vladimir Putin's election. Putin, plucked from a little-seen position of power in the FSB by outgoing president Boris Yeltsin's wealthy supporters and named prime minister, seemed destined to lose. Authorities blamed Chechens, Putin attacked, and the populace rallied around the Kremlin and voted in Putin as president. In the increased vigilance that followed the initial bombings, though, a bus driver returning home to a fifth apartment building, in Ryazan, on September 22 noticed a white Lada with a partially obscured license plate parked in front while a woman in the main entryway nervously looked around. He called police, who found a bomb in the basement with a detonator set to go off at 5:30 A.M. They evacuated hundreds from the building in a panic. The local bomb squad defused the device and found it contained hexagen, a hard-to-obtain explosive that the government said had been used in the previous attacks. Using witness descriptions of people seen in and around the Lada, police arrested two suspected terrorists within days. But they produced FSB identification and were ordered released. As questions

mounted, the FSB, which had previously congratulated the building residents on escaping certain death, abruptly switched course. On September 24 the agency declared that the apparent bomb had been planted as part of an official training exercise and contained only sugar. The bomb squad's testing equipment must have malfunctioned. The squad leader explained to journalists why that was impossible, but all the evidence was seized by the FSB. Without access to the bomb materials, there can be no proving what happened. But former *Wall Street Journal* and *New York Times* Moscow correspondent David Satter, in his 2003 book, *Darkness at Dawn*, makes a compelling case that the apartment residents correctly concluded that the FSB had intended to murder everyone in the Ryazan building, and therefore most logically had been behind the four bombings that had already killed hundreds.

131 **the one on the Houston machine:** Sources for this and similar sections include Crocker, Russian legal documents, and interviews with Russian law enforcement.

134 **"I trust you":** Sources for the dynamic between Crocker and Yakovlev include Crocker, his colleagues, and people Yakovlev confided in.

135 **the world's third most expensive city:** According to Mercer Human Resource Consulting's March 2004 Cost of Living Survey.

CHAPTER 8

139 **Webmoney funds sent to an account there:** Major sources for this section include Crocker, documents related to the arrests and prosecution, and interviews with Russian law enforcement.

145 **Stran had organized DDoS attacks for extortion:** Major sources for this section include Crocker, documents related to the arrests and prosecution, and interviews with Russian law enforcement.

147 **most likely from local or national police:** Sources on the RBN include Crocker, others in U.K. and U.S. law enforcement, Jart Armin, Kaspersky Labs, Paul Ferguson, Kim Zenz, and Zenz's report for VeriSign, "Global Threat Research Report: Russia," available at http://cicentre.com/Documents/verisign_idefense_russia_Jan%2007.pdf.

149 **That meant Zet, Milsan, and Bra1n:** Sources include Crocker, Crocker's colleagues, Russian law enforcement, and Russian and U.K. documents.

151 **drove back to the hotel:** Sources include Crocker and Russian law enforcement.

154 **every time Andy made progress:** Sources for this and following sections include Crocker, Russian law enforcement, Crocker's former colleagues, and documents related to the investigation.

CHAPTER 9

161 **crawled through the Net to collect them:** Interviews with dozens of law enforcement officials, among others.

163 **decided to open the site for business:** The dozens of sources on Carder-Planet and Shadowcrew include former FBI Agent E. J. Hilbert.

164 **more than 9,000 people had registered:** Among other sources, a federal complaint against Script in *U.S. v. Dmitry Golubov*, U.S. District Court in Los Angeles.

164 **Douglas Havard:** Sources for the material on Havard include Dickey, transcripts of Havard's chats, documents from the British court file, and coverage in the Texas press, including a *Dallas Observer* article at www.dallas observer.com/2002-12-26/news/crazy-white-mother/.

166 **"will need services of another person":** www.crime-research.org/interviews/Interview_carder2/.

166 **antivirus firm McAfee:** Interview with McAfee's Dmitri Alperovitch.

167 **according to someone who worked the case:** Sources on Stepanenko include U.S. law enforcement, the U.S. indictments in San Francisco and New York, and related press releases.

169 **"go out and hire them for hacking":** Additional sources include other FBI and Secret Service agents and those who worked closely with them.

169 **Crabb told Wired.com:** "Tracking the Russian Scammers,"www.wired.com/politics/onlinerights/news/2007/01/72605.

170 **David Appleyard:** Sources include the Shadowcrew court file, *U.S. v. Andrew Mantovani* in U.S. District Court in Newark, and law enforcement on the case. There was also extensive media coverage.

171 **a Secret Service agent investigating Shadowcrew:** Cavicchia's downfall was described by those who worked with him, the press, and court papers from *U.S. v. Nicolas Lee Jacobsen* in U.S. District Court in Los Angeles.

172 **Ashcroft said in a press release:** The October 28 announcement is at www.usdoj.gov/criminal/cybercrime/mantovaniIndict.htm.

172 **Tyukanov was never brought to justice:** Interviews with U.S. law enforcement. Andrew Mantovani got less than three years.

173 **he could tell if it was true:** Sources for the material on Thomas include his own comments on various Web pages, a podcast interview available at http://smallworldpodcast.com/?p=41, and an excellent *Wired* article by Kim Zetter, "I Was a Cybercrook for the FBI," at www.wired.com/politics/onlinerights/news/2007/01/72515.

173 **effectively of the governments themselves:** Sources include numerous law enforcement officials in the U.S., U.K., and Russia, as well as Zenz's VeriSign report.

175 **"Will pay with Western Union":** Chat witnessed by the author.

175 **a payment processor owned by the Royal Bank of Scotland:** Press accounts include http://voices.washingtonpost.com/securityfix/2009/02/data_breach_led_to_multi-milli.html?wprss=securityfix.

175 **that a CarderPlanet guru named BigBuyer had ordered from Outpost.com:** The Zetter article in *Wired* noted above.

176 **rippers who stole from other thieves:** Sources include interviews with Mularski and Shawn Henry.

177 **with more than fifty others in multiple countries:** For more on Cha0, see "Turkish Police Arrest Alleged ATM Hacker-Kidnapper," www .wired.com/threatlevel/2008/09/turkish-police/.

178 **an executive of a top encryption firm:** Interview with Phil Dunkelberger, chief executive of PGP Corporation. The T.J. Maxx indictments came in Boston, against Gonzalez and others, and San Diego, against Yastremskiy and others, www.usdoj.gov/usao/ma/Press%20Office%20-%20Press%20 Release%20Files/Aug2008/TJXPressRelease.html.

178 **persuaded authorities there to make an arrest:** Interviews with U.S. law enforcement.

178 **He had gone by both Soupnazi and Segvec:** An engaging account of Gonzalez's multifaceted career appeared in Brad Stone's *New York Times* story "Global Trail of an Online Crime Ring," at www.nytimes.com/2008/ 08/12/technology/12theft.html?.

CHAPTER 10

181 **high-ranking officials in the area:** Major sources for this chapter include Crocker for events before the SOCA takeover of his agency, Pohamov, U.K. and Russian documents, the judge's ruling, and Russian law enforcement.

186 **"the papers will disappear":** Interview with Pohamov. Crocker wouldn't comment on anything after the point in the trial when he began working for SOCA.

191 **"Absolutely," Barrett said:** According to Lyon.

193 **brought no changes:** Interviews with U.K. law enforcement and private security experts. Some of the complaints were aired in public, and SOCA's travails have been reported in the British press.

193 **the ending of *Raiders of the Lost Ark*:** According to people Crocker confided in.

CHAPTER 11

196 **as high as possible, at King Arthur:** Sources include Pohamov, others in Russian and U.K. law enforcement, and Lyon.

196 **a man in his early twenties living in the Russian republic of Dagestan:** A U.S. official with another federal agency confirmed that identification for its publication here, as did a colleague of Crocker's at the NHTCU.

196 **signaling an end to the subject:** Crocker described this scene to colleagues,

196 **The committee never pursued the case:** Interviews with Russian law enforcement.

198 **much to Andy's amusement:** Sources for this section include Lyon and another person at the party.

199 **give his country another chance:** Interview with Pohamov.

200 **had to be numbered by hand:** Crocker described the Russian format when discussing previous submissions. Other details are from Crocker's law enforcement allies.

200 **including Milsan:** U.S. law enforcement sources.

201 **within days of its release:** According to security firm Commtouch.

201 **Small businesses were increasingly targeted in account transfers:** See such Brian Krebs articles on the topic as http://voices.washingtonpost.com/securityfix/2009/09/more_business_banking_victims.html?.

201 **far less than half of 1 percent of the perpetrators:** The Gartner study by Litan.

202 **the top country for hacking:** Interviews with Zenz, Henry, and others.

203 **"political protection at a very strong level":** Interviews with U.K. and U.S. law enforcement, private researchers including Jart Armin, Paul Ferguson, David Bizeul, Don Jackson, and Zenz, along with written reports from those five and others. Some say the key protector is not Flyman's father but his uncle.

204 **the Soviet government's anti–organized crime bureau:** Interviews with Serio and his book, *Investigating the Russian Mafia.* For more on organized crime and the government, see *Darkness at Dawn* by David Satter and *Godfather of the Kremlin* by murdered *Forbes* journalist Paul Klebnikov.

206 **one researcher who was able to log onto the home site:** Jackson. For more on Gozi and the evolution to hacking as a service, see Scott Berinato's "Who's Stealing Your Passwords?" in *CIO Magazine*, at www.cio.com/article/135500/Who_s_Stealing_Your_Passwords_Global_Hackers_Create_a_New_Online_Crime_Economy.

206 **the biggest American identity thief ever accused:** As of October 2009.

206 **"They have had many opportunities":** Interviews with Jackson and the prosecution source.

206 **including identity-theft tools:** The Bank of India hack was described in multiple places. A good account was provided by Sunbelt Software.

207 **security firm Secunia:** Available at http://secunia.com/blog/37/.

207 **half a million bank credentials:** According to a report from security firm RSA. See www.rsa.com/blog/blog_entry.aspx?id=1378.

208 **evade blocking:** A description of the Asprox alliance by RSA is at www.rsa.com/blog/blog_entry.aspx?id=1338.

209 **police officials as the most corrupt:** Both findings were cited in Zenz's report.

210 **centralizing corruption:** See the books by Satter and Klebnikov.

210 **ATM cards en masse as well:** Peretti interview.

211 **attempted coup there:** The *CompSec* story is available at www.compseconline.com/analysis/040121419fraud.html.

211 **was directed from Russian computers:** The *LA Times* article, "Cyberattack on Defense Department Computers Raises Concerns," appears at http://articles.latimes.com/2008/nov/28/nation/na-cyberattack28.

212 **"it was state sponsored":** Interviews with Schmidt and McConnell.

212 **all foreign Internet traffic:** Interview with Ilves. The Estonian attack received substantial press coverage.

213 **"cybercrime to cyberwarfare":** Alexander spoke at the 2009 RSA security conference in San Francisco.

213 **RBN operatives Alexander Boykov and Sergey Smirnov:** McQuaid interview and his written report at http://securehomenetwork.blogspot.com/2008/09/rbn-operatives-part-ii.html. Such bogus security software was one of the fastest-growing criminal markets in 2009.

214 **"some of the attacks":** Jackson interview and his blog postings. The nonprofit U.S. Cyber Consequences Unit at Tufts University produced a more than one hundred–page analysis of the Georgia attack on its first anniversary, though it has distributed only a less sensitive summary to the members of the press. That summary concludes that organized crime and ordinary citizens conducted the attack but had "advance notice of Russian military intentions."

214 **knocked the popular messaging site Twitter offline:** A *Financial Times* story on the attack is at www.ft.com/cms/s/0/e21434ac-83b0-11de-a24 e-00144feabdc0.html.

215 **shot in the head:** Evloev's death was reported on by *Kommersant* at www.kommersant.com/p1018915/Evloev_killed/. Zenz and Rohozinski spoke in interviews.

215 **DDoS attacks on Palestinian sites:** Press accounts include this one, www.theregister.co.uk/2009/01/09/gaza_conflict_patriot_cyberwars/, in *The Register*.

216 **worthy of respect:** The FSB statement was reported in Russian media and at www.rferl.org/content/article/1142607.html.

216 **redirecting traffic to anti-Chechen sites:** Some of Soldatov's findings are summarized in English at http://windowoneurasia.blogspot.com/2007/05/window-on-eurasia-fsb-encourages-guides.html.

216 **"not become any less productive":** A photo of Kuryanich's proclamation is in Zenz's report.

217 **would likely continue:** Jim Lewis of the Center for Strategic and International Studies, who was also on the panel, described the comments in an interview.

217 **a means of raising funds:** As reported in the *Washington Post* in a story available at www.concordmonitor.com/apps/pbcs.dll/article?AID=/2004 1216/REPOSITORY/412160328/1003/BUSINESS.

217 **cashed out the winnings:** Krebs recounted al Daour's exploits in "Three Worked the Web to Help Terrorists," www.washingtonpost.com/wpdyn/content/article/2007/07/05/AR2007070501945_pf.html.

217 **"soft ribs and strategic weaknesses":** Wang Huacheng's paper was cited on page 166 of the 2008 U.S.-China Economic and Security Review Commission report to Congress, available at www.josephmenn.com/FatalSystemError.

218 **contained in the Library of Congress:** Titan Rain was exposed in a 2005 *Time* magazine article available at www.time.com/time/magazine/article/0,9171,1098961,00.html.

218 **"even detect the efforts"**: U.S.-China Economic and Security Review Commission report.

218 **knock it offline for months:** Congressional testimony by, and interview with, Joe Weiss. Other experts have issued similar warnings, and the *Wall Street Journal* reported deep penetration of the power grid by Chinese reconnaissance.

219 **some of the most important organizations:** VeriSign and others have produced in-depth reports on the evolution of Chinese hacking.

219 **the hand of Chinese government:** Interviews with Hypponen, Rohozinski, Tethong, and others.

220 **3322.org:** The Booz Allen Hamilton anecdote comes from *Business Week*, "The New E-Spionage Threat," at www.businessweek.com/magazine/content/08_16/b4080032218430.htm.

220 **earning enough to leave school:** The report by iDefense is available from its corporate parent VeriSign. Former iDefense expert Ken Dunham elaborated on it in an interview.

220 **hacking the Pentagon:** The *Time* article "Enemies at the Firewall" is at www.time.com/time/magazine/article/0,9171,1692063,00.html.

221 **"ministries or international organizations":** The GhostNet report, "Tracking GhostNet: Investigating a Cyber Espionage Network," is available at www.scribd.com/doc/13731776/Tracking-GhostNet-Investigating-a-Cyber-Espionage-Network.

221 **a broad and distinguished group was so concerned:** A copy of the letter is at www.uspcd.org/letter.html.

221 **Congress did authorize hundreds of millions:** Through the Cyber Security Research and Development Act of 2002, aimed mainly at the National Science Foundation. Actual appropriations were handled separately, but the bill didn't envision developing a new Internet architecture. The "mixed" comment comes from a 2003 *Frontline* interview at www.pbs.org/wgbh/pages/frontline/shows/cyberwar/interviews/saydjari.html.

222 **"trying to figure it all out":** Schmidt interview, along with interviews of many security company executives.

222 **according to Congress's Government Accountability Office:** The GAO report is at www.josephmenn.com/FatalSystemError. See also a critical report by the DHS's inspector general posted there

222 **cut off all Internet access for a time:** According to congressional testimony.

222 **would have been ten times worse:** According to a person at the meeting.

223 **raised their hands:** The author was in attendance and interviewed Dixon later.

223 **"global jihad":** The CSIS report is available at www.josephmenn.com/FatalSystemError.

224 **"strategic national asset":** A transcript of Obama's speech is posted at www.josephmenn.com/FatalSystemError.

CHAPTER 12

225 **boasting of the attack on an IRC channel:** Adelson saw the transcript. The teen was not arrested.

226 **the billing address assigned to those cards:** Interviews with multiple people involved in the case.

228 **said Steve Santorelli of Team Cymru:** Santorelli interviews.

228 **"foundation is there":** Interviews with Henry. Others were skeptical of serious progress, noting that the arrests had not been publicized.

229 **more urgency in developing offensive cyberweapons:** This comes from interviews with top defense cyber officials and advisors. In general, the *New York Times* has been providing good ongoing coverage of the development of offensive cyberweapons.

230 **$140 billion the previous year:** Blair's testimony came in a February 12 hearing on "current and projected national security threats."

231 **the SANS Institute:** Paller interviews.

232 **spam dropped by 10 percent:** Interviews with Armin, McQuaid, and spam researchers. The two Armin reports are reproduced at www.josephmenn .com/FatalSystemError.

233 **gave Belize as its base:** Leibowitz interview and documents from *Federal Trade Commission v. Pricewert*, U.S. District Court in San Jose.

233 **he only dealt with over ICQ:** Law enforcement interviews.

234 **credit card fraud and forgery:** Krebs's stories appeared at http://voices .washingtonpost.com/securityfix/2008/09/estdomains.html and http:// voices.washingtonpost.com/securityfix/2008/09/estdomains_a_ sordid_history_an.html.

234 **The potential for bad publicity reached Eastern Europe:** The *Financial Times* account is at www.ft.com/cms/s/0/a95420aa-8545-11de-9a64- 00144feabdc0.html.

235 **computer security research:** The National Academies made one such plea at book length, www.nap.edu/catalog.php?record_id=10274.

236 **top twenty-five mistakes:** The SANS report is posted at www.sans .org/top25errors/.

237 **quadrupled in the previous six months:** Jim Lewis interview.

237 **focus on it:** This idea originates with Gartner's Litan.

238 **any government involvement must come with oversight:** The NSA has the capability to scan all Internet traffic entering the U.S., weeding out at least DDoS attacks and possibly more, but that might require new legislation because of laws against domestic spying. The *Wall Street Journal* has covered the issue well in places such as http://online.wsj.com/article/ SB124657680388089139.html.

239 **the version ready for prime time:** Interviews with Cerf.

240 **"real progress":** Interview with McConnell.

EPILOGUE

243 **insufficient evidence to proceed:** Interview with a U.S. law enforcement
source.

AUTHOR'S NOTE

249 **stop letting it use the Manas air base:** This decision was later reversed.

INdEX

DOUG PIBURN

Joseph Menn covers cybersecurity and other technology issues for the *Financial Times*, after a decade on the same beat for the *Los Angeles Times*. He is the author of 2003's *All the Rave: The Rise and Fall of Shawn Fanning's Napster* and a two-time finalist for the Gerald Loeb Award, the top prize in business reporting.

PublicAffairs is a publishing house founded in 1997. It is a tribute to the standards, values, and flair of three persons who have served as mentors to countless reporters, writers, editors, and book people of all kinds, including me.

I. F. STONE, proprietor of *I. F. Stone's Weekly*, combined a commitment to the First Amendment with entrepreneurial zeal and reporting skill and became one of the great independent journalists in American history. At the age of eighty, Izzy published *The Trial of Socrates*, which was a national bestseller. He wrote the book after he taught himself ancient Greek.

BENJAMIN C. BRADLEE was for nearly thirty years the charismatic editorial leader of *The Washington Post*. It was Ben who gave the *Post* the range and courage to pursue such historic issues as Watergate. He supported his reporters with a tenacity that made them fearless and it is no accident that so many became authors of influential, best-selling books.

ROBERT L. BERNSTEIN, the chief executive of Random House for more than a quarter century, guided one of the nation's premier publishing houses. Bob was personally responsible for many books of political dissent and argument that challenged tyranny around the globe. He is also the founder and longtime chair of Human Rights Watch, one of the most respected human rights organizations in the world.

· · ·

For fifty years, the banner of Public Affairs Press was carried by its owner Morris B. Schnapper, who published Gandhi, Nasser, Toynbee, Truman, and about 1,500 other authors. In 1983, Schnapper was described by *The Washington Post* as "a redoubtable gadfly." His legacy will endure in the books to come.

Peter Osnos, *Founder and Editor-at-Large*